To interpret art is a
do so theologically
collection powerful
significant, at times da.... , contribution to the burgeoning study
of art at the boundaries of faith. I thoroughly enjoyed this book!

**Christopher Pramuk**, University Chair of Ignatian
Thought and Imagination at Regis University,
author of *The Artist Alive: Explorations in Music,
Art, and Theology*

*Walk the Line* explores an ambitious and underexplored highway
leading us often to astonishing routes in the journey to God.
These top-notch theologians lend their vast experience by
interrogating the wonderful bridge that joins rock music and
its spiritual undercurrents. Fr. Christian has gathered an eclectic
collection which maps connections as fascinating as Dylan
and the Donatists on the one hand and Leonard Cohen and
pneumatology on the other. These essays would make a fine
textbook and deserve a wide readership for anyone interested
in the cultural space which inhabits theological inquiry.

**Fr. Guerric DeBona**, professor of Homiletics
at Saint Meinrad Seminary and School of Theology,
co-author of *Savior on the Silver Screen*

*Walk the Line*, a compilation of essays written by a diverse
assembly of today's most insightful theologians, is a compelling
and fascinating study of the sometimes hidden and other times
hit-you-over-the-head spiritual and theological themes of some
of the most captivating and inspired rock music of the past
50 + years. Traditional as well as contemporary rock music
and Christianity are often seen as being at direct odds with
each other, but in this fascinating study of a number of the
most prolific and brilliant musical artists in our lifetimes, these
riveting essays examine the intertwined relationship between the
lives and lyrics of secular musicians and the inspirations of the
saints and the beauty and truth of the Gospels. *Walk the Line* is

not meant as an evangelization tool for rock lovers, but rather a luminescent and genius unearthing of the orthodoxy of our faith that cannot be separated from the yearnings and desires of the secular heart that magnetically draws humanity to rock and roll. This book will be a must-read for all educators of the faith and theologians who desire to touch the hearts of the people. Rock music may not be designed to "save your soul," but these insights into the journeys and longings of secular society can unquestionably provide a map to illuminating a path to God by shining a light in the world.

**Jeannie Gaffigan**, television and comedy writer, co-host of U.S. Catholic's *Field Hospital* podcast

# Walk
# the Line

# Walk the Line

## Rock Music and the Christian Imagination

Edited by
### Christian Raab, OSB

NEW CITY PRESS

Published in the United States by New City Press
202 Comforter Blvd., Hyde Park, NY 12530
focolaremedia.com

Walk the Line
Rock Music and the Christian Imagination

Edited by Christian Raab, OSB

ISBN 978-1-56548-568-6 (paperback)
ISBN 978-1-56548-569-3 (e-book)

Library of Congress Control Number: 2023940679

Printed in the United States of America

# Contents

# Foreword

Until around the middle of the twentieth century, if one wished to hear music reflecting on ideas of Christology, salvation, moral theology, or eschatology, the pickings at the local record store were slim. Were one inclined toward the great Catholic liturgical compositions, which were mostly choral in nature, well, Mozart's *Ave Verum Corpus* (or even Byrd's) would certainly bring about a serious contemplation of the salvific nature of the blood of the crucified Christ. Along similar lines, nothing might surpass Bach's *Mass in B minor* (or his *St. Matthew's Passion*). Likewise, the sweeping treatments given the liturgical storm of the *Requiem* could drive one to one's knees in awestruck wonder, led bar by bar, musical phrase by extended interlude, to ponder the promise of either redemption or a severe and everlasting judgement, until the end of the world.

But if one were looking for somewhat lighter fare—something oriented toward the Christian tradition, only in English; a bit more singable but not precisely "churchy" (nothing, then, from the mainline Protestant hymnody)—one's choice was largely to be taken from the moving traditional spiritual songs of the enslaved African peoples of the American South, or from the death-heavy catalogue of the impoverished Scots-Irish living deep within the Appalachian Mountains. The first genre, haunting and tribal-tinged, was usually performed by descendants of the suffering men and women who lived under the lash of human traffickers, and is notable for the profound sense of life—even liveliness—that is expressed within the unique combination of ancestral tones joined to lines from Scripture or sentiments originating there. These traditional spirituals, whose melodies were sometimes edged with a bit of Euro-Celt influence picked up during treacherous ocean voyages, are unique to a specific sort of suffering humanity and yet are capable of communicating themes that touch all of us. They speak of loneliness, injustice, separation, secrets, and weary hearts, yet come forth, even from the descendants of these stricken people, with verve and authentic, soaring hope. Listen to Sam Cooke and the Soul Stirrers perform "He'll Make a Way" or The Mighty Clouds of Joy sing "I Ain't No Ways Tired"—or any accomplished African American church choir belt out "Ride On, King Jesus," and it is easy to see why the music is so valued and beloved. Likewise, the music of Appalachia—with its "devil's breath or deliverance"-heavy themes—often boasts an ironic jauntiness that leaves a listener curiously uplifted amid the hoots and keening tension found between the tones and tongues, the darkness and the light.

Both forms comprised the bulk of what might arguably be called the first "popular Christian" musical fare consumed by listeners until people like Elvis Presley, Chuck Berry, Jerry Lee Lewis and Little Richard drew that music out of the churches and choral groups, dressed it up with a blazing, hard-edged sexual component, and thereby brought rock and roll into the mainstream, where it has never stopped evolving.

That a marriage between sex and church music, two such potent forces, created something so ground-breaking, compelling, and ultimately lasting really shouldn't surprise us. The quest for God—for something to believe in and worship that is bigger than the self—seems hard-wired into humanity. Where belief in a supreme being does not exist, movements and ideologies often fill that God-sized hole, complete with their own versions of sins, sacraments, sacred observances and even ersatz popes. In 1996, Bono, U2's front man, succinctly explained why rock music, in all of its myriad forms, has been the dominant secular soundtrack of our lives for nearly seventy years: "Sex and music are still for me places where you glimpse God. Sex and *art*, I suppose, but unless you're going to get slain in the spirit by a Warhol or Rothko, I think for most of us art *is* music."[1]

One suspects he is on to something.

U2, of course, has the distinction of being one of the biggest bands in the world to also—for much of its nearly 50-year existence—wear faith on its sleeve, routinely ending concerts

---

1.  Bill Flanagan, *U2: At the End of the World*, (New York: Dell Publishing, 1996), 81.

with a song based on Psalm 40, and bringing religious allusions (that could rather puckishly be denied or affirmed seemingly at whim) into its lyrics. That is something the reader will find explored in this book by theologian Keith Lemna.

But U2 is neither the first nor the last rock act to bring spirituality into its work. Joseph Quinn Raab discusses how one member of the Beatles (who began an "invasion" that economically colonized the world for Britain) found relief from the emptiness of hyper popularity and seemingly endless material gain in the teachings of Hinduism and the music of India. George Harrison, raised an indifferent Catholic, ended up something of a syncretic believer, bringing elements of his mother's devotions and his own explorations into a faith that he could not avoid adding to his art.[2]

Syncretism—the joining of elements taken from disparate religious traditions in order to accommodate a search for God that "fits" one's own longings and limits—is something that pops up often in the spiritual expressions of rock artists, right along with Gnosticism, angst, and often brutal honesty. Within this collection of essays offered by theologians, historians and philosophers who, importantly, are also *fans*, the reader will find examinations of musical artists who have come to define their era, like Bob Dylan, or have remained in the stubborn margins of fame, like Judee Sill and Kurt Vile. Some, like Taylor Swift and Sara Bareilles, have contributed to the common lexicon or evolving social mores, while the band Genesis has brought virtuoso innovation to the industry. All have managed to share

---

2.   In 1989 the Congregation for the Doctrine of the Faith delivered a Letter to the Bishops of the Catholic Church on Some Aspects of Christian Meditation. In Section V of that document, then-Cardinal Joseph Ratzinger (later Pope Benedict XVI) wrote, "Just as 'the Catholic Church rejects nothing of what is true and holy in [the great religions]' neither should these ways [of prayer] be rejected out of hand simply because they are not Christian. On the contrary, one can take from them what is useful so long as the *Christian conception of prayer, its logic and requirements are never obscured*" (paragraph 16, emphasis added).

snapshots of the states of their souls—or how they have viewed the soul of the world—at a given moment; they show us their often-rocky quests to reach, or to reconcile with, God. Like Jacob with the angel, they bring that search for the Omnipotent One, the Creator who loves, into their work and wrestle with a world that has driven their search (The Hold Steady), fueled their passionate hunger for justice (Nina Simone), or simply tried to make sense of the paradoxical constants of light and dark, continually at war all about us (Leonard Cohen, Switchfoot).

This is an unusual textbook—a needed and refreshing gift to theology students, as it showcases instances of sometimes willfully confused spiritual wandering and gives insight into how such meanderings can demonstrate the cost of poor catechesis or, conversely, expose a Christ-consciouness reached via surprising routes.

Beyond students, though, this book may well speak to many who call themselves "nones," though not because they especially want to. Studies have shown that most "nones" are not deliberate atheists but rather are poorly catechized, or too scandalized to see beyond headlines and troubling social narratives.[3] They are often disillusioned; many of them oppose church positions—usually without a full understanding of the theology upon which complex teachings are founded. Perhaps some of them are simply bored. For certain, they "still haven't found" what they're looking for, but—encouraged by such essays as these—perhaps they may at least begin their own search, their own quest, and take their own turn at wrestling with angels.

And if the Churches can stand it, it could be a gift to them, as well. Let us pray!

Elizabeth Scalia
Montauk, October 2022

---

3. Pew Research Center, "Why America's 'nones' don't identify with a religion," August 8, 2018, available online.

# Introduction and Acknowledgements

*Walk the Line: Rock Music and the Christian Imagination* came about in the midst of the Covid-19 pandemic of 2020–2021. With more leisure time and fewer places to go than usual, I started listening to music avidly in a way that I had not done since my teen years. My perception had changed, however, since the 80s and 90s. I still loved the rock music of my youth, but my ears were now the ears of a Christian, a monk, a priest, and a theologian. I was struck now by the ways many rock artists incorporated spiritual and theological themes in their work with varying degrees of relationship to the truth and beauty of the gospel. I thought it would be interesting to put together a book about rock music's persistent but, shall we say, rocky relationship to Christian truth. Since I knew a number of theologians who were also rock music fans and also a little less busy than usual, I thought it would be fun to make the book a multi-author volume. I reached out and quickly discovered that many of my theologian friends were eager to collaborate.

The governing idea for this project has been to create a book that, rather than using rock music to get people into religion (a pandering tactic of the Christian rock industry), uses theological reflection to help people listen to secular music in a new way, with ears able to discern the presence of the true, the good, and the beautiful, in this perhaps most unlikely of places. The book approaches rock music somewhat how now-Bishop Robert Barron used to approach popular movies in his early Word on Fire videos. He would analyze films in light of his theological background, and this opened a door for viewers to watch movies in a different way, picking up themes they might have otherwise overlooked. In *Walk the Line*, we hope to open similar doors for listeners to rock music.

The book is organized into four parts. The first three chapters deal with Christological themes. Here we find Joseph Quinn Raab investigating the relationship between the Sacred Heart devotion George Harrison learned in his Catholic upbringing and the Indian mysticism he later espoused. Next, Dawn Eden Goldstein takes a measure of Judee Sill's gnostic-tinged portrayal of Christ and finds her to have an "accidental orthodoxy." Then Keith Lemna examines how U2's public positioning on social justice issues relates to their understanding of Christ as liberator.

The second set of chapters focuses on the Holy Spirit, the Church, and the sacramental economy of salvation. Thomas Malewitz illuminates Leonard Cohen's pneumatological vision. My chapter on The Hold Steady asserts that the band's 2005 album *Separation Sunday* is best viewed as a creation-fall-redemption narrative with an authentic Catholic vision. Robert Alvis portrays Bob Dylan as a qualified Augustinian figure whose consistent challenging of rigid fan expectations parallels Augustine's contest with the ancient Donatist heresy.

The third part of the book brings together three chapters concerned with moral theology. Philosopher William C. Hackett's chapter proposes Kurt Vile as a witness to the ontological goodness of being. Brian Pedraza brings Taylor Swift's articulation of the meaning of love into dialogue with Pope Benedict XVI. Elizabeth Woodard investigates the relationship of Sarah Bareilles' song "Brave" to contemporary moral relativism.

The final three chapters focus on eschatology. Nathaniel Marx presents Nina Simone's heart-wrenching "Sinnerman" as an invitation for white Christian listeners to reflect on social sin in light of eschatological judgment. My second contribution to the book discusses Switchfoot, a Christian band who've had mainstream success, as revealing the potentiality for Christian faith to be countercultural in a post-Christian age primarily through witness to hope. Finally, Lawrence King makes a case that Peter Gabriel's vision of the last things, as presented in Genesis's "Supper's Ready," fits an orthodox eschatological schema.

A book with this title needs to say a word about how it is using the term "rock." Rock began as rock and roll, piano- and saxophone-based dance music, played by African Americans in post-war juke joints. By the end of the 1960s it was most commonly associated with guitar-based groups of white men, many of whom were English. In that morphing it had integrated influences as disparate as Indian classical music, English skiffle,

Appalachian country music, and the Delta blues. Historian Andrew Hickey, in his podcast "A History of Rock Music in 500 Songs," said that rock music has "no essence in the Aristotelian sense"; it can only be identified prototypically and has "fuzzy boundaries." Furthermore, it is historical. What seems to be closest to the center of the type changes over time.[1] This book shares Hickey's broad approach to what might be included in the category of rock music. During rock's twentieth-century peak of cultural influence, musicians like Dylan, Harrison, Genesis, and U2 were at the center of what most people thought of when they used the word "rock." Sill, Simone, and Cohen were more eccentric but nonetheless part of rock's story, the latter two members of its hall of fame. The Hold Steady, Switchfoot, and Vile ascended in more recent decades, but represent a small sample of the many different ways rock's family tree has continued to evolve and branch out. Swift and Bareilles are more often referred to as pop artists rather than rock, but in truth, the catalogs of both women are genre crossing, and both can be considered worthy heirs and developers of the pop side of the rock tradition—a line that has included giants such as the Beatles, Carole King, and Billy Joel.

Despite the sonically inclusive approach of this volume, it is important to acknowledge more Black artists could be engaged here, especially since rock's roots are in Black music. Similarly, though we did attempt to recruit a wide range of authors, there could be more female authors and authors of color. The authors who did choose to contribute have naturally written from their own perspectives and backgrounds. A potential second volume would hopefully engage other perspectives.

I am very grateful to all the authors who contributed to this volume for their hard work and patience. Thanks in a special way to Dawn Eden Goldstein who served as a great sounding board in the early days of the project, helping it along with

---

1. Hickey, "July 2022 Q&A," *A History of Rock Music in 500 Songs*, July 30, 2022, https://500songs.com/wp-content/uploads/2022/07/July2022QandA.mp3.

encouragement and clear-sighted advice. She served as a second set of eyes on some of the chapters and helped with pitches to publishers. Thanks as well to my brother Joseph Raab, who not only contributed a great chapter of his own but also supplied important editorial assistance.

Thank you finally to everyone at New City Press. This book would not have been possible without the support of Gary Brandl, Greg Metzger, and their coworkers. Thanks especially to Susanna Seibert for the exceptional job she did as copy editor of this volume.

# Trying to Reach the Light
## George Harrison's Quest for a Holy Communion

Joseph Quinn Raab

George Harrison's search for God and for his own authentic identity took a deliberate turn after he tried LSD for the first time. Though raised a Catholic, Harrison had distanced himself from the Church and become an agnostic in his early teens. In April of 1965, at the age of 22, he unwittingly consumed some coffee spiked with the psychedelic drug and found himself surprised by an overwhelming realization.[2] Sounding a bit like Thomas Merton recalling his Louisville experience,[3] Harrison said, "I felt in love. . . . Everything was perfect, in a perfect light, and I had an overwhelming desire to go around . . . telling everybody how much I loved them—people I had never seen before."[4] That pivotal experience moved him beyond his momentary doubt to a firm belief in God and in an underlying unity of being—a belief that would persist until his death.

The fleeting quality of drug-induced euphoric fugues sparked a deeper longing for a communion with the God he came to know as Love. Within two years, Harrison would give up psychedelics and become a serious student of Indian music and culture under the tutelage of Ravi Shankar, and of meditation practices under Maharishi Mahesh Yogi. His music in the late 1960s through the 70s blended influences from gospel, rock, and Indian classical genres in ways that still speak to both fans belonging to a variety of religious traditions and those belonging to none.

---

2. The Beatles, *The Beatles Anthology* (Chronicle Books, 2000), 177.
3. See Thomas Merton, *Conjectures of a Guilty Bystander* (Image, 1968; first published by Doubleday, 1966), 156–59. The original journal entry draft is recorded in Merton, *A Search for Solitude*, ed. Lawrence S. Cunningham (HarperCollins, 1996), 181–82.
4. Quoted in Steve Turner, *The Gospel According to the Beatles* (Westminster John Knox, 2006), 16.

In this chapter, I first frame Harrison's spiritual journey in *Sanskrit* terms, as an accelerated shot through the *purusharthas:*[5] briefly seeking happiness in *dharma* (living dutifully within societally prescribed constraints), then in *kama* (sensual pleasure) and *artha* (wealth and fame), only to discover the ephemeral nature of their rewards. Finally, disillusioned, he turned with ardent yearning toward the blissful peace of *moksha*, "liberation" from all snares and illusions, from all the idols that turn out to be empty.[6] Next, I seek to understand that journey from within a theological tradition open to affirming what is true and good in it, but also equipped to address its difficulties. Harrison's journey, I suggest, proves valuable, not because it offers a model to follow, but because it bears witness, in its own fascinating way, to "the true light, which enlightens everyone" (John 1:9).[7] I close the chapter with an anecdotal illustration of how Harrison's lyrics can offer a language of prayer for modern pilgrims, even Catholic ones.

## Ditching *Dharma* and Losing His Religion (1943–1959)

The German *Luftwaffe* decimated Liverpool just before George Harrison was born there on February 25, 1943.[8] War would

---

5.  The four legitimate "aims of life" recognized by Hindus.
6.  Using this frame as a literary device helps to illustrate the organizing values that conditioned Harrison's priorities at different points in his life. However, the framing should not suggest clean demarcations; he never renounced all pleasures, nor did he relinquish all his riches, and in the last decade of his life, he tended to the conventional duties of marriage and fatherhood more than he had in previous years.
7.  Vatican II's document *Nostra Aetate* employs this passage to frame its discussion of non-Christian religions and to affirm that they "often reflect a ray of that Truth which enlightens all men [*sic*]" (*NA*, 2).
8.  "The Liverpool Blitz" transpired intermittently between 1940 and 1942. See "The Blitz on Merseyside," E. Chambré Hardman Archive, https://web.archive.org/web/20120612082511/http://

continue for two more years, and its aftermath cast a lengthy shadow over the working-class town, where mandated rationing continued until 1954.[9] Often called "the most Catholic city in England," Liverpool hosted a large population of Irish immigrants. Three of the four scousers[10] who would become Beatles had Irish last names, but did not grow up in observantly Catholic homes. Harrison, the only one with an English name, had an Irish Catholic mother who made sure that he did. Louise Harrison had her son baptized as an infant, and at age 11, he received his first Holy Communion. Though indelibly impressed by his mother's devotion to the Sacred Heart, young George was not so impressed by "the Church."

As a pre-teen, George began to dress in Teddy boy[11] fashion and to learn to play guitar in the style of jazz legend Django Reinhardt. Louise, a music enthusiast herself, encouraged her son's passion. By the time George turned thirteen he had met Paul McCarthey at school. Paul, who was a bit older, was already in a band called the Quarrymen with John Lennon, a student at the Liverpool College of Art. Eventually, when Paul learned

---

www.mersey-gateway.org/server.php?show=ConNarrative.153, accessed on October 20, 2021.

9.   Ina Zweiniger-Bargielowska, "Rationing, Austerity and the Conservative Party Recovery after 1945," *The Historical Journal* 37.1 (1994), 173–97.

10.  "Scouser" is a term for someone from Liverpool.

11.  The Teddy boys, or "Teds," were working class dropouts who donned jackets and ties, drainpipe pants, and "brothel creeper" socks. Like the Beats in the U.S., only more violent and nativist, the Teds in Liverpool represented non-conformity and a rebellious impulse. It was not their anti-immigrant nativism that attracted George, but the music they listened to, their blues, jazz, and rock and roll. The defiance, vibrancy, and raw sensuality of that sound spoke to him and symbolized an alternative to the world of his elders, a world that, for George, had crumbled along with the bombed-out churches of Liverpool. See Mitch Mitchell, "A brief history of the Teddy Boys," in *Revolutionary Socialism in the 21st Century*, February 19, 2019, https://www.rs21.org.uk/2019/02/19/a-brief-history-of-the-teddy-boys/.

that George had some prowess on the guitar, he introduced him to John, who invited George to join the band. George was then fifteen and the Quarrymen were playing the Cavern Club in Liverpool to growing crowds. At sixteen, George dropped out of school and began working as an electrician's apprentice during the day and playing the Cavern at night. The music, however, soon overshadowed everything, and he quit his day job.

Along with his schoolbooks and his tool belt, George dropped his church. Catholic theologians like Pope Benedict and Cardinal Dulles have lamented the fact that for many pre-conciliar Catholics "the Church" was something other than the laity, exclusively clerical, and it seems to have been that way for young George.[12] Speaking of the Church, he told biographer Graeme Thomson " . . . they blind you with ignorance, like a government does, as if [the Church's] power . . . has become reason enough for you not to question anything it says. It's like, 'You don't know anything about Christ and God because we're the ones who own the franchise.'"[13] In another interview, Harrison stated, "They tried to make me a Catholic" and "They told you to just believe what *they're* telling you" without question and without appealing to any experience.[14]

Although drawn to the Christ engraved in the Stations of the Cross, George was put off, even as a child, by what seemed

---

12. Dulles discusses this "institutionalist ecclesiology" as an aberration that "identifies the Church itself with the governing body or hierarchy" so that the laity become passive recipients of the Church's teaching, sacraments, and governance. See *Models of the Church* (Doubleday, 1974), 34. In "The Ecclesiology of Vatican II" Cardinal Ratzinger (later Pope Benedict XVI) wrote, "If until that time we had thought of the Church primarily as a structure or organization, now at last we began to realize that we ourselves were the Church." The full text is available here: https://www.ewtn.com/catholicism/library/ecclesiology-of-vatican-ii-2069.

13. Graeme Thomson, *George Harrison: Behind the Locked Door* (London: Omnibus Press, 2016), 11.

14. *Anthology*, 233. See also *George Harrison: Living in the Material World*, Martin Scorsese (Grove Street Productions, 2011).

to him to be the prevalence of hypocrisy. He was annoyed when the parish priest would go door to door asking parishioners for cash and George's mother, hardly scraping by, would "stuff two crowns in his sweaty little hand and off he'd go to build another church."[15] Harrison said:

> [O]n every corner they'd have a church and on the other corner a pub. Everybody's out there getting pissed and then just goes in the church, says three Hail Marys and one Our Father and sticks a fiver in the plate. It felt so alien to me. . . . I just didn't like the bullshit. After Communion, I was supposed to have Confirmation, but I thought, "I'm not going to bother with that, I'll just confirm it later myself."[16]

## Exhausting *Kama* and *Artha* (1960–1967)

In 1960, George was seventeen and in Hamburg, Germany, for his band's first tour. They stayed in a room behind the Bambi Kino porn theater while they performed at the Indra and Kaiserkeller Clubs.[17] Beatles biographer Hunter Davies claimed that this section of the city, on and around the Reeperbahn, "had more strip clubs" than anywhere else in the world.[18] At first, the Beatles barely made ends meet, but as George said, "being right in the middle of the naughtiest city in the world . . . was kind of exciting."[19] Pete Best, who played drums on that tour, recalled, "We got drunk a lot . . . [and] we had a lot of girls."[20] While the bandmates sought pleasure in squalid conditions, some

---

15. Scorsese, *Material World*.
16. *Anthology*, 26.
17. Scorsese, *Material World*.
18. Hunter Davies, *The Beatles: The Authorized Biography* (McGraw-Hill, 1968), 75.
19. Scorsese, *Material World*.
20. Davies, *The Beatles*, 77.

money began to roll in. The five Beatles[21] were collectively making close to thirteen pounds a day, about two and half pounds apiece—more in a day than George had made in a week as an apprentice electrician, and more than George's father made as a bus driver back in Liverpool.[22]

In 1962, just before their second Hamburg tour, the Beatles signed a management contract with Brian Epstein. Stuart Sutcliffe had quit the band and by November of that year Ringo Starr had replaced Pete Best on the drums. The "Fab Four" would soon make far more money in under a decade than most people would in an entire lifetime, or even ten. Early Beatles hits like "Please Please Me" and "Money (That's What I Want)"[23] were celebratory anthems to pleasure and mammon, and their fame grew so great that their very presence could cause fans to faint or riot. There are even reports of families bringing their lame and crippled loved ones to receive blessings from a Beatle in hopes of a cure.[24] This sounds like hagiographical hyperbole, but it is not.

The relentless attention, however, was annoying and oppressive. Harrison, sometimes called "the quiet Beatle," did not want to be idolized and felt alienated from his public image.[25] As early as 1964, Beatles songs like "I'm a Loser" and "Can't Buy Me Love" began to signal a realization that fame fed falsity and that the love they longed for was much more than a commodity.

---

21. At this point the band was comprised of Lennon, McCartney, Harrison, Stuart Sutcliffe, and Pete Best.
22. Joshua M. Greene, *Here Comes the Sun: The Spiritual and Musical Journey of George Harrison* (Hoboken, NJ: Wiley, 2006), 42. See also Matt Adomeit, "The Fascinating History of the Beatles in Hamburg," available at https://www.iamexpat.de/lifestyle/lifestyle-news/fascinating-history-beatles-hamburg.
23. John Lennon wrote "Please Please Me," which became the title track of their first LP. Berry Gordy, Jr., and William Robinson, Jr., wrote "Money (That's What I Want)"; Barrett Strong recorded the song in 1959 and the Beatles recorded their version in 1963.
24. Greene, *Here Comes the Sun*, 49.
25. Scorsese, *Material World*.

Meanwhile, the idea that one could consume a substance and subsequently experience God was part of the atmosphere of the 1960s counterculture. Acid, though by no means a mainstream drug, was still legal before 1968 and its usage since the publication of Huxley's *The Doors of Perception* (1954) had been growing. In 1962, Alan Watts published *The Joyous Cosmology: Adventures in the Chemistry of Consciousness*; both of these books emphasized points of convergence between psychedelic experiences and the accounts of a transcendent, non-dual reality found in contemplative traditions of all stripes, but especially Eastern ones. In 1965, the Beatles began experimenting with LSD, and George claimed that his experience with acid, at least initially, gave him "the realization of God."[26] It led him to a firm belief that God was real, and that anything other than God was ultimately illusory. That same year he began exploring Eastern philosophy and experimenting with the sitar.

The first two Harrison songs that the Beatles recorded which revealed his growing interest in the East were "Love You To" (1966) and "Within You Without You" (1967). The first is a reflection on the impermanence of life with a corresponding urgency to "make love all day long" and "make love singing songs"—still transparently revealing the writer's aim as *kama*. The second, however, is a more sober evocation of a *universal* love, a love that "we all could share" and that can "save the world." It hints at a need for repentance—for a change in the direction of our search for fulfillment. Alluding to the words of Christ, Harrison cautions the people who "gain the world" yet "lose their soul[s]"[27] by getting trapped in selfish desires. Instead, he concludes "When you've seen beyond yourself then you may find / Peace of mind is waiting there / And the time will come when you see we're all one / And life flows on within you and without you." Perhaps one reason the second song begins to link mortification with mysticism is that it comes after Harrison had spent six weeks in Mumbai (then known as

26. *Anthology*, 263.
27. Cf. Mark 8:36.

Bombay to the English-speaking world) doing formal study of the sitar with Ravi Shankar, practicing yoga, and reading the works of Swami Vivekananda.[28]

Harrison's fascination with Indian music and culture continued to grow, but his excitement over the promises of LSD utterly vanished after visiting Haight-Ashbury in August of 1967 with his first wife, Pattie Boyd. The Haight was the epicenter of hippie culture, and the Harrisons expected to find a utopian oasis there, where peace, love, and understanding abounded and creativity flourished. Instead, they saw many "spotty youths" aimlessly addicted to hedonistic pursuits. Boyd recalled, "It was horrible, full of ghastly drop-outs . . . all out of their brains. Everybody looked stoned—even mothers and babies."[29] Harrison said, "It showed me what was really happening in the drug culture. . . . That was a turning point for me—that's when I went right off of the whole drug cult and stopped taking the dreaded lysergic acid."[30] On their flight from San Francisco to Monterey, they encountered terrible turbulence and George saw lights flashing "DANGER" on the pilot's control panel.

---

28. In September of 1966 George and Pattie Boyd went to India to learn more about yoga and so that George could get some formal training on the sitar from Ravi Shankar. Through Shankar, Harrison learned that practicing *yama*, self-restraint, chastity, and cultivating awareness of one's total dependence on God were essential foundations for realizing union with God. Raju Shankar, Ravi's brother, gave Harrison of copy of Vivekananda's *Raja Yoga* (originally published in 1896). Vivekananda's exegesis of the *Chandogya Upanishad* strengthened Harrison's conviction that one could realize the union of *atman* (soul, or one's immanent reality) with *Brahman* (the ultimate reality, as it is transcendent). Swami Vivekananda was a disciple of Sri Ramakrishna and a cultural ambassador of India. He attended the Parliament of World Religions in Chicago in 1893. See *Here Comes the Sun*, 69, and *Anthology*, 233.
29. Pattie Boyd, *Wonderful Tonight: George Harrison, Eric Clapton, and Me* (New York: Crown, 2008), 98.
30. *Anthology*, 259.

He initially felt that this was the end, and he started chanting "Om, Christ, Om."[31] However, as the plane stabilized, he sensed a providential confirmation of the dangers of drugs and an impulse to seek God, or enlightenment, in more disciplined, ascetic ways.[32]

## Aiming for *Moksha* (beyond 1967)

After the disillusioning experience in San Francisco, Harrison's commitment to yogic practice and meditation intensified. Later in August 1967, the Beatles attended a meditation seminar in Wales hosted by Maharishi Mahesh Yogi, and though they had to cut their time short due to the death of Brian Epstein,[33] the lads initially remained determined to continue formal training and practice. In February of 1968, they journeyed to Rishikesh in northern India to participate in a Transcendental Meditation course conducted at the Maharishi's *ashram* (hermitage). George focused on the meditation and progressed admirably. John Lennon said, "The way George is going, he'll be flying a magic carpet by the time he's forty."[34]

After Rishikesh, the Maharishi—who was able to extend the reach of his ministry because he had become the guru to the Beatles, the Beach Boys, and other artists and celebrities—came under scrutiny in the press as a charlatan. Rumors of sexual misconduct, which Harrison and Lennon initially believed, but which Harrison later dismissed as unsubstantiated, created a rift. In an undated letter to his mother, Harrison wrote:

---

31. Ibid.
32. Scorsese, *Material World*. Note, however, that even though Haight-Ashbury changed George's attitude toward LSD, it did not make him renounce all drug use. Alcohol and cocaine became a problem for him, temporarily, on his Dark Horse tour in 1974. See Thomson, *Behind the Locked Door*, 281–82.
33. Brian Epstein died on August 27, 1967, of a drug overdose. He was 33 years old.
34. Greene, *Here Comes the Sun*, 95.

Don't think anything negative about Maharishi. He's not a phony. It's only the shit written about him that's phony. . . . All he's doing is teaching us how to contact God. And as God is not divided into different sects . . . it does not affect my dedication to Sacred Heart in any way. It only strengthens it. . . . Don't think that I've gone off my rocker because I haven't. But I now love you and everybody else much more than ever. So it's not that bad, is it?[35]

By the end of 1970 the members of the Beatles had liberated themselves from the group. The factors contributing to their breakup are too numerous to recount, but the dissolution likely started in the early wake of Brian Epstein's death. The formal end, however, came in December 1970 when Paul McCartney filed suit to dissolve the partnership. Though Harrison's relationship with the Maharishi was temporarily strained after the Rishikesh retreat, his devotion to Eastern wisdom and practice continued unabated. He found a new community with the International Society for Krishna Consciousness founded by Swami Prabhupada, and in August of 1970 he invited members of the Radha Krishna Temple in London to record "Hare Krishna Mantra" at Apple studios.[36] In November of the same year, George released *All Things Must Pass*, a triple album containing many previously unrecorded compositions from his days as a Beatle, and many that reflected his fascination with Hinduism. The project's most successful song, "My Sweet Lord," is a *bhajan*, or devotional song, that blends familiar gospel refrains (My Sweet Lord, Hallelujah) with Hindu devotional chants (Hare Krishna, Gurur Brahma, Gurur Vishnu). Remarking on the song, George said, "I wanted to show that 'Hallelujah' and 'Hare Krishna' are quite the same thing. . . . I don't feel guilty about it, in fact it

35. Scorsese, *Material World*.
36. Gary Tillery, *Working Class Mystic: A Spiritual Biography of George Harrison* (Quest Books, 2011), 72–3, 161.

saved many a heroin addict's life . . . and its effect far exceeded the legal hassle."[37]

While George's solo career was taking off, Ravi Shankar called on him to put his celebrity status at the service of human suffering. What was happening in Bangladesh was a full-scale humanitarian disaster,[38] but it remained only a peripheral concern for many Europeans and Americans—until Harrison agreed to help. Harrison and Shankar put together a star-studded benefit concert at Madison Square Garden, which included appearances by Ringo Starr, Bob Dylan, Eric Clapton, and others; they also produced an album and a film documenting the event. All told, they raised in excess of 12 million dollars and collaborated with UNICEF to distribute the aid to victims of the crisis.[39]

Harrison's next album, *Living in the Material World* (1973), continued voicing his beliefs and sharing his prayers. The song "Give Me Love (Give Me Peace on Earth)" is characteristic, and Harrison called it "a prayer and a personal statement between me, the Lord, and whoever likes it."[40] By 1974, however, his confidence in the dawning of a new age of peace and love was beginning to wane. The war in Vietnam continued, Bangladesh was still suffering, and George's first marriage was coming apart. His next album, *Dark Horse* (1974), and the tour that followed, disappointed many critics and fans. The title track is Harrison's confession, directed to Pattie Boyd, that he had never been

37. George Harrison, *I, Me, Mine* (Chronicle Books, 2007), 176. The "legal hassle" refers to the plagiarism lawsuit brought by the publisher of the Chiffons' 1963 hit "He's So Fine" that Harrison lost.
38. The Bengalis were largely Hindu citizens of what was Pakistan's eastern region. After decades of marginalization, they declared independence from Pakistan on March 26, 1971. The resultant war included genocidal retribution from Pakistani forces; its devastation was compounded by famine and a refugee crisis.
39. Alan Clayson, *George Harrison* (Sanctuary, 2003), 308.
40. Harrison, *I, Me, Mine*, 246.

faithful to her.[41] On the Dark Horse Tour, Harrison abused cocaine and brandy and broke off his religious practice.[42]

His marriage to Pattie Boyd officially ended in 1977, and she married Eric Clapton in 1979. George married Olivia Trinidad Arias, following the birth of their son, Dhani, in 1978. Through the 80s and 90s George continued to create music as a solo artist and then with his supergroup, the Traveling Wilburys. At the same time, he returned to his daily practice of meditation, chanting *bhajan*, and frequenting his gardens. In 1990, Olivia started the Romanian Angel Appeal to provide aid to children orphaned by violence after the deposing of Romania's communist leader, Nicolae Ceausescu. George supported Olivia's relief work, and he produced the charity album *Nobody's Child* to raise money for the project.

In 1997, Harrison was diagnosed with throat cancer; radiation treatments initially rendered promising results. In 1999, however, "a deranged fan" broke into the Harrisons' Friar Park home and "stabbed Harrison through a lung" before Olivia subdued the attacker.[43] The number of times Harrison was actually stabbed remains unclear, and internet reports range from four to forty.[44] Cuts deep enough to count as stab wounds, however, are likely on the low side, but the one to his chest

41. Harrison said, "Dark Horse is the old story. 'Mr. Penguin's poking Mrs. Johnson from the Co-Op.' 'Oh really! Who'd have thought that—he's a bit of a dark horse isn't he?' I didn't know 'til later the other idea of a dark horse—the one that wins that nobody has put any money on. I'm a bit thick really" (*I, Me, Mine, 288*).
42. Thomson, *Behind the Locked Door*, 282.
43. Brian Hiatt, "The Private Life of George Harrison," *Rolling Stone*, September 15, 2011, https://www.rollingstone.com/feature/the-private-life-of-george-harrison-238017/.
44. *Rolling Stone* reported the number at four (see https://www.rollingstone.com/music/music-news/harrison-back-at-home-after-attack-250092/), and Cheatsheet.com claims it was forty. See https://www.cheatsheet.com/entertainment/former-beatle-george-harrison-survived-near-fatal-stabbing-aide-changed-him.html/.

resulted in serious damage. Dhani continues to suspect that it weakened his father's ability to fight the cancer that attacked Harrison's lungs and brain in early 2001.[45] Though Harrison had hoped for more time on this earth to be there for his son, his friends and family testify that he was at peace when his death finally arrived on November 29, 2001. Olivia said, "George lit the room" when he died.[46]

## Seeking to Understand George's Faith

As a self-styled non-conformist, George's journey was, technically speaking, heterodox. It would therefore be unfair to both Catholic Christians and Vaishnavite Hindus to look to Harrison as a reliable representative for either tradition. Nonetheless, Harrison was a person of deep faith, as much Christ-haunted as he was salvation-seeking.[47] To recognize him as such is to acknowledge an important distinction between faith and belief, or as Paul Tillich would put it, between the subjective aspect of being grasped by ultimate concern and one's objectified, formulated beliefs about such.[48] Without this distinction, one could read George's adolescent rejection of his belief in the "man in the sky" as a loss of faith; in light of it, one can see this

---

45. Hiatt, "The Private Life of George Harrison."
46. Scorsese, *Material World.*
47. Andrew Ferguson wrote: "Religious devotion of the most intimate sort pre-occupied him, and his oscillation between guilt and redemption had a Catholic look to it." See "George's God," *Washington Examiner,* November 21, 2011, https://www.washingtonexaminer.com/weekly-standard/georges-god.
48. Tillich defined faith as "the state of being grasped by ultimate concern" and he referenced Deut 6:5 to illustrate what surrender to the subject/object of ultimate concern meant. Tillich, *The Dynamics of Faith* (1957). Vincent Williams provides a helpful summary of Tillich's understanding of the relationship between faith, doubt, and belief in his article "Paul Tillich on the Nature of Faith" on his blog *Curating Theology.*

rejection as a symptom of the doubt inexorably tied to being grasped by an ultimate concern. When one is concerned with the ultimate, one begins to doubt whether a finite "concept" can be of spiritual service, or whether it will turn into an idol that serves to separate.

As Vatican II acknowledged, sometimes the non-believer has "such a faulty notion of God that when they disown this product of their imagination their denial has no reference to the true God" (*GS*, 19). When George was asked whether the word "God" had changed its meaning since he began practicing meditation, he said, "It means all sorts of things to me. I mean, the first concept of a man in the sky, well, I kicked that . . . years ago, but I've got back to that now, because it's a man in the sky as well if you like. . . . It's everything, every aspect of creation is part of God."[49] If George's brief stint as an agnostic corresponded with his kicking the concept of God as a "man in the sky" to the curb, well, who would cast a stone over his lost allegiance to that puerile image?[50] It may just be, as James Fowler would say, that George's mythic-literal faith from early childhood had temporarily failed to mature along with him.[51]

---

49. Scorsese, *Material World*. George's assertion here can sound pantheistic, and maybe that is how he intended it, but his use of the term "creation" pushes back against pantheism. Saying that every aspect of creation is part of God can imply a sacramental view of creation, insofar as creation is of God and in God. For example, Aquinas's assertion that creation has no being *per se*, but only in relation to God, compels a sacramental view of creation (*Summa Theologica*, Q45, A. 2).

50. At the beginning of the third episode of his *Catholicism* series, Bishop Robert Barron recalls conversations he has had with non-believers in which he discovered that the images of God they are rejecting are images he himself rejects. Yet he does not discount the possibility that in those "atheists" is a hunger for truth, a concern for the ultimate, that is sincere. *Catholicism* DVD series, WordOnFire.org (2010).

51. See James Fowler's *Stages of Faith: The Psychology of Human Development and the Quest for Meaning* (HarperSanFrancisco,

It was, in fact, George's inability to *understand* his mother's Catholicism, along with his negative perceptions of the institutional Church, that moved him out of it. "I was raised a Catholic," he said, "but even as a kid I couldn't understand the claim that Jesus was the only Son of God when, in fact, we all are."[52] Given that George experienced the Church as discouraging any questions, he likely never asked for any clarification of what was meant by that claim—how being "eternally begotten before all ages" might differ from our "being begotten" temporally through the gift of God's love (1 John 4:7)—but George's affection for Jesus never seemed to waiver. Still, the question of *how* he understood Jesus is a difficult one.

It seems to me that George's Christology was not so much shaped by an understanding of dogmas and the contexts that influenced their formulations, but more so by the way devotion to Jesus had been assimilated in the context of Hindu culture. That is to say, he did not read Hinduism through the lens of a well-formed Christological hermeneutic, as Thomas Merton, Bede Griffiths, Jacques Dupuis, or Raimon Panikkar might have;[53] rather he came to interpret Jesus through a monistic lens.

Such an approach appears to embrace a Monophysite or Docetic Christology, denying the hypostatic *union* of two natures in the one Christ and the reality of his physical body. However, while both Monophysites and Docetists were concerned with securing Christ's divinity as a *difference* over and against the humanity of mere mortals (seeing aspects of that humanity as irredeemably opposed to divinity), monists intend to affirm his *sameness* with mortals. For monists, in terms of nature, or substance, God alone is. From this point of view, Jesus is different not as a matter of substance but as the enlightened differs from

---

1981), 135–50.

52. Greene, *Here Comes the Sun*, 6.

53. See Peter C. Phan, "Multiple Religious Belonging: Opportunities and Challenges for Theology and Church," *Theological Studies* 64 (2003), 495–519, especially 504–16.

the unenlightened, as an *arhat*[54] differs from those bound by karmic entanglements.

Jacques Dupuis, in his seminal work *Jesus Christ at the Encounter of World Religions*, discerned six different types of Christologies among Hindus who exhibit deep devotion to Jesus.[55] In these models, there are Christologies from above and from below, but they are rendered against a background not of Jerusalem and Athens but of Mumbai and Kolkata. Jesus, no doubt, has many friends among the Hindus, but as Dupuis noted, "It is perfectly possible for Hindu[s] to integrate Jesus into [their] vision of the world and reality—to assimilate him— without necessarily involving faith in Jesus Christ *as Christianity understands that faith*," thus making it easy to befriend and follow Jesus without joining his church.[56] Even George's guru, Maharishi Mahesh Yogi, had immense fondness for Jesus, claiming "I love Christ very much," though he worried that Christianity tended to foreground the crucifixion to the point where Christ's message about finding the kingdom, becoming like children, etc., could fall into the background.[57]

---

54. *Arhat* (never-returner) refers to a person who is no longer bound to "again becoming." One who attains moksha/nirvana has become eternal.
55. These are: the *ethical* model of Jesus as a proponent of non-vi- olence (Mahatma Gandhi); the *devotional* model of Jesus as the perfect union of humanity and divinity (Keshub Chandra Sen); the *philosophical* model of Jesus as the highest stage of humanity's evolution toward its highest realization (Sarvepalli Radhakrish- nan); the *theological* model of Jesus as an incarnation of Brah- man (Swami Akhilananda); the *ascetical* model of Jesus as a yogi (Manilal C. Parekh); and the *mystical* model of Jesus as a guru (Brahmabandhab Upadhyaya). See Dupuis, *Jesus Christ at the En- counter of World Religions* (New York: Orbis Books 1989), 18–42.
56. Ibid., 17, italics added.
57. See the interview with Maharishi Mahesh Yogi recorded on No- vember 23, 1971, in Mallorca, Spain. Available on YouTube as "Maharishi on Christ and Meditation."

Since Catholics such as Abhishiktananda,[58] Aloysius Pieris,[59] and others could immerse themselves in the wisdom of India, and affirm it, while retaining their own Catholic faith, it raises the question of whether Harrison could have done the same had he any theological training. The hypothetical is unanswerable, but it is important to understand that George was barely a teenager, hardly even catechized, when he turned away from the Tiber and journeyed toward the Ganges. Nonetheless, his Catholic tradition could have aided him, I suspect, in dispelling the vestiges of dualism that seemed to surface when he talked about "the material world."

According to Olivia, George would frequently remind Dhani, "you are not your body," and speak of his own death as a release from the body and from the material world.[60] Such apparent disregard for material existence can seem Manichean, a point made by Andrew Ferguson, who described Harrison as a "a rock star buried in a pile of cocaine one minute and a *sadhu* renunciant fingering his beads the next."[61] But to be a Manichean is not simply to distinguish matter and spirit, but to reify each as an eternal existent locked in primordial conflict as an irreducible *two*; this is not Shankara's *advaita*,[62] nor is it

---

58. Swami Abhishiktananda (Henri le Saux, 1910–1973) was a Benedictine monk who moved to India in 1948 and became a serious student of *Advaita Vedanta* and later founded an ashram. See *Swami Abhishiktananda: Essential Writings*, ed. Shirley du Boulay (New York: Orbis Books, 2006).
59. Aloysius Pieris is a Sri Lankan Jesuit priest and theologian and the founding director of the Tulana Research Center for Encounter and Dialogue. See Pieris, *Fire and Water: Basic Issues in Asian Buddhism and Christianity* (New York: Orbis Books, 1988).
60. Scorsese, *Material World*.
61. Ferguson, "George's God."
62. *Advaita* (Sanskrit for "not-two" or non-dual) is the experience in which all separations dissolve, are recognized as illusory, between subject and object, perceiver and perceived, etc. Shankara (788–820), the chief proponent of *Advaita Vedanta* philosophy, advocated for a radical monism that ultimately denies all differences, so that distinctions themselves become meaningless. See the en-

fair to dismiss George as a dualist. George imagined that matter was mere *maya* (illusion) and spirit was God (Ultimate Reality) in a way that *did* oppose the two, but he remained monist, not dualist, in his belief that the latter eliminates the former for the *arhat*, who realizes identity as "the One without a second." For, if one of two contraries be absolute, the other is annihilated. The Christian tradition, however, not only affirms the reality of matter, but beholds it sacramentally, not as a *contrary* existing independently in competition with God, but as an outpouring of God's grace, as being contingent upon the absolute, incapable of existing on its own. The material world is not mere illusion, but a reality that subsists contingently upon the Absolute. The Incarnation and the Resurrection reveal the eschatological indissolubility of matter and spirit as a non-dual unity (not separate), but George never appeared to go that far.

Harrison evinced, in later years, a conciliatory posture toward the religion of his boyhood, beginning to find again in the reconciling wonder of *advaita* a non-duality between the wisdom of the *Upanishads* and the religious tradition that first shaped him. Whatever evidence we have of any integration he achieved, however, suggests that while his foray into Eastern wisdom traditions proved personally advantageous in his own search for God, it was not catholic enough, that is to say not inclusive enough, for him to affirm the *advaita* that ultimately obtains between the spiritual and the material a non-dual unification that preserves rather than annihilates.[63]

In his song "The Light That Has Lighted the World," George sings "I'm grateful to anyone / That is happy or 'free' / For giving

---

tries for "Advaita" and "Shankara" in *Oxford Concise Dictionary of World Religions*, ed. John Bowker (Oxford University Press, 2000).

63. It is important to recognize that non-monistic interpretations of *advaita* exist within Hindu traditions. Tantric and Shaivistic interpretations of *advaita*, such as those Abhishiktananda utilizes in his reading, emphasize that the denial of separateness does not equate with a denial of all distinctions. See John Glenn Friesen's *Abhishiktananda's Non-Monistic Advaitic Experience* (PhD Dissertation, University of South Africa, 2002).

me hope / While I'm looking to see / The light that has lighted the world." I have no idea if he intended a reference to John 1:9–10—"The true light, which enlightens everyone, was coming into the world. He was in the world, and the world came into being through him; yet the world did not know him."—but it seems clear that George was sincerely seeking that Light and had, at times, glimpsed it.

## Mary's Funeral: A Post-script

In September of 2011, I attended the funeral Mass of Mary Talaga, a dear family friend who had died of cancer. During a meditative interlude after Holy Communion, her son John, his daughters, and two of his nieces, performed George Harrison's song "Give Me Love (Give Me Peace on Earth)." Now, I am neither a priest nor a liturgist, but I am aware that the use of this song in this way would likely offend some liturgical sensibilities since it was not composed for liturgical use and its sacred object is ambiguous.[64] Nonetheless, on this day I found it incredibly moving. "Give me love, give me love / Give me peace on earth." It was a mantra oddly reminiscent of the hymn "Take, Lord, Receive"—only more intimate in this context.[65] The significance was in the yearning for ultimate fulfillment in Love, for freedom from the heavy load of life's burdens. Later, I asked John about his decision to sing Harrison's song, and not surprisingly, his answer was intensely personal.

I had already known that Mary and her late husband, Tom, were both Beatles fans and that their kids, while growing up, played Beatles records in the basement with near reverence, wonder, and awe. What I learned, however, was that throughout

---

64. The Church provides general guidelines for sacred music. Some of the most important documents are: Pius XII, *Musicae Sacrae* (December 25, 1955); and Second Vatican Council, *Sacrosanctum Concilium,* Chapter VI (December 4, 1963).
65. "Take, Lord, Receive" was written by the St. Louis Jesuits and first recorded on their *Earthen Vessels* album (1975).

the week before Mary's death, John and his siblings had been holding vigil at her bedside. Because of the advanced stage of her illness, she had become non-communicative. When John briefly left her side to run an errand, he got in his car and "Give Me Love" began to play on the radio. "At that moment," John said, "I immediately heard the lyrics as if my mom were speaking." It seemed providential, that the lyrics could be her prayer. John was overcome with emotion. "Give me hope, help me cope / With this heavy load / Trying to touch and reach you / With heart and soul." He decided then to sing it for her at her funeral.

In this context, the song was Mary's prayer: seeking final passage into the eternally perfect triune Love of God. I doubt anyone at Mary's funeral was thinking about the line "keep me free from birth" as an allusion to *moksha* as a liberation from *samsara* (the cycle of life, death, and rebirth)—an idea whose corollary in Christianity essentially evaporated with the formal condemnation of Origen of Alexandria's teachings on reincarnation.[66] Still, the basic belief that complete liberation may take more than a single earthly lifespan undergirds the hope that even though we die still woefully imperfect, an opportunity for post-mortem purification awaits. Hindus conceive it as another birth allowing another opportunity to cleanse karmic residue; for Catholics, the purgation transpires beyond the constraints of calendar dates, of births and deaths. The overall sentiment and message of the song, however, concerns the desire for ultimate fulfillment in loving union with God. The faith and hope that such desire will find fulfillment is perfectly appropriate for a funeral. For Mary and George, then, and all the faithful departed, "Eternal rest grant unto them, O Lord, and let perpetual light shine upon them. May they rest in peace. Amen."

---

66. On Origen's teaching and its condemnation see Charles Stang, Harvard Divinity School's Price Lecture "Flesh and Fire: Reincarnation and Universal Salvation in the Early Church" (2019), https://hds.harvard.edu/news/2019/03/19/flesh-and-fire-reincarnation-and-universal-salvation-early-church.

# "Resurrection Waits Within":
## The Accidental Orthodoxy of Judee Sill

Dawn Eden Goldstein

Gnosticism, with its distaste for embodiedness, came naturally to Judee Sill. As a teenager, bearing the wounds of a childhood spent in an abusive household, she sought solace through drugs—first marijuana, then LSD, and finally heroin. Her addictions in turn led her to suffer further trauma as she ran with criminals, underwent arrests and jail time, and—in a desperate bid to feed her heroin habit—prostituted herself. In 1972, looking back at her heroin abuse from a few years' distance, Sill told *Rolling Stone*, "I see why people got hooked: the opiates afford an exclusive type of relief for people who have a certain quality in their unhappiness. It's a kind of horror of air on your flesh."[1]

Sill's interest in the ancient gnostic heresy—which she encountered in the late 1960s through her studies of Rosicrucianism, Theosophy, and Carl Jung—thus served a psychological function for her. It provided her with a rationale for her longing to be freed from a body capable of feeling. As a fellow survivor of abuse, I can relate to that longing, even though I found my answer to it in the Catholic faith that Sill herself cast aside as a youth.[2]

---

1.    This quote is from a transcription on a Judee Sill fan website of an article listed simply as "Rolling Stone, March 2, 1972" (no author or headline given). See kneeling.co.uk/pages/jsill/rollingstone.php.

2.    Strangely, although nearly every review of Sill's music describes it as having religious content, it does not appear that any account of her life mentions the faith tradition in which she was raised. Although Sill's parents' religion is unknown, her stepfather Kenneth Lee Muse—who married Sill's mother, Oneta, when Sill was ten—was Catholic. So Sill would likely have been exposed to Catholicism from at least age 10 onward. Additionally, although Oneta's funeral was at a funeral home and not a

Yet Sill's recordings, despite their many explicit references to gnostic spirituality, for me served effectively as *praeambula fidei*. When I discovered her work as a college student in the late 1980s—by which time I had drifted from the Jewish faith of my childhood—it gave me a new language to express my desire for God.

As I grew older, Sill's music, unlike that of many other artists who then struck me as profound (such as Big Star), refused to be consigned to nostalgia for my spiritual adolescence. Instead, her music continued to unfold its wisdom at every stage of my faith journey. Today, thirty-six years after my discovery of Sill—with eight of those years spent pursuing a doctorate in sacred theology—songs of hers that I once appreciated for their unorthodox approach to belief now give voice to my orthodoxy.

## A Religious Artist with a Secular Cult

In saying that Sill's music moves me on a deep spiritual level, I am by no means unique. During the decades since she died at thirty-five in 1979 from a drug overdose, and especially since the internet era made it easy for listeners to hear her after reading critics' rave reviews, Sill has gained recognition as a songwriter's songwriter. Her recordings on YouTube have tallied several million views, which is particularly impressive given that she sold less than one hundred thousand records during her lifetime. Celebrities who admire her, such as Liz Phair, Greta Gerwig, and Fleet Foxes singer Robin Pecknold, are identifiable more by their high level of artistry than by any shared religious affiliation. XTC's Andy Partridge, an atheist with pagan leanings, told *Rolling Stone* in 2021, "Unfortunately, I can't listen to [Sill's] 'The Kiss' anymore because it just presses the 'sob your heart out' button.

Catholic church, the death notice mentions that a rosary was to be prayed there. It is therefore possible that Oneta was Catholic as well, and that she was denied a funeral Mass because she was in an irregular marriage (since Muse was divorced and his first wife was still living).

I'm just destroyed for the next hour. I actually think it's the most beautiful song ever written by anybody."[3]

One afternoon in 1986, I visited the Greenwich Village record shop It's Only Rock 'n' Roll and found a promotional copy of Sill's eponymous debut album in a plain white cover—the original apparently having gone missing long ago. The lack of a cover, as well as Sill's not being a "collectable" artist at the time, was probably why the shop was offering the disc for the rock-bottom price of $1. Sill's name was familiar to me as the writer of the Turtles' minor hit "Lady-O." When I saw that "Lady-O" was listed on the album's label, I figured it was worth the dollar if only to hear the song interpreted by its author.

Upon taking the album back to my dorm room at New York University's Weinstein Hall and dropping the needle on the first track, "Crayon Angels," I immediately recognized that here was no ordinary singer-songwriter. Although the seeming affectation of Sill's Southern-tinged accent grated on me at first (as when she sang "forgit" for "forget"), her astonishingly pure tone was irresistible.

Unlike contemporaries such as Joni Mitchell or Judy Collins, Sill did not seem interested in accentuating her vulnerability or her *eros* in a feminine manner. But neither did she seek to project the aggressive genderbending force of a Janis Joplin. Her singing style has been compared to the presentation style of a teacher or professor. There's no vibrato and no theatrics—just a plaintive voice crying out in the wilderness about the "one truth [that] survives death's silent starkness" ("My Man on Love").

A great deal more could be said, particularly within a religious context, about Sill's talent as a composer, arranger, and musician. While in college she became fascinated by Pythagorean music. "That's where you learn how to fit rhythms and melodies to emotions," she later explained.[4] Her other musical influences

---

3.    Angie Martoccio, "The Many Lives of Judee Sill," *Rolling Stone*, March 16, 2021, rollingstone.com/music/music-features/judee-sill-songwriter-profile-1130869/.

4.    John Weisman, "She's Given Up Earthly Love for Music," *Detroit*

included Ray Charles, Carmen McRae, and, most of all, Bach. ("I get knocked out by Bach," she told *Rolling Stone*.[5]) But here I wish to focus on her lyrics, because Sill consciously made them carry the burden of her songs' spiritual import. Inside the gatefold sleeve of her first album, alongside the printed lyrics, she gave her fans the dictum, "May you savor each word like a raspberry."

## Judee Sill: Following Her Gnosis

As one who does savor Sill's words, I would like now to analyze lyrics from her two studio albums, *Judee Sill* (1971) and *Heart Food* (1973). My aim is to demonstrate how, even as they employ conceptual categories drawn from neo-gnostic sources, they express a spiritual longing so clearly genuine that they become more orthodox than Sill may have even intended.

Beyond the beauty of its vocals, *Judee Sill*'s leadoff track "Crayon Angels" won me over because its lyrics reflected my own experience as a teenager who felt the absence of the confidence I once had in God's care for me. I knew what Sill meant when she began the song with the words, "Crayon Angel songs are slightly out of tune," for I too, having once drawn crayon angels, now found that their hymns no longer resonated with me. And I, like the singer, having lost that innocent sense of nearness to the divine, was now "waitin' for God" and "hopin' for truth."

But Sill herself was not content to merely pine for lost innocence. In "Crayon Angels," she pondered the reasons why something was off in her perception of the heavenly host. Her conclusion was that she had traded the truth for lies: "Magic rings I made have turned my finger green / . . . Phony prophets stole the only light I knew." Left without "holy visions," she could only hear the angels' laughter in her dreams.

When an interviewer asked her the meaning of the song, Sill began by saying that the "phony prophets" were "astral

---

*Free Press*, June 30, 1972, 6B.
5.  "Rolling Stone, March 2, 1972."

deceptions"—a term she took from her studies of Theosophy. But she added that she intended the song to be hopeful. "The angels know I'm hung up in astral deceptions, and they're laughing at me because they know I'm going to work my way out of it. I don't know it, of course. I'm only 51 percent sure, but at least I'm leaning on the positive side."[6] (She also said in the same interview, "I'm not concerned with astral things because they're cheap thrills.")

In *Judee Sill*'s second track, "The Phantom Cowboy," the songwriter introduces the central character of her *oeuvre*: a lone man on horseback who is vulnerable, courageous, desirable, and just out of reach. Each of the many times he appears in her songs, he bears some resemblance to Christ. However, although Sill did not deny that some of her songs were about Jesus, she saw her "elusive lover" character as being immanent rather than transcendent: "You see, I'm English and Irish, and while my religion is unspeakable, it's not unsingable. . . . The 'elusive lover' in my songs is really my vision of my animus. Every woman [has] an animus; it's your internal male counterpart, just as every man has an anima. It's archetypal. You'll find it in all occult sources."[7]

Sill drew her understanding of her inner *animus* from Jung, particularly from his *Archetypes and the Collective Unconscious*,[8] and it suffused practically the entirety of her debut album. The third track of *Judee Sill* is, in fact, called "The Archetypal Man." Although Sill would later claim she wrote the song about an ex-boyfriend who was not a cowboy but only a garden-variety Los Angeles lawyer,[9] it begins with explicit Jungian animus language: "Fleeter even than Mercury / He flies inside the walls he calls his own." Mercury, under his Greek name of Hermes,

---

6.   Ibid.
7.   Ibid.
8.   C. G. Jung, *The Archetypes and the Collective Unconscious*, 2nd ed. (Princeton, NJ: Princeton University Press, 1968).
9.   Grover Lewis, "Judee Sill: Soldier of the Heart," *Rolling Stone*, April 13, 1972, rollingstone.com/music/music-news/judee-sill-soldier-of-the-heart-233809/.

messenger of the gods, is for Jung the highest level of the animus. He is also one of the gods whose symbolism was appropriated by early Christians; during the time of Roman persecution, statues of Hermes carrying a sheep were used to represent Christ the Good Shepherd.

What follows "The Archetypal Man" is one of Sill's best-loved songs, and certainly one of her most explicitly Christological compositions: "The Lamb Ran Away with the Crown." As she said when introducing it at a concert for the BBC, the song is "about good winning over evil." The protagonist of the song is Sill herself. She strives to rule, bless, and guard her battleground, only to be deceived at every turn by creatures that symbolize (or are) the devil: a "serpent," a "beast," and a "demon." At the climax of each verse, her grand scheme is foiled when she discovers that, while she was distracted by delusions of grandeur, "the lamb ran away with the crown."

Interestingly, as with "Crayon Angels," "The Lamb Ran Away with the Crown" can be read as Sill's self-critique of her occult obsessions. This is particularly evident in the serpent's temptation: "If you try to evoke the spark / You can fly through the dark." The image of the "divine spark" within the human person that longs to be released from its fleshly prison was central to gnostic traditions and was also taken up by Theosophical Society co-founder Helena Blavatsky. In that light, when Sill makes herself out to be a buffoon while the lamb runs away with the crown, she seems to be admitting that her efforts at gnostic self-deification are bound to fail.

*Judee Sill*'s next track, "Lady-O," is among the songwriter's most beautiful and most mysterious works. To a melody that evokes Bach's "Air on the G String" (which was also an inspiration for Procol Harum's "A Whiter Shade of Pale"), Sill sings to a woman who has a "crescent moon" at her feet: "I'll see you in my holiest dreams, Lady-O."

The song's Marian imagery is obvious, and it is interesting in this light to note that Sill was herself born on October 7—the Feast of Our Lady of the Rosary (or, one might say, Lady O' the Rosary). However, "Lady-O" also has other levels of meaning that resist a simple interpretation. It can be seen as a wistful tribute to Sill's mother Oneta, who died of cancer in 1964, when Judee was nineteen. And here too the Jungian imagery is present, as Sill sings, "So on my heels, I'll grow wings"—another apparent reference to her animus, Hermes, known for his winged sandals.

At the close of side one of *Judee Sill* comes Sill's best-known track, produced by Graham Nash: "Jesus Was a Cross Maker." Whenever the songwriter was asked about the song, she was quick to explain that it concerned a failed love affair. "It's not about Jesus. It's about the bandit who ripped me off for my heart. I wrote the song to reconcile my lust and my divine love."[10] At the same time, she added that she genuinely believed that Jesus had manufactured crosses, having read that claim in Nikos Kazantzakis's *The Last Temptation of Christ*. Given her fondness for Gnosticism, it is not surprising that she was attracted to the author's depiction of Jesus as being unable to avoid cooperation with evil. "Kazantzakis touches my heart more than any other author ever touched my heart," she said.[11]

On side two of the album, following another song about the elusive lover/animus ("Ridge Rider"), is a song that Sill told an interviewer "most people have misinterpreted": "My Man on Love." "They don't realize it's about Jesus, because I don't ever say his name in the song," she said.[12] I find it surprising that listeners failed to understand the song, since its lyrics refer explicitly to "agony," "passion," and "resurrection." But perhaps they were distracted by its overarching nuptial spirituality, which, although profoundly biblical, in Sill's hands fits neatly into the love song mold: "One star remains in the false darkness / Have you met my man on love?"

---

10. "Rolling Stone, March 2, 1972."
11. Ibid.
12. The quote is from an interview for Frank H. Lieberman in the Los Angeles *Herald-Examiner*, transcribed online at kneeling. co.uk/pages/jsill/herald.php under "Herald and Examiner" (no headline or date is given).

The nuptial spirituality continues into the third track on side two, "Lopin' Along Thru the Cosmos," in which Sill introduces an image that will loom large in her second album: the divine kiss. Here, too, for the listener familiar with Sill's gnostic leanings, there is a hint of self-critique as she sings, "I'm hopin' so hard for a kiss from God / I missed the sweet love of the air." Could this be the same woman who once identified with "people who have a certain quality in their unhappiness . . . a kind of horror of air on your flesh"? Now she realizes that the "sweet love of the air" is itself a kind of "kiss from God." It is a revelation of God's love through nature akin to that which Lewis Carroll put in the mouth of Alice in chapter one of *Through the Looking-Glass* (which enjoyed wide popularity at the time Sill was writing): "I wonder if the snow *loves* the trees and fields, that it kisses them so gently?"

After "Enchanted Sky Machines," a lighthearted gospel-tinged vision of a rapture in which the titular machines "take all the gentle home," *Judee Sill* closes with another animus song, "Abracadabra." Here her masculine self "fears the great truth / That would free him with its mercy." The answer, she tells him, is to accept "the key to the kingdom" and "See through the eyes that be behind yours."

Sill's explanation of "Abracadabra" to *Rolling Stone* indicates that she had thoroughly absorbed the Jungian concept of "alchemy":

> Abracadabra was originally the term they used in alchemy when they wanted to turn base metals to gold, but that's the lowest form of alchemy. It was really about reaching to open up your heart and eyes to the Christ spirit within us, and to expand it. Those lines refer to the moment when the bottom drops out of your consciousness, the moment of inspiration. It's as if you'd just discovered the you behind the crummy "you" you thought you were stuck with.[13]

---

13. "Rolling Stone, March 2, 1972." I have added the quotation marks around the word "you."

It is not difficult to find in Sill's words the claim put forth by Jung that "Christ himself is the perfect symbol of the hidden immortal within the mortal man."[14]

## Heart Food: A Meal of Mercy

Whereas the lyrical motifs of *Judee Sill*—particularly its "elusive lover" songs—were broad enough that I could listen to the album without feeling as though I were being catechized, I had a considerably different reaction upon hearing her second album, *Heart Food*. When, after some searching, I finally managed to obtain a copy of *Heart Food* in 1988 at an indoor flea market in New Jersey, I listened to it a single time before putting it aside for good—or so I thought. My excuse for dismissing the album, I told a friend at the time, was that it was too Jesus-y.

By the time Rhino Handmade released *Heart Food* on CD in 2003, I had become a Christian, and so was willing to listen to it anew. When I did, I discovered the real reason it had been too much for me. It was not the album's Christianity that had put me off; it was its *nuptiality*.

Although most of *Heart Food*'s tracks are in the same elusive-lover vein as *Judee Sill*, its standout tracks, "The Kiss" and the eight-minute epic "The Donor," are nuptial in the truest sense of the word. That is to say, they express sheer, almost brutal vulnerability. And, until my conversion, when I began to learn how to be transparent before God, I could not stand to be reminded of my vulnerability. It was too painful. Like Andy Partridge, I felt destroyed by "The Kiss"—and in some sense, I still do.

The song begins: "Love, risin' from the mists / Promise me this and only this / Holy breath touchin' me like a wind song / Sweet communion of a kiss." The same songwriter who, in "Lopin' Along Thru the Cosmos," was "hopin' so hard for a

---

14. Jung, *Archetypes*, 121.

kiss from God" was now no longer merely hoping but crying out to heaven for the promise and fulfillment of communion.

When she performed "The Kiss" on a British television show, Sill said, by way of introduction: "This song is about the union of the opposites that we all have, and the kiss is the symbol of the union." The "union of the opposites" is yet another image drawn from Jung, which Jung himself drew from his twin interests in Rosicrucianism and alchemy. In *Memories, Dreams, Reflections,* he described the imagery on his family crest:

> Just as cross and rose represent the Rosicrucian problem of opposites (*'per crucem ad rosam'*), that is, the Christian and Dionysian elements, so cross and grapes [on the crest] are symbols of the heavenly and the chthonic spirit. The uniting symbol is the gold star, the *aurum philosophicum.*[15]

Another likely source of inspiration for "The Kiss," which I have not seen mentioned in connection with Sill elsewhere, is a scholarly book by University of California, Berkeley professor Nicolas J. Perella, *The Kiss Sacred and Profane: An Interpretative History of Kiss Symbolism and Related Religio-Erotic Themes.* In the book's introduction, the author writes:

> [The idea of breath or spirit] is also the notion that lends itself most readily to the concept of the possibility of communion and union between two human creatures as well as between man and the source of life. . . . Besides the importance of breath in Indian speculation, one need only think of the Stoic concept of the World Soul, *anima mundi,* and of the Holy Breath that is one of the Persons and *traite d'union,* the very osculant, as we shall see, of the Christian Triune God.[16]

---

15. C. G. Jung, *Memories, Dreams, Reflections* (New York: Vintage Books, 1973), 232. The *aurum philosophicum* is the philosopher's stone of alchemical legend.
16. Nicolas J. Perella, *The Kiss Sacred and Profane: An Interpretative History of Kiss Symbolism and Related Religio-Erotic Themes*

Here, in a single paragraph, we have many of the terms already seen in the opening lines of "The Kiss": the "communion" of a kiss and the mention of "Holy Breath." Perella goes on to treat extensively of these concepts within the writings of Church Fathers as well as later mystics such as Bernard of Clairvaux. Although Perella also writes about occult and gnostic understandings of the kiss, Sill's lyrics make clear that she was particularly taken with his explication of its Christian meaning. For her, this "sweet communion" represented the love that was "gonna wipe all your tears away"—a clear reference to Revelation 21:4.

"The Donor" is a remarkable cry of the heart. Much of the recording consists of a swirling, multipart choral arrangement of the *Kyrie*. The remainder of the lyrics express Sill's thoughts as she lies in her bed, like the psalmist, pleading for divine mercy: "Now songs from so deep / While I'm sleepin' / Seep in / Sweepin' over me / Still the echo's achin' / 'Leave us not forsaken.'"

When she introduced "The Donor" during a BBC performance, Sill said:

> I thought I would take a different approach when I wrote this song, in that most of my songs, I always try to write them so they'll make people feel better, or make them feel that their warm, human spirit is affirmed. But I thought one day when I was real depressed, you know when you're real depressed and you see everything comes to nothing, well, I thought, maybe I ought to take a different approach, and write a song that, instead of directed at people, would somehow musically induce God into giving us all a break.[17]

As she indicated, such an approach was indeed unique for her. Although other songs of hers such as "Crayon Angels" and "The Kiss" make reference to a world of spirit, "The Donor" is

---

(Berkeley, CA: University of California Press, 1969), 5.

17. Judee Sill, "The Donor" (introduction), *Live in London: The BBC Recordings 1972–1973* [compact disc] (Water, 2007).

Sill's only song that explicitly addresses God as a being who is transcendent and not merely immanent. At the end of *Judee Sill*, she addressed her own animus, which feared "the great truth / That would free him with its mercy." Now, in the final lyrics of *Heart Food*, she was addressing Truth itself, pleading for its merciful love.

Sill may have felt herself in a worse place emotionally when she recorded *Heart Food* than when she recorded her first album. In her BBC performance of "The Donor," after saying she hoped the song would "would somehow musically induce God into giving us all a break," she added, "I've decided that I shouldn't get any more breaks [from God], 'cause I already squandered them in weird places."[18] Yet, in terms of spiritual depth, "The Kiss" and "The Donor" show considerable growth since *Judee Sill*. The artist's God is now not merely the interior "divine spark" of the gnostics, but the enfleshed, incarnate Lord of the Gospels. One can only hope that, even as she struggled in her final years with physical infirmities and addictions, Sill retained her vision of a Christ who is as high above as the angels and as near as a kiss.

18. Judee Sill, "The Donor" (introduction).

# Christ the Liberator:
## The Gospel According to U2

Keith Lemna

For decades, U2 have been in perennial running for the unofficial title "World's Biggest Rock Band." In many years, the title could have been easily ceded to them without serious competition or complaint. At the same time, they have been the most overtly Christian rock band among viable contenders, without applying the label "Christian" to themselves. The size of their influence is related to the religious power of their musical expression and lyrical message. Their music and lyrics herald the prospect of liberation from self-enclosed immanence and isolation.

This heralding of liberation is marked with a sense of the realism and ambiguities of the human condition, and the person of Jesus Christ figures large in the band members' musical and personal histories. Christ is truly a figure of liberation for them. The message and music of this group are coherently intertwined in an often elevating, anthemic sound that has had mass appeal for decades, the very aesthetics of which are an indication of deep religious inspiration.

However, certain notes in their message have rankled with some Christians. Others have suggested over the years that U2 may have a thing or two to teach these naysayers about the real truth of Christ, but there is at least one population whose liberation the rock band grotesquely neglects—even opposes—in a manner that is difficult to describe as anything but anti-Christian, namely, the unborn. I suggest that this and other ambiguities and negligences in U2's public witness are rooted in a problematic understanding of Christ as Liberator. I shall first briefly explore in this chapter the role of Christianity and religion in the history of U2's musical output and then address in a critical manner a troubling blindness in their Christian self-understanding.

## Expressing Faith

The music of U2 has been marked from the beginning by the Christian practice that was formative for Paul Hewson (Bono), David Howell Evans (The Edge), and Larry Mullen, Jr.[1] Only bassist Adam Clayton did not share in the Christian faith common to the other three members of the group at its foundation. Their first hit single, from the 1981 album *October*, was "Gloria," which seems to speak imperatively of the need to praise God. They sing: "Gloria, in te domine [in you Lord] / Gloria, exultate [exult] / Oh, Lord, if I had anything / anything at all / I'd give it to you." While many have taken this song to be rather straightforwardly religious or Christian, Bono himself speaks of it as a loving allusion to Van Morrison's 1964 hit single by the same name. But U2's song is, he says, about "a woman in the spiritual sense and . . . God in the sexual sense." If before U2's "Gloria" one could "actually sing to God, but it might be [about] a woman," after it, "you can pretend it's about God, but not a woman."[2] The song is in fact about both God *and* a woman.

Already we see a symbolic polyvalence that will characterize the music of U2. It lends their art a poignancy and depth lacking in many musical groups who operate explicitly under the appellation "Christian rock." In this, they show how Christian rock 'n' roll can exude a catholicity that attracts an immense audience. U2 does not turn their music into apologetics or dogma, which would surely ruin its artistic merit and limit the scope of their reach. Yet the Christian message is assuredly present all the same. "I Still Haven't Found What I'm Looking For," the second number one hit from 1987's *The Joshua Tree*, is certainly an expression of faith, even deemed by some popular Christian musicians to be one of the most important of contemporary Christian hymns.

---

1.  See Steve Stockman, *Walk On: The Spiritual Journey of U2* (Orlando, FL: Relevant Books, 2005). Stockman gives a good summary of the background of U2's spirituality and argues in defense of the Christian inspiration of their political activism.
2.  John Waters, *Race of Angels* (Newtownards, UK: Blackstaff Press, 1994), 148–49.

The Edge referred to it as a "gospel song," and U2's performance of the song with the New Voices of Freedom Choir in Harlem verifies at least its compatibility with the gospel genre.[3]

In a *New Yorker* piece, Joshua Rothman makes a strong case for U2's religiosity. He points out that U2 frequently talk about God, even without seeming to do so—and knowing this helps us understand all their work at a deeper level: "Previously opaque or anodyne songs turn out to be full of ideas and force." The group, he notes, has "a few straight-up love songs," but usually, "when Bono uses the words 'love,' 'she,' 'you,' or 'baby'—which he does often—a listener can hear 'God' instead."[4] Often Bono writes lyrics evocative of the Song of Solomon, the biblical book that expresses and gives praise to love.

One can interpret "With or Without You," "The Fly," and "Until the End of the World" in Solomonic vein. Rothman suggests that U2's most poignant example of this sort of nuptial writing is "Ultra Violet (Light My Way)," from 1992's *Achtung Baby*:

> You bury your treasure
> Where it can't be found
> But your love is like a secret
> That's been passed around
> There is a silence that comes to a house
> Where no one can sleep
> I guess it's the price of love
> I know it's not cheap

Rothman interprets this song as being only seemingly about "desperate romance." In actuality, he suggests, it is "about the cruelty of God's reticence." It is a perfect example of what Rothman takes to be a spiritual tension fruitful for genuine artistic inspiration. This tension was especially present in U2's work between 1987, with the recording of *The Joshua Tree*, and 1997, with the recording of *Pop*. In these years, U2 inhabited

---

3. Paramount Pictures, *U2: Rattle and Hum*, 1988.
4. Joshua Rothman, "The Church of U2," *The New Yorker* (September 16, 2014), https://www.newyorker.com/culture/cultural-comment/church-u2.

a *between*: "between discipline and vulnerability, order and openness, being willful and giving in." This tension "became U2's central preoccupation, and gave it its aesthetic."[5]

Rothman in fact bemoans what he takes to be U2's increasing overtness and self-confidence in their religious faith in recent years. They have, in his view, lost the poetic vulnerability of their earlier days. This is an interesting twist of interpretation, because some commentators go so far as to make the opposite claim, namely, that U2 have left their religious roots behind in recent years. Rothman suggests by contrast that whereas until the late 1990s the band was dramatically ambiguous with respect to their religious convictions, they have in more recent albums become straightforwardly religiously positive in their message, with songs like "Every Breaking Wave" and "Song for Someone." Perhaps he gives these more recent songs too religious an interpretation. Nevertheless, he preferred the group in an earlier incarnation, which he deems to have been more ambiguously religious.

## Spiritual but not Religious?

Other sides to the religious message of the group have sometimes put them at loggerheads with traditional and more conservative Christians. For one thing, there is a liberationist aspect to their thinking which allies them at times with the radical political left and which shows the influence of leftist versions of Christianity.[6] For another thing, the group has never embraced the importance of belonging to a church or ecclesial community. Certainly, a good portion of the members' instincts with respect to liberation,

---

5. Ibid.
6. For example, in "Bullet the Blue Sky" (on *The Joshua Tree*), Bono decried the treatment of El Salvador's communists. Though Bono later described the one-sided position of the song as "naïve," it fits a pattern with the group that has in many ways never abated. See Bono, "Bono Interview: Behind 'Bullet the Blue Sky,'" Rock & Roll Hall of Fame, May 8, 2020, https://www.rockhall.com/bono-interview-behind-bullet-blue-sky.

social justice, and ecclesial membership can be explained by their origins in sectarian, war-torn Ireland during "the Troubles" in the 1960s and 70s. The group members were prone to be disaffected with the religious affiliations of their parents: Bono's father was Catholic and his mother Anglican; Adam Clayton and David Evans (The Edge) are both from fully Protestant backgrounds; Larry Mullen is from a fully Catholic background. Bono, Evans, and Mullen got involved with a "spiritual but not religious" Christian group in high school that called itself "Shalom." Over time, they became disaffected with this group as well as with the broader world of institutional Christianity.[7]

The members of U2 proudly sniffed out hypocrisy, corruption, and lack of honest self-dealing in religious institutions. Yet the Christian religiosity or spirituality they have tended to support has been an incoherent mixture of radical individualism in the concrete and communitarianism in the abstract. *Christianity Today*, in a 2003 editorial, called out U2, and Bono in particular, for the hypocrisy of this stance. Bono had been going about the world criticizing Christian churches, both Catholic and Protestant, for—in his estimation—refusing to combat social injustice, particularly with respect to the AIDS crisis in Africa. The editorial criticized the incoherence of Bono's message as well as his blindness toward what Christians were in fact contributing to alleviate the suffering of people in Africa:

> Never mind that many Christians were bringing relief to suffering Africans in the same decade that U2 poured millions into its bloated Zoo TV and PopMart tours (keeping the latter on the road cost $1.3 million a week). If Americans fail to persuade the Bush administration to increase foreign aid to the percentage of gross domestic product that Bono finds acceptable, then Bono finds the

7. See Greg Garrett, *We Get to Carry Each Other: The Gospel According to U2* (Louisville, KY: Westminster John Knox Press, 2009), 1–23.

church guilty of standing by, like Germans watching Jews being hauled away to the death camps.[8]

Bono's commitment to social justice is commendable, the editorial insists, but he has so tied it to an individualistic activism without communion in the corporate worship of Christianity that he has rendered it empty. Thus his version of Christianity is targeted as "thin ecclesiology."

The tension between U2 and traditional Christians reached successive breaking points when the group backed, first, the 2015 referendum supporting gay marriage in Ireland, and second, the 2018 repeal of the Eighth Amendment of the Irish Constitution, which had recognized the right to life of children in the womb. The latter is the grotesque negligence to which I referred in the opening section of this chapter. U2 seem to have always had a desire for a return to a purer, idealized version of Christianity closer to how they think it was lived in the first century. Now, they were giving their imprimatur to an activity that first-century Christians vehemently and prophetically denounced: the murder of children in the womb. Writing in *First Things*, John Waters denounced the crass and unambiguous materialism into which the band had fallen, the origin of which he locates in *Achtung Baby*: "Once a band uniquely capable of standing against the seduction of the material, U2 has become indistinguishable from the herd it has latterly so assiduously courted, volunteering for enslavement to fashion, cool, and emptiness."[9] Waters and others interpreted U2's actions as an overt consecration of nihilism and a stark transgression of the gospel message at its most fundamental level.

All the same, Rothman is correct, in my view, to hold that U2 has become—if anything—more overt, open, calm,

---

8.   See "Bono's Thin Ecclesiology," unsigned editorial, in *Christianity Today*, March 1, 2003, christianitytoday.com/ct/2003/march-web-only/29.37.html.

9.   John Waters, "How U2 Betrayed Rock 'N' Roll," *First Things*, May 7, 2018, https://www.firstthings.com/web-exclusives/2018/05/how-u2-betrayed-rock-n-roll.

and confident in their own self-understanding as Christians. Certainly, Bono has given interviews in recent years in which he has made the point forthrightly. He has said explicitly that he views Christ as the Messiah and Son of God. He speaks in traditional-sounding terms of the meaning of Christ's death: "The point of the death of Christ is that Christ took on the sins of the world, so that what we put out did not come back to us, and that our sinful nature does not reap the obvious death."[10] Christ is the Liberator, in this view, in that he takes on the sins of the world and saves us from death. However, for much of the message of U2, this belief relates to a socio-political understanding wherein the "death" in question is reduced to socially imposed constraints on personal identity.

The message of U2 consistently promotes liberty as transcendence from the constraints of socialized identity, particularly with respect to "gender" and the body. Communally, their message speaks of liberation as the aspiration to draw all the people who have fallen through the cracks of orthodox Christian neglect—all of those who have been "Christianly" marginalized—into a new, common community.[11] U2 becomes the center or home of a new community of marginalized post-Christians. *Christianity Today* complained that Bono promoted a "thin ecclesiology" by measuring "the church's mission . . . almost exclusively in geopolitical terms."[12] Rothman argues, by contrast, that U2's ecclesiology has become quite thick indeed. They are their own church now, he insists: the church of U2.

Rothman's description strikes me as accurate. U2 have come to view themselves as a rock-band-*cum*-mystical-body in which isolated, wayward misfits—victims of conformist institutional Christian churches that persecute misfits—can find liberating transcendence. Daniel DeForest London associates the liberating

---

10. Michka Assayas, *Bono: In Conversation* (New York: Riverhead Books, 2005), 204.
11. Here I refer to Bono's "Songs that Saved My Life" segments on U2 radio, especially his paean to Lady Gaga's "Born this Way."
12. "Bono's Thin Ecclesiology."

message of the "church of U2" with *apocatastasis* (a belief that at the end of time all of creation, including the devil, will be restored to perfection and reunited to God), albeit, I would add, so long as one rejects the pomp and circumstance of one's pharisaical ways. U2, in his understanding, plays a central role in eschatological restoration, "furthering the reign of the Kingdom of Heaven on earth."[13] They welcome the marginalized, particularly the LGBT+ community.[14] Sexual liberation as transcendence from the normativity of institutional Christianity is seemingly a crucial dimension of this new kingdom. Liberation, here, is therapeutic self-acceptance in a community of the like-minded that heals one from the social wounds of orthodox Christian judgment. Traditional Christianity as the marginalized often experience it tends to lay up heavy burdens on human shoulders, causing those who do not heed its dictates to be shunned. The priority, in U2's "restoration," is especially shifted away from sexual sin. If my interpretation here is accurate, this shifting priority is what enables U2 to justify in their own minds the legality of abortion: The orthodox Pharisees have laid too heavy a burden on humanity. The stigma of sexual sin or sexual diversity must be erased so that a sort of gospel of authenticity may replace it.

## Rohr and the Universal Christ

Bono's recent friendship with Richard Rohr helps to make some connections on the theological plane that could verify the assertions made above and permits a deepened approach to U2's vision of Christ as Liberator.[15] Rohr is a Franciscan friar and priest who

---

13. Daniel DeForest London, "Sympathy for MacPhisto: Finding Apocatastasis in U2," *Daniel DeForest London* (blog), June 6, 2015, https://deforestlondon.wordpress.com/2015/06/06/sympathy-for-macphisto-finding-apocatastasis-in-u2/.
14. Ibid.
15. Eliza Griswold, "Richard Rohr Reorders the Universe," *The New Yorker* (February 2, 2020), https://www.newyorker.com/news/on-religion/richard-rohr-reorders-the-universe.

is the founding head of the Center for Action and Contemplation in New Mexico. He is a popular spiritual counselor who counts several famous friends among his spiritual clientele, including Oprah Winfrey and Bono.[16] For the singer of "Love Is Bigger Than Anything in Its Way," Rohr's own message of the universal love of God present in Christ beyond the narrow constraints of a too-limited Jesus-centered religion must be quite attractive.

On the front cover of Rohr's 2019 New York Times bestseller, *The Universal Christ: How a Forgotten Reality Can Change Everything We See, Hope For, and Believe*, the reader finds a blurb from Bono: "I cannot put this book down."[17] The book is Rohr's summary synthesis and testimony to his own life's work. He argues that modern Christianity has become too Jesus-focused and has lost sight of the cosmic, salvific presence of the Universal Christ. As St. Paul teaches in Colossians 3:11, all humanity and the cosmos are "*en Cristo*" (in Christ): "there is no longer Greek and Jew, circumcised and uncircumcised, barbarian, Scythian, slave and free; but Christ is all and in all!" For Rohr this Christocentric rather than Jesus-centric emphasis means that there "is only Christ. He is everything and he is in everything."[18]

Rohr insists that Christians have not adequately understood the marvelous truth of the universality of the Gospel. The "independent divinity" of Jesus has been overemphasized, from the time of the first ecumenical councils of the church.[19] This emphasis has had the net effect through the centuries of promoting anthropocentrism and individualism. We need, Rohr counsels, a paradigm shift, a recognition of the Universal Christ beyond the particularity and concreteness of the Jesus of history: "*Jesus can hold together one group or religion. Christ*

---

16. Ibid. Bono occasionally sends Rohr little messages that Rohr sees as "love notes."
17. Richard Rohr, *The Universal Christ: How a Forgotten Reality Can Change Everything We See, Hope For, and Believe* (New York: Convergent Books, 2019).
18. Ibid., 43.
19. Ibid., 45.

*can hold together everything.*"[20] Christ as universal liberator is an inclusive savior, not a judge trapped in the hidebound mores of an ancient society, aiming to exclude people from life with him based on their peccadilloes. What the Gospel message boils down to for Rohr is that true religion is not at all about individual moral reform in the sexual sphere but primarily about waking up to the truth of one's inherent election by God.[21] It is not by establishing moral perfection within us that Christ awakens us. It is by making us whole, accepting who we are on the level of everyday wishes and affections. There is no place for shame in Christ's kingdom, because Christ is not punitive, at least when it comes to matters involving human sexuality.

Rohr appears to participate in today's religious revival of the legacy of Carl Jung.[22] Despite a professed disdain for Gnosticism of a body-denying variety, Rohr gladly promotes such body-denying Gnosticism as would claim that the notion of sexual sin has no place in the concern of a follower of Christ. In line with Jung, he embraces a turn inward, toward the inner archetypes, where, he says, God speaks to us. Certainly, this turn inward bears a surface resemblance with the tradition of early Christian Platonism represented by figures such as St. Gregory of Nyssa (fourth century), who held that to see God we must turn inward to the divine image that we bear in our soul. However, this strand of early Christianity promoted the turn inward in line with an ascetical reading of the beatitudes of Jesus Christ, according to which we cannot behold the image of God within without being open to God's cleansing grace in Christ to clear away the filth that covers it.[23]

20. Ibid., 47. The italics are Rohr's.
21. Ibid., 72–74.
22. See Chase Padusniak, "Jungianism and the Proliferation of Meaning-Seeking Esotericism," *Church Life Journal*, February 2, 2022, https://churchlifejournal.nd.edu/articles/jungianism-and-the-proliferation-of-meaning-seeking-esotericism/.
23. See Matt 5:28: "But I say to you that everyone who looks at a woman with lust has already committed adultery with her in his heart." Bono is, of course, not entirely naïve on this front. See his

Rohr can also be said to evince the age-old gnostic self-assurance that he has discovered a deeper form of Christian understanding than what one finds in the churches aligned with bishops in apostolic succession. We turn inward, discover our inner depths, and find that our own inner experience is a surer path to the truth than dogmatic Christianity.

The theology and spirituality I am describing is a form of "meaning-seeking esotericism."[24] This expression references individualistic forms of spirituality set within the context of a kind of religion of consumerism. However, Rohr holds that spirituality must be embodied in the quest for social liberation. It must take a socio-political form. On this point, he is assuredly very different from the ancient Gnostics and from Jung. For Rohr, as for U2, there can be no such thing as a non-political religion that is spiritually true. Rohr's vision promotes the "correct" kind of political action, namely, whatever the vanguard of the contemporary left is putting forth as a moral exigency, such as the need to defeat "racism, sexism, homophobia, militarism, lookism, and classism."[25] Rohr describes his retreat center as the Center for *Action* and Contemplation—with action taking the primary place. Like many, he views Pope Francis as a figure who is re-founding Christianity based on notions of self-acceptance and political transformation. This view of the Holy Father is false, of course, but it is remarkable how Rohr ties his gnostic anthropology to a commendation of papal authority in one particular pope whom he thinks is re-starting Christianity according to Rohr's own liking.

Surely it is a bridge too far to entirely identify the theology and spirituality of Bono, or U2 as a whole, with Richard Rohr—not least because we cannot fully know or judge their beliefs—but it seems to me U2 has always tended in the direction of thought to

---

lyrics for "God, Part II": "Don't believe in rape / But every time she passes by / Wild thoughts escape."

24. See Padusniak, "Jungianism and the Proliferation of Meaning-Seeking Esotericism."

25. Rohr, *The Universal Christ*, 67.

which Rohr's *The Universal Christ* gives voice: Christ liberates us from the rigid, moralistic, legalistic bondage of the narrowing of the Christian vision through centuries of Christendom. This approach opposes what its proponents take to be the reassertion of Christendom in the last half of the twentieth century in Evangelical Protestantism and the Roman Catholicism of Pope John Paul II, which supposedly focused the moral attention of Christians on the sexual sphere and ignored the plight of the poor, the maliciousness of the wealthy, the destruction of the environment, and the scourge of racism.

Perhaps U2 does not go as far as Rohr in divorcing the Universal Christ from the historical Jesus of Nazareth. The way Bono has spoken about the person of Jesus Christ and his work of atoning expiation seems foreign to Rohr's perspective. Nevertheless, whether or not Bono's understanding of Jesus Christ perfectly aligns with that of Rohr, his inherent ecclesiology (or lack thereof) has a deep underlying congruency with the pop Franciscan spiritual master.

## The Concreteness of Christ

What is missing in the theology of Rohr (and Bono/U2) is a sense of the *concreteness* of the universality of Jesus Christ. A proper *ressourcement*, or re-sourcing, of the cosmic Christology of the Jesuit paleontologist, Pierre Teilhard de Chardin, S.J., may be in order to redress this imbalance. In the work of Teilhard—a figure of decisive reference for Rohr—is found a deeper understanding of Christ. The great theologian Henri de Lubac, S.J., a confrère of Teilhard, explains:

> We should therefore make no mistake. Any misunderstanding would be fatal, and Père Teilhard would have protested against it with all the ardour of his faith. "Alpha and Omega, Beginning and End, Foundation Stone and Keystone"—even in this cosmic role Christ was still for him the one and only Jesus of history and dogmatic tradition—"the historic and transhistoric Jesus," the Jesus

of the Gospel, the son of the Virgin Mary, he whose hands "were pierced," the "Jesus" whose name comes so often in his prayers. . . . "By ascending into heaven, after having descended into hell, You have so filled the universe in every direction, Jesus, that henceforth, to our joy, it is impossible for us not to be within You."[26]

Teilhard recovered the idea, present in the Eastern Church Fathers of Christianity, that it is precisely the glorified, *individual* humanity of Jesus Christ, in its concrete particularity, that opens us to transcendence in the universal communion and reconciliation of humanity and cosmos that Rohr envisions. The historical teachings and singular exemplarity of Jesus of Nazareth and the dogmatic tradition that interprets the meaning of the intimate, unbreakable unity of Jesus and God in Christ are conditions *sine qua non* of catholic and ecumenical peace and social communion. Perhaps orthodox believers have stingily neglected to embrace the inherent catholicity and ecumenicity of Jesus of Nazareth, even while affirming that Jesus is always perfectly united to the divine Word and so can be the "cosmic Christ." However, the solution to overcoming this stinginess cannot be found by detaching the Universal Christ from the singular humanity of Jesus of Nazareth and the individual specificities of his teaching and example.

The loss of a sense of this abiding union of the individual humanity of Jesus with the Divine Word can be catastrophic in the moral and social domains. What is at stake is a realistic grasp of how the message of the gospel is truly communicated in the embodied condition of human existence in its finite particularity. God is universal not simply in the way of an archetypal paradigm dimly present in the depths of the subconscious mind but as a concrete historical person who lived in our midst, truly uniting us to himself in mystical union through his suffering, death, and resurrection. What is missing in the arguably gnostic Christianity of Rohr is a grasp of the deep intimacy of the unity of opposites

---

26. Henri de Lubac, *Teilhard de Chardin: The Man and His Meaning*, trans. René Hague (New York: Burns and Oats, 1965), 51.

in Christ, of the infinite with the finite, the above with the below, God with creation, and the universal with the particular that the full union of God with man in *Jesus* Christ makes possible.

Whether or not U2 is wholly "Rohrian," perhaps they, too, need a reminder. They preach transcendence and universality, but it does not seem to have to come for them through the intimate concreteness of personal individuality in its givenness, particularly in fleshly embodiment. An essential part of Jesus' teachings is dismissed. Is it not better to affirm, with creedally orthodox Christianity, that the Universal Christ in Jesus of Nazareth enters the suffering flesh through the personal singularity of his unique, once-and-for-all existence, and that his total message is authoritative for transcendence and universality? He forms a universal body out of the blood and water of the Cross, sending his Spirit so that his followers may be really united to him in and through his glorified humanity by virtue of the transformation of their own embodied individuality. The universal principle of creation is a singular *Person*, and he enters the darkness of humanity's self-imposed wretchedness by taking on the particular destiny of an individual humanity in fully personal embodment, actualizing its openness to the totality of human society as well as to the cosmos from within the individual specificity of a concrete, finite, unrepeatable, personal life on earth. It is true that Jesus Christ gives us much more than the "moral God" of modern idolatry, but through his unique humanity he issues a universal call to holiness to be embraced by each individual human person on earth in accordance with the totality of their personal identity in the gift of their embodied condition. Engraced personal holiness enables fruitful universalism, or extension of Christ's body to the totality of the human race.

## Seeking Liberation without Compromise

The Universal Christ took "the form of a slave" (Phil 2:7). In doing so, he identified himself with the poor, the weak, and the defenseless, and with all people who have no legal rights for self-determination simply because they are deemed nothing more than property. The Christian Left is correct to cry out against the sins of racism, economic oppression, and (somewhat ambiguously) sexual exploitation. But the church of U2—the Christian Left expressing itself in anthemic musical delight—is not infallible. It does not speak for the weak and oppressed taken as a totality. It allows for the turning of a vast group of defenseless human beings into property to be wiped out by the scalpels of "proper" medical authorities.[27] The truly Universal Christ, uniquely present in Jesus of Nazareth, keeps everyone in loving view. I find it difficult not to be sympathetic to those who turned away from U2 in disgust at what they consider to be the band's arrogant stance on abortion. The church of U2 has too much reconceived Christ the Liberator as a sexual liberator in the contemporary understanding of sexual liberation, promising transcendence from the concrete particularity of one's embodiment and that of one's dependents. They have failed to heed the liberating message of Jesus Christ in its totality, through which we are drawn into the universal communion of charity, of free and perfect personal self-gift, to make a gift of ourselves, body, heart, and soul, unhindered by inner desires that may keep us locked up within ourselves.

Can rock and roll be a platform for a truer form of liberation, even of the sexual variety? Can it proclaim the "freedom of the children of God," the charity that prophetically opposes the oppression that mangles the body and turns people into property over which the powerful have absolute rights, even to the point of murder? The message of U2 is mixed. They embrace a form of Christianity in which the principles of the Universal Christ have become detached from the singularity of the Way of the Cross

---

27. See Waters, "How U2 Betrayed Rock 'N' Roll." Waters says: "More and more, their public stances seemed to be about attitude, about being cool, about remaining top of the league. Gradually, heartbreakingly, they went native, nestling deeper and deeper into the cultural Marxist groupthink. The band's corporate Repeal gesture is but the culmination of all that, a banal and self-disgracing embrace of the very antithesis of the music they had redeemed."

on the path to personal holiness that true encounter with the living Jesus Christ in the concrete existence of his church alone enables. We await a more authentic, catholic, and ecumenical voice of Christian liberation to call out for us in the milieu of contemporary popular music, with all its ambiguities—which certainly should not be avoided, but, at the same time, should not force one into a position of such blatant moral compromise.

# The Order of the Soul:
## Leonard Cohen's Pneumatological Vision

Thomas Malewitz

Often associated with images of fire and wind throughout Scripture (Exod 13:17–14:29; Acts 2:1–4), the Holy Spirit has traditionally been understood as an Advocate, refining and purifying the human heart through the journey toward knowing and living the will of G-d.[1] Reception of the Spirit existentially changes lives, animating and renewing individuals toward a deeper calling of prayer, repentance, and unity.[2]

Leonard Cohen, poet and songwriter, permeated his creative writings with pneumatological images, specifically with reference to the purification of the soul and the search for human unity. Known as "the poet of despair,"[3] Cohen's poetry and lyrics often offered stark dystopian images of a world that has "overturned the order of the soul" ("The Future"), establishing a life of discord fueled by egocentric desire. To contrast this dark imagery, Cohen used images of light and fire to signify restorative and unifying grace, especially in his song-prayers. Through his search for holistic order, Cohen explored the role of

---

1.  John Paul II, *Dominum et Vivificantem* (On the Holy Spirit in the Life of the Church) (1986); Yves Congar, "The Renewal in the Spirit: Promise and Questions," in *I Believe in the Holy Spirit*, trans. David Smith (New York: Herder & Herder, 2016), 213–28.
2.  Raniero Cantalamessa, *Contemplating the Trinity: The Path to the Abundant Christian Life*, trans. Marsha Daigle-Williamson (Ijamsville, MD: The Word Among Us Press, 2007); Yves Congar, "The Spirit Is the Source of Life in Us Personally and in the Church," in *The Spirit of God: Short Writings on the Holy Spirit*, trans. Susan Mader Brown et al. (Washington, DC: Catholic University of America Press, 2018), 36–51.
3.  Steve Turner, "Depressing? Who? Me?" in *Leonard Cohen on Leonard Cohen: Interviews and Encounters*, ed. Jeff Burger (Chicago: Chicago Review Press, 2015), 51–56.

the Spirit as a force for purifying the soul and establishing human unity.[4] This chapter will examine Cohen's album *The Future* as an exemplar of his search for purification from the disorder of the world, to a unitive order in the Spirit that binds one with G-d and neighbor, and brings fellowship, liberty, and wisdom.

## Poet and Spiritual Seeker

Leonard Cohen the novelist, poet, preeminent lyricist, and popular musician was a lifelong seeker of relationships of intimacy with G-d and neighbor. Cohen was born in the French-speaking province of Quebec, Canada, in 1934. He was raised in a deeply rooted Jewish family who claimed lineage to Aaron, the High Priest—an aspect of his pedigree that underlines his transmutation into a wisdom figure and icon in popular culture, as a pseudo-ecumenical high priest and "pop-saint," or modern-day prophet.[5] This early formation in Jewish Scripture and midrash directly molded a lens of his lyrical imagery throughout his life.[6]

His first written manuscript was a book of poetry, *Let Us Compare Mythologies* (1956). After moving to a semi-secluded lifestyle on the island of Hydra, Cohen wrote several novels

---

4. Aubrey Glazer, *Tangle of Matter & Ghost: Leonard Cohen's Post-Secular Songbook of Mysticism(s) Jewish & Beyond* (Brighton, MA: Academic Studies Press, 2017).

5. Thom Jurek, "The Prophet of Love Looks into the Abyss: A Conversation with Leonard Cohen" in *Leonard Cohen on Leonard Cohen*, 362–68; Shaul Magid, "Preface" in Glazer, *Tangle of Matter & Ghost*, 13; Yvette Nahmia-Messinas, "An Ecumenical High Priest: A Tribute to Leonard Cohen coming up in Athens," *The Jerusalem Post* (January 6, 2019); Michael Posner, *Leonard Cohen, Untold Stories: The Early Years* (New York: Simon & Schuster, 2020).

6. David Brinn, "Leonard Cohen Concert Proceeds to Benefit Reconciliation Work," *The Jerusalem Post* (July 28, 2009); Liel Leibovitz, *A Broken Hallelujah: Rock and Roll, Redemption, and the Life of Leonard Cohen* (New York: W. W. Norton, 2014); Michael Posner, "That's How the Light Gets In," *Queen's Quarterly*, 124(4), 2017.

and books of poetry, including a bildungsroman manuscript entitled *The Favourite Game* (1963). In 1966, Cohen turned his attention toward songwriting, but continued to intermittently publish books of poetry.[7] He became a recognized and accomplished lyricist in the folk music scene of the late 1960s, where his songs were brought to prominence by musicians like Judy Collins and Joan Baez. Throughout his lyrical corpus, Cohen intertwined lyrics of personal relationships and physical intimacy with lines expressing a transcendent spirituality and divine intimacy. The spiritual side of his work—and one could argue that it is all spiritual—is expressed with a deeply Jewish lens and narrative,[8] but also includes prominent imagery from Christianity.[9] Cohen was attracted to Buddhist spirituality for some time as well, and in 1994, he entered the Mt. Baldy Zen Center outside Los Angeles. After two years of living in the monastery he was ordained a monk and took the name *Jikan*, which is translated "noble silence."[10] He continued to live on the monastic grounds until 1999, when he returned to the musical circuit after finding that he was in relative poverty due to financial embezzlement by his then-manager.[11] Cohen took up global touring again and continued to write poetry and compose songs until his death in 2016.

The spiritual dimension of Leonard Cohen's works has been well established and widely discussed.[12] Cohen's lyrics

---

7. Posner, *Untold Stories*.
8. Glazer, *Tangle of Matter & Ghost*; Jiří Měsíc, "The Nature of Love in the Work of Leonard Cohen," *Popular Romance Studies* no. 7 (2018), 1–21.
9. Leonard Cohen, *Beautiful Losers* (New York: Vintage Books, 1966/1993).
10. Shozan Jack Haubner, "Ode to Leonard Cohen, From a Fellow Zen Monk," *The New York Times* (December 6, 2016).
11. Leibovitz, *A Broken Hallelujah*.
12. Jiří Měsíc, "The Song of Initiation by Leonard Cohen," *Ostrava Journal of English Philology* 5, no. 1 (2013), 69–93; Timothy P. Jackson, "The Prophetic Mr. Cohen," in *Leonard Cohen and Philosophy*, ed. Jason Holt (Chicago: Open Court, 2014), 217–29;

include allusions to people from the Hebrew Scriptures, such as David, Ruth, and Samson.[13] Cohen also authored songs about the lives of Christian religious figures, such as "Joan of Arc" and "Song of Bernadette." He even wrote song-prayers that act as contemporary midrash-like dialogue of Jewish spirituality, including "Born in Chains," "Come Healing," "If It Be Your Will," and "Show Me the Place." Rabbi Jonathan Sacks, author and theologian, acknowledged that the song "You Want It Darker" was likely the most Jewish song Cohen ever wrote, as it contains the Kaddish[14] and an isomorphic view of the Abraham and Isaac story and the struggle between obedience, sacrifice, abandonment, and resistance (see Gen 22).[15]

Cohen was no stranger to the history of the Jewish people and included stark reminders of the history of Jewish oppression in songs like "Born in Chains" and "By the Rivers Dark." He presented the continuation of the human struggle between the order of the soul and the order of the world in songs like "Almost Like the Blues," "Everybody Knows," "The Future," and "Puppets," where his lyrics examined a post-war reality through the eyes of suffering and human pathos. Cohen wove narratives that yearned for an intimate relationship with G-d and longed for life defined within a divine order, from the view of a life of brokenness and suffering; he stated: "Real spirituality has its feet in the mud and its heart in heaven."[16]

Cohen's literary and lyrical catalogue is too vast to explore in a single chapter. The following will examine one specific album that showcased his wrestling between hope and anxiety about the

---

Jiří Měsíc, "Leonard Cohen, the Priest of a Catacomb Religion," *Moravian Journal of Literature and Film* 6, no. 1 (2015) 29–47.

13. For example, see "Halleluiah," "Story of Isaac," "Samson in New Orleans," and "Whither Thou Goest."

14. The Kaddish is a hymn of praise of G-d, usually associated with services of mourning in Judaism.

15. Jonathan Sacks, "Rabbi Sacks on Leonard Cohen and Parsha Vayera," *YouTube*, November 18, 2016, 1:50–7:39, https://www.youtube.com/watch?v=2s3kQSZ_Qxk.

16. Leonard Cohen, as quoted in Leibovitz, *A Broken Hallelujah*, 223.

present and future events of the world, through a pneumatological lens. Although Cohen directly references the Spirit through lyrics on other albums (such as the holy dove in "Hallelujah" and healing of the body and Spirit in the context of the prayer-song "Come Healing"), I chose the album *The Future* for this analysis because of its concentrated search for authentic intimacy with G-d and neighbor throughout the album as a whole.

## The Future: A Prophetic Call for Repentance and Order

The blizzard, the blizzard of the world
Has crossed the threshold
And it's overturned / The order of the soul
"The Future"

In 1992, Cohen released a seminal album, *The Future*, which germinated amid the context of national and global events of monumental social awareness and dramatic change, namely, the Los Angeles riots and the fall of the Berlin Wall. The lyrics were charged with raw emotion, trying to make sense of the hope and anxiety that defined the world of that time, sifting through events of chaos and order.[17] Throughout the original lyrics, written by Cohen, a concentrated focus of pneumatological imagery creates contrasts between wholeness and brokenness, light and darkness, clarity and confusion, and order and chaos. The album contains only nine songs, two of which are covers. Of the seven originals, one is a strictly instrumental piece. The remaining six numbers are: "The Future," "Waiting for the Miracle," "Closing Time," "Anthem," "Democracy," and "Light As the Breeze," all of which evoke a nuanced progress in yearning for the Spirit's bringing of healing, integrity, and unity in contrast to the present chaos of the world and dis-order of the soul.

The cover art of the album establishes the mission and focus of Cohen's work, as it includes three objects: a pair of

---

17. Alberto Manzano, "The Future," in *Leonard Cohen on Leonard Cohen*, 322–24.

handcuffs, a heart, and a hummingbird. The opened pair of handcuffs lies beneath the heart. In the foreground of the heart, the hummingbird is in ascent. The hummingbird is a prominent figure throughout Cohen's canon; he created drawings, lyrics, and poetry of the bird throughout his career. Scholars of Cohen's work have indicated that the hummingbird is a representation of compassion, wisdom, and liberation for him.[18] We note too that a bird is a common image of the Spirit. If it is an accurate interpretation of Cohen's use of imagery, the cover art for *The Future* itself may serve as an iconic summary of the longing for the Spirit of freedom, peace, and wisdom present in the journey of the lyrics within the album itself.

**The Future.** The opening song is one of Cohen's most vivid and challenging songs. Some scholars have called it an apocalyptic vision, while others declare that it parallels an ancient prophetic challenge of social injustice; either way, it illustrates concurrently a present and a future view of a world in moral chaos.[19] Cohen lays out a blueprint of the state of the world, off-kilter and disordered, a world of isolation and war, devoid of authentic relationship. This disorder is explored through a vision of individualism, violence, and vice. The chorus alone cries out for repentance, as a prophet from the wilderness, for a reordering of the soul—though it is unclear what that means to the author, leaving the listener in suspense and waiting for a miracle of an answer to the nightmarish scene. The song indicates that there is some choice to be made between "Stalin" and "Saint Paul," and between "Christ" and "Hiroshima." The future, like the past, could go either direction.

---

18. Manzano, "The Future," in *Leonard Cohen on Leonard Cohen*, 318–36; Allan Showalter, "Between the Hummingbird and the Handcuffs: Leonard Cohen's Avian Symbolism of Liberating Wisdom," August 15, 2020, https://allanshowalter. com/2020/08/15/between-the-hummingbird-and-the-handcuffs-leonard-cohens-avian-symbolism-of-liberating-wisdom/.
19. Heidi Hochenedel, "A Reading of The Future," *The Leonard Cohen Files*, 1996; David G. Whiteis, "Leonard Cohen: The Future," *The Leonard Cohen Files*, 1997.

**Waiting for the Miracle.** The second song of the album continues with a sense of listlessness and apathy of disillusion because of the state of the world as well as a perceived lack of an answer or action from G-d to the pain and suffering present in the world. Cohen presents an individual tired from expecting an answer to their prayer, recognizing that a better order, built on blessing and relationship, is possible. Similar to the challenging questions throughout the biblical books of Wisdom literature, Cohen poses an indirect question of why G-d is waiting to reveal the divine presence in a post-World War II existence of struggle and unfulfilling relationships.

**Closing Time.** In this song, Cohen creates an image of a feast of dancing, drinking, and partying through hedonistic celebration, similar to Belshazzar's feast (Dan 5). In the second verse, though, he interjects the voice of the Holy Spirit, as the writing on the wall, through the words of a popular fast food advertisement catchphrase from 1980s and 90s: "And the Holy Spirit's crying, 'Where's the beef?'" Cohen's lyrics directly evoke the Spirit as the voice of conscience and wisdom advocating for a return to the question of where the substance and meaning is in the midst of a life full of debauchery and passion. Here the Spirit embodies the gifts stated in the prophet Isaiah: "the spirit of wisdom and understanding, / the spirit of counsel and might, / the spirit of knowledge and the fear of the LORD" (Isa 11:2). Midway through the song Cohen includes a fascinating line: "And I just don't care what happens next / Looks like freedom but it feels like death / It's something in between, I guess / It's closing time." The lyrics again indicate the lack of fulfillment from the superficial aspects of the world.

**Anthem.** The fifth song on the album creates a glimmer of hope in a broken world with the image of a type of sanctification coming from a light beyond the darkness. Through the metaphor of the crack in the Liberty Bell, and the bell's engraved message of liberty (Lev 25:10), Cohen juxtaposes the blessing of renewal from the natural beauty in morning bird calls with the terror of war, fear, and even the control of buying and selling religious beliefs. Again, the bird and the light are images of the

Spirit, and Cohen more directly references the Spirit as "the holy dove." Ultimately, the lyrics show little regard for lawless worldly honors but focus instead on G-d's vindication of those suffering and broken who authentically depend on the Spirit to enter and bring light into the darkness of the world. The scene is reminiscent of the proclamation of liberty and good news the prophet Isaiah declared through the Spirit of the Lord (Isa 61).

**Democracy.** The sixth song on the album again explores the hope in a changing world through an upbeat but thought-provoking philosophical reflection. The song takes place as democracy spreads across eastern Europe after the fall of communism. Not blindly committing to a new ideology over a previous one, Cohen remains hesitant to jump on the bandwagon for the end goal of the experiment of democracy but hopes that, in the change, liberty and freedom will be possible for the future.[20] The line "From the war against disorder" again evokes an image of the role of the Spirit of G-d as one of order over chaos (Gen 1).

**Light As the Breeze.**[21] In the seventh song on the album, Cohen explores, through the metaphor of intimacy, the grace of healing and wholeness as a blessing from heaven from "the alpha and the omega." The lyrics serve as a culmination of gratitude

---

20. Manzano, "The Future," in *Leonard Cohen on Leonard Cohen*, 319–21.
21. Cohen often uses a metaphor of erotic intimacy to explore the mystical relationship; see "Hallelujah," "Lover Lover Lover," and "Who by Fire." Although intimacy is often used as a metaphor in prophetic and wisdom literature in the Hebrew Scriptures (Ezek 22–23, Hosea, Isa 57, Song of Songs), the metaphor is always bound within the context of covenant relationship, where breaking the covenant through idolatry is similar to committing adultery within an intimate relationship. Likewise, in the Christian spiritual perspective, mystics such as Teresa of Ávila and John of the Cross clearly state that mystical intimate experiences do not have any type of sexual experience associated with them. For more on rightly relating the mystical and erotic, see C. S. Lewis's essay "Transposition," 91–116, in *The Weight of Glory and Other Addresses* (New York: Harper Collins, 2001).

and praise for the wholeness previously longed for, a prayer answered. Cohen brings an allegory of unity through a consummation of an intimate relationship of body, mind, and Spirit. As is common throughout Cohen's poetry and lyrics, there is multivalent meaning where the spiritual and sexual dovetail in the romantic. In the tradition of the Song of Songs and much of Western mysticism, Cohen turns to physical intimacy as a metaphor for divine relationship.[22] So, the ambiguity remains in these very intimate lyrics, but what is clear is the joy found in authentic unity and relationship.

Throughout his original lyrics on the album *The Future,* Cohen masterfully wove together Judeo-Christian imagery, secular philosophy, and a holy longing for intimacy in relationship: from a world of disorder in "The Future" to an intimate communion with the other in "Light As the Breeze." Throughout the progression of the lyrics Cohen longs for a new heart and the order of the soul through the Spirit of G-d, much like the prophetic promise in ancient Judaism: "I will give them one heart, and put a new spirit within them; I will remove the heart of stone from their flesh and give them a heart of flesh" (Ezek 11:19). To explore this concept further, we will look at how the reception of a heart and the order of G-d can find roots and a tangible expression in Scripture through the celebration of the Jewish and Christian feast of Pentecost.

## The Ordering of the Soul: Encountering Pentecost

*Celebrating the harvest of freedom: Establishing an annual feast of encounter and order*

Shavuot, the Feast of Weeks (later known from the Greek translation as Pentecost), was a dedicated ritual established in ancient Judaism, focusing on a celebration of gratitude and thanksgiving for the first fruits of the harvest (see Exod 34:22). The date for the celebration of Shavuot is directly connected to Passover;

---

22. Měsíc, "Nature of Love."

it occurs fifty days after that predominant Jewish celebration. The pilgrimage feast of Shavuot consisted of an offering that included wheat, barley, grapes, figs, pomegranates, olives, and dates taken to and sacrificed at the Temple after being blessed by the *kohen* or *cohen*, the Hebrew term for priest.

Today, Jewish tradition celebrates Shavuot as the commemorative anniversary of the reception of Torah by the Israelites at Mount Sinai. Central to the feast of Shavuot are the concepts of order and relationship—the Torah, a sign of the covenant between G-d and Israel, created an order of righteousness after the freedom from slavery in Egypt—as well as an annual remembrance of that gift illustrated through Israel's offering of the first fruits of the work of their hands from the land of freedom offered back in gratefulness for G-d's abundant generosity.

In Christian tradition, the feast of Pentecost also holds a powerful ritual and symbolic meaning. Before Jesus of Nazareth's Passion, he promised his followers that he would send them an advocate. This advocate would be a Spirit of truth and righteousness:[23] "Nevertheless I tell you the truth: it is to your advantage that I go away, for if I do not go away, the Advocate will not come to you; but if I go, I will send him to you" (John 16:7). After his Ascension, Jesus' disciples were gathered in Jerusalem for Shavuot when the Spirit descended upon them as tongues of fire. The events surrounding the descent of the Holy Spirit at Pentecost (Acts 2:1–42) created a crux and existential change for the message and mission within the hearts of the followers of Jesus of Nazareth, and a new vision for righteous order for the future of humanity. Through the intercession of this Advocate of wind and fire, the Apostles emerged as living witnesses of word and truth, through signs and wonders, establishing a future of re-unification for humanity, a new order of the soul.[24] Central

---

23. Raymond Brown, *The Community of the Beloved Disciple: The Life, Loves, and Hates of an Individual Church in New Testament Times* (New York: Paulist Press, 1979), 139.

24. Congar, "The New Testament: The Johannine Writings," in *I Believe in the Holy Spirit*, 49–62; Mathias Thelen, *Biblical Founda-*

to the feast of Pentecost, also in Christian perspective, are the concepts of order and relationship, where the Spirit re-orients the world from a position of isolation and separation to one of unity, a fellowship of persons in heart and language, through the joy of evangelization.[25]

*Written on our heart: Recognizing the Spirit and the order of the soul*

> But this is the covenant that I will make with the house of Israel after those days, says the Lord: I will put my law within them, and I will write it on their hearts; and I will be their God, and they shall be my people. (Jer 31:33)

In the religious perspectives of both Judaism and Christianity, the feast of Pentecost marks the annual remembrance of an encounter of a treasured blessing of G-d's presence, a gift that sustains and strengthens relationship within divine authority, charism, and structure.[26] Torah, the law, offered to the newly freed Israelites a way of life that allowed them to have right relationship with G-d through an order of justice; then the descent of the Holy Spirit upon the disciples of Jesus of Nazareth recalls the encounter of liberty and restoration of G-d's right order in the world, and the birth of the Church, a unitive body of Christ. To recall this through ritual, on the eve of Pentecost the Evening Prayer of the Daily Office includes a reading from Exodus chapter 19, where "God gave a law, the Decalogue, and established a covenant with the people, who then became a 'royal and priestly people' on the basis of that law."[27]

---

*tions for the Role of Healing in Evangelization* (Eugene, OR: Wipf & Stock), 36–40.

25. Congar, *The Meaning of Tradition* (San Francisco: Ignatius Press, 2004), 51–58; Pope Francis, *Evangelii Gaudium* (The Joy of the Gospel) (2013), 21, 259.
26. Congar, "The Pneumatology of Vatican II," in *I Believe in the Holy Spirit*, 167–73.
27. Raniero Cantalamessa, *Sober Intoxication of the Spirit: Filled with the Fullness of God* (Cincinnati, OH: Servant Books, 2005), 118.

The gift of liberty found in the sacred law, through order and Spirit, lays the foundation of communal relationship with G-d, as illustrated through the evangelical mission and ministry of the followers of Jesus of Nazareth.[28] The feast of Pentecost serves as a point of definition and illustration of pneumatological significance within both Judaism and Christianity. So too, the very heart of intimate unitive fellowship with G-d and others, seeking the righteous order of the soul, and gratitude for authentic liberty are prominent themes throughout the works of poet and singer/songwriter Leonard Cohen. Cohen clearly draws a deep influence from Judeo-Christian imagery throughout his album *The Future*, in his struggle to achieve the order of the soul while living in the order of the world. Cohen's poetry and lyrics offer an uncanny insight into the beauty and mystery of the Spirit present and active in our intimate and tangible fellowship with G-d and neighbor.

> Ring the bells that still can ring
> Forget your perfect offering
> There is a crack, a crack in everything
> That's how the light gets in
> "Anthem"

---

28. Congar, "The Spirit Is the Source of Life in Us Personally and in the Church," in *The Spirit of God*, 36–51.

# The Hold Steady's Tale of Two Transcendences:
## Sin and Salvation on Separation Sunday

Christian Raab

The Hold Steady is an obvious subject for a chapter in a book bringing together Catholic theology and rock music. The group is led by Craig Finn, a Boston College-educated cradle Catholic, who writes the band's lyrics and serves as its singer and rhythm guitarist. Though Finn has acknowledged that his religious practice is on-again and off-again,[1] Catholic themes and cultural references are ubiquitous throughout The Hold Steady's body of work.

Finn's Catholic imagination is especially apparent on 2005's *Separation Sunday*.[2] The album tells the story of Holly, a young woman from a Catholic family caught in a tug of war between sensuality and spirituality. Through Holly's experience, *Separation Sunday* broaches universal topics such as fall and redemption while making explicit Catholic cultural references to "CCD," various saints, and "the 5:30 folk Mass." These details concretize Holly and the other characters who populate *Separation Sunday* as working out their destinies in a Catholic milieu and with the faith in view as an important orientating touchstone.[3]

---

1.  Bruce Headlam (host), "Craig Finn Holds Steady," *Broken Record*, episode 106, Pushkin, June 22, 2021.
2.  Looking back on the record in 2021, Finn identified *Separation Sunday* as a peak point in his exploration of Catholic themes (Headlam). At the time of its release, Finn unapologetically stated: "Catholicism is a big part of everything I do" (Joe Gross, "The Gospel According to the Hold Steady," *The Village Voice*, April 26, 2005, https://www.villagevoice.com/2005/04/26/the-gospel-according-to-the-hold-steady/).
3.  For these reasons *The Village Voice* called *Separation Sunday* one of the most "egregiously" Catholic albums in rock history

While the Catholic allusions on *Separation Sunday* are obvious, the exactitudes of Holly's story and its ultimate meaning are more difficult to ascertain. The story's vagueness comes from its non-linear time progression, its lack of clarity about which characters are speaking, and the potential unreliability of their testimony. Accordingly, it has been compared to T.S. Eliot's similarly disorienting poem, *The Wasteland*.[4] While I don't claim to have the authoritative key to interpreting *Separation Sunday*, I do contend that a biblical and theological lens can shed light on what is happening. I propose that *Separation Sunday* is best heard as a salvation drama which follows the basic pattern of creation-fall-redemption and unfolds in five acts, each containing sequences of two or three songs apiece and mirroring the biblical narrative in important ways.

In what follows, I will recount the basic story told on *Separation Sunday*, explaining the many biblical and Catholic allusions Finn makes and demonstrating how they support the overall narrative of Holly's fall, God's work on her behalf, and her final redemption. Then, I will highlight and evaluate some theological claims that the record seems to be making, showing that the album does, for the most part, represent an orthodox Catholic view of creation, fall, and redemption. This will show that *Separation Sunday* isn't just Catholic in setting; it is Catholic in its worldview.

(Gross). Meanwhile, Rob Sheffield of *Rolling Stone* loved the album for being full of "Catholic angst" and "grappling with a lot of Catholic issues" while still being "rock." See James Breig, "A Rock Critic Talks Faith," *Franciscan Spirit Blog*, Franciscan Media, May 14, 2020, https://www.franciscanmedia.org/franciscan-spirit-blog/a-rock-critic-talks-faith.

4.    Shawn Westfall (host), "*Separation Sunday* Track 1: Hornets! Hornets!," *A Positive Jam*, Season 2 Episode 1, Shortman Studios, January 6, 2021.

## *Separation Sunday*: An Exposition

### Act One

Act One consists of the first two songs, "Hornets! Hornets!" and "Cattle and the Creeping Things." These songs provide the setting in which the drama will unfold. "Hornets! Hornets!" takes its title from the school mascot of Edina High, a suburban Minneapolis high school near where Craig Finn grew up.[5] The high school setting is typical rock and roll fare, but Finn is up to more than repeating tropes. He is setting up for a biblically themed drama and giving it the perfect backdrop.

In the public imagination, high school is simultaneously a place of innocence and of rebellion. As such, it is something like the garden of Eden—and Edina sounds a lot like Eden. It is in this Edenic/Edinic setting that we first meet the protagonist of the record, an adolescent girl named Holly. She appears at first as a typical teen who likes skateboarding videos and rock concerts. She's also recently been introduced to sex and drugs, though she has not yet "done much of this." Thus, Holly seems, in this opening track, to be relatively innocent but teetering on the edge of rebellion.

Holly has a song called "Running Up That Hill" running through her head. Finn emphasizes that Holly doesn't just sing this song; it is "scratched on her soul." "Running Up That Hill" is a song by 80s English singer Kate Bush. For our purposes, it is fascinating that "Running Up That Hill" is parenthetically titled "A Deal with God." This, it seems, is an important clue about how to understand what is going on with Holly in biblical terms. She has "a deal with God" "scratched on her soul." In this place of innocence and rebellion, she eventually chooses rebellion, but the deal with God will not just disappear.

The "deal with God" being scratched on Holly's soul is evocative of an important scriptural motif: the permanent mark which

---

5.  Craig Finn, "I was no longer a loser," *The Guardian*, May 11, 2007, https://www.theguardian.com/music/2007/may/11/po-pandrock2.

links us to God. In the opening chapters of Genesis, humanity is said to be created in God's "image" and "likeness" (Gen 1:26). God is non-corporeal, so the *imago dei* must be understood as a spiritual reality. A patristic tradition compares the creation of humanity *imago dei* to the inscription on a coin: the inscription indicates one's resemblance to and belonging to God.[6] St. Gregory of Nyssa made a distinction between the image and the likeness. He explained that the likeness is one's acquired virtue, whereas one's being *image* is a matter of one's possession of a free, rational soul. The likeness to God can be lost (as virtue can be lost), but the image remains. It is never lost, even if one strays.[7]

The Bible returns to the theme of the permanent mark in the story of Cain. After Cain murders his brother Abel, God punishes Cain by exiling him to wander the earth. Before doing so, however, God puts a special mark on Cain so that Cain can be recognized as one protected by God (Gen 4:15). Finally, there is the permanent mark of circumcision. Throughout Genesis, God makes a series of covenants: first with Adam and Eve (Gen 1:26–2:3), then with Noah (9:1–17), then with Abraham (12:1–3; 22:16–18), and so on. The parties in covenant relationships become family to one another and are bound by promises of fidelity to one another. Covenants are accompanied by signs of some sort.[8] The sign of the covenant that God makes with Abraham is circumcision, which he also commands of all Abraham's male descendants (chapter 17). Circumcision is a

---

6. Tertullian and Augustine interpreted Christ's teaching about rendering the coin with Caesar's image to Caesar as an implication that the human person should be rendered to God because the human person is inscribed with God's image. For references see Thomas C. Oden and Christopher A. Hall, eds., *Ancient Christian Commentary on Scripture: New Testament II: Mark* (Downers Grove, IL: InterVarsity Press, 1998), 167.

7. Andrew Louth, ed., *Ancient Christian Commentary on Scripture: Old Testament I: Genesis 1-11*, (Downers Grove, IL: InterVarsity Press, 2001), 33.

8. See John Grabowski, *Sex and Virtue* (Washington, DC: CUA, 2003), 29–32.

permanent mark which serves as a sign and reminder of the covenant relationship between God and Abraham and all the descendants of Abraham. In the covenant relationship between God and human beings, human beings often fail to uphold their end of the partnership. God, however, is always faithful to his side of the covenant. Over and over again Scripture attests that even when humanity strays, God continues to be there for his partner, and does so for the sake of the covenant he made with them.[9]

The lyrical reference to "Running Up That Hill (A Deal with God)" comes at the end of "Hornets! Hornets!," but it retroactively illuminates Holly's statements at the beginning of the song. There she says, "Always remember never to trust me." In the context of the "deal with God" it suggests that in this primordial Edenic covenant, one of the parties (the human) cannot be trusted quite as much as the other (the divine). Holly won't hold onto her last threads of innocence for very long. If this is Eden, she is Eve, and Eve is soon going to use her God-given freedom to rebel.

Holly's second statement points to such an inevitability. She says, "There's gonna come a time when I'm gonna have to go / With whoever's gonna get me the highest." Insofar as this is a story about an adolescent in the midst of an experimentation phase, Holly is announcing that she is eager to "get high" and that she plans on following her appetites. Through a biblical lens, the line recalls Eve's conversation with the serpent in the garden. The serpent tells Eve that if she eats of the tree God forbade her to eat from, she will become "like God" (Gen 3:5). The serpent thus promises to get her very high indeed! Sadly, like Eve, Holly will follow a serpent. Thankfully, this will not be the end of the story. Already the language of following "whoever" can get her the highest suggests that there may come a different avenue toward a different transcendence than the one the serpent offers and the one Holly initially takes.

---

9. See Exod 2:24, 6:5; Lev 26:9, 26:52, 26:45; Deut 7:9, 7:12, 8:18; Judg 2:1; Neh 1:5, 9:32; Pss 105:8–11, 106:45, 111:5; Isa 54:10.

"Hornets! Hornets!" is followed immediately by "Cattle and the Creeping Things." Since the title phrase comes from Genesis 1:24, describing the sixth day of creation, its use here, as well as the song's multiple explicit scriptural references, confirms for the listener that *Separation Sunday* is a record which must be interpreted with reference to the Bible. While the phrase "cattle and the creeping things" harkens back to the beginnings of the biblical story, the song seems to take us far forward in time with respect to Holly's personal narrative. How far forward is unclear, but possibly several years. The setting is a 12-step meeting where a conversation about Scripture is taking place. The interlocutors interpret events of their lives through the Bible stories: Cops catching criminals are like one of the plagues of Egypt. Holly's recovery from a drug overdose is compared to the resurrection. There are also references to the final judgment of the apocalypse, to Jesus driving money changers out of the temple, to Adam and Eve, and to Cain and Abel. Notably, most of the Bible stories mentioned here center on the notions of sin, judgment, and consequences. As such, "Cattle and the Creeping Things" suggests where the choices Holly was about to make when we left her in "Hornets! Hornets!" will ultimately land her. If "Hornets! Hornets!" alludes to a rebellious choice for a false transcendence, "Cattle and the Creeping Things" indicates that that choice will lead her down a road of addiction and self-destruction before recovery.

## Act Two

Act Two encompasses the songs "Your Little Hoodrat Friend" and "Banging Camp," which explain how Holly eventually reaches her low point. At the same time, they provide a ray of hope through symbols of God's grace and fidelity.

It is unclear which song comes first chronologically, but both seem to take place in the time between "Hornets! Hornets!" and "Cattle and the Creeping Things." "Your Little Hoodrat Friend" never uses Holly's name, but a later track indicates that the song is indeed about her.[10] In "Your Little Hoodrat Friend," Holly is in a much worse place than when we saw her in "Hornets! Hornets!" She is described as "broke" and "heartbroken," and she has taken to cutting herself. Where before she was being led into the world of substance abuse, she is now a leader in that world, getting others high.

The sad portrait of Holly in "Your Little Hoodrat Friend" invites us to ask what happened to her, and "Banging Camp" might provide an answer. In this track, Holly is part of a seedy underground scene that gathers in a public park and on the banks of the river. Among this populace are "great white sharks" and "killer whales." Possibly, these are men who use women's drug dependencies as a way of gaining control over them toward sexual ends.[11] When the narrator spots Holly on a particular evening, she is "half naked," "shaky but still trying to shake it," and "completely alone." Something has clearly happened to her. The next verse may introduce the culprit, a dark figure eerily portrayed in priestly terms. On the bank of the river, "He was breaking bread and giving thanks / With crosses made of pipes and planks / Leaned up against the nitrous tanks." He advertises the "hit" he offers as something that will make one "high as hell and born again." This drug dealing pimp is called Charlemagne, and we will hear more about him in the next song.

"Your Little Hoodrat Friend" and "Banging Camp" are two of the darkest songs on *Separation Sunday*. Importantly, though, the songs each provide a sign of hope. In "Your Little Hoodrat Friend," the sign is Holly's tattoos. On her neck are the words "Jesus lived and died for all your sins" and on her lower back are the words "Damn right, I'll rise again." Together, these phrases express the good news of forgiveness and hope of

10. "How a Resurrection Really Feels" contains the line, "Holly was a hoodrat / Now you finally know that."
11. This interpretation is supported by The Hold Steady fan website *Clicks and Hisses*, https://clicksandhisses.com/lyrics/banging-camp/great-white.

resurrection. They reflect Christ's conquering of sin and death and the application of Christ's victory to the individual soul.

Tattoos continue the permanent mark motif already introduced in "Hornets! Hornets!" Some of the Church Fathers used the metaphor of the tattoo to explain the spiritual reality effected by baptism.[12] In the ancient world, tattoos were branded on livestock and soldiers. A brand served "as a sign of ownership and belonging" but also "as protection for the one who bears it."[13] Similarly, in baptism one receives a spiritual mark on the soul that identifies him or her as a member of the Body of Christ, belonging to God, and being under God's protection. According to St. Gregory of Nazianzen, the seal of baptism is "a guarantee of preservation and a sign of ownership."[14] And, like a tattoo, the baptismal "character" is never lost. If a person falls into sin, they remain indelibly marked by baptism as a child of God.[15] So, while they may have strayed from God, God remains committed to them. Furthermore, baptismal character not only signifies one's relationship with God, it also functions in a causal way to recall, maintain, and strengthen that relationship. It is not just a mark; it is a link.[16] With their explicit Christian messaging, Holly's tattoos recall her baptismal status. They show that she is marked by the forgiveness of sins and sealed with the hope of resurrection. Indeed, by the end of the record we will know

---

12. Among these were Theodore of Mopsuestia, John Chrysostom, and Basil of Caesarea. See Robin M. Jensen, *Baptismal Imagery in Early Christianity: Ritual, Visual, and Theological Dimensions* (Grand Rapids, MI: Baker Academic, 2012), 66, 86–88; Jean Daniélou, *The Bible and the Liturgy* (Notre Dame, IN: University of Notre Dame Press, 1956), 54–69.
13. Jensen, *Baptismal Imagery*, 87.
14. Daniélou, *The Bible and the Liturgy*, 56.
15. *Catechism of the Catholic Church*, 1272.
16. For a precise treatment of the causal role baptismal character plays in one's relationship with God, see Paul Palmer, "The Theology of the *Res et Sacramentum*," in *Readings in Sacramental Theology*, ed. C. Stephen Sullivan (Englewood, NJ: Prentice Hall, 1964), 104–23.

that, as bad as things get for Holly, God has continued to pursue and protect her.

In "Banging Camp," the sign of hope is a string tied around Holly's finger. The ring has obvious connotations of marriage. In the Old Testament, the covenant between God and Israel is portrayed in spousal terms,[17] and in the New Testament the Church is the bride of Christ.[18] Though humanity sometimes strays from God, God remains faithful to his bride and continues to pursue her. Considering the trials Holly goes through in these two songs, the string on her finger is a hope-filled symbol that Holly is not abandoned and God has not given up on her.

The image of the ring of string may also be a nod to the famous Catholic novel *Brideshead Revisited* by Evelyn Waugh. The novel describes the journeys of two rather wayward siblings, Julia and Sebastian. At one point, their younger, more faithful sister Cordelia remarks that "God won't let them go for long."[19] She then goes on to interpret their situation through the lens of a G. K. Chesterton story where a detective catches a thief "with an unseen hook and an invisible line which is long enough to let him wander to the ends of the world and still to bring him back with a twitch upon the thread."[20] The second half of the book, in which the characters are drawn back to God, is titled "A Twitch upon the Thread."[21] It is a powerful image of God's grace "as an invisible, inescapable line" that allows humanity room to err but never cuts them off and also initiates their return.[22]

---

17. Hos 1–3; Jer 3:6–24; Ezek 23:4.
18. Eph 5:21–33; Col 3:18–4:1; 1 Pet 2:13–3:7. Cf. Michael G. Lawler, *Marriage and Sacrament: A Theology of Christian Marriage* (Collegeville, MN: Liturgical Press, 1993), 36–47.
19. Evelyn Waugh, *Brideshead Revisited: The Sacred and Profane Memories of Captain Charles Ryder* (Boston: Little, Brown and Company, 1945), 220.
20. Chesterton, quoted in Waugh, *Brideshead*, 220.
21. Waugh, *Brideshead*, 223.
22. Annesly Anderson, "'A Twitch Upon the Thread': Grace in Brideshead Revisited," *Faith and Culture: The Journal of the Augustine Institute*, January 24, 2020, https://www.faithandcul-

Before and after describing the darkness Holly has wandered into, "Banging Camp" reminds us twice that "there are strings attached to every single lover." It is a sign of hope recalling the truth expressed by the psalmist in Psalm 139: "If I make my bed in Sheol, you are there. / . . . even there your hand shall lead me, / . . . If I say 'Surely darkness shall cover me, / and the light around me become night,' / even the darkness is not dark to you" (verses 8, 10, 11–12).

## Act Three

The next two songs are about other characters: "Charlemagne in Sweatpants" and "Stevie Nix." Charlemagne personifies evil and Stevie is a good figure, though a bit ambiguously. The juxtaposition of these characters at the midpoint of the album has the effect of contrasting two roads a soul can take.

Charlemagne is characterized as "running numbers between bars" and "girls between the cars." He is carrying something that will meet the needs of a man in the corner "asking for a dance" and the "speed shooters driving 'round" in search of an "entrance ramp." Finn emphasizes Charlemagne's wickedness by describing his icy eyes. In Dante's inferno, the lowest level of hell is cold rather than hot.[23]

Since Charlemagne is a pimp and a drug dealer, he could be the same person who ruined Holly at the end of "Banging Camp." In this song, Holly remains in Charlemagne's orbit. She is coming to him, looking "for something / she could take up to a party." We are told that Holly is not "enslaved"; rather, she is "enthralled." This is actually a more frightening description—an enslaved person is trapped but may still retain the will and desire for liberation. An enthralled person is bewitched, hypnotized such that the will is compromised. To be enthralled is to be further down the road of dehumanization.

---

ture.com/home/2020/1/24/a-twitch-upon-the-thread-grace-in-brideshead-revisited.

23. See Dante Alighieri, *The Divine Comedy I: Hell*, Canto XXXIV.

By the time we reach "Charlemagne in Sweatpants" we have now heard a lot about Holly's hard-luck story. We might begin to feel pessimistic, even despairing for Holly's future. Perhaps to save us from becoming too discouraged, Finn interjects to tell us that this story he's been telling is not "boy meets girl," or a "murder mystery," but a "comeback story." The shift in tone is reinforced by the bright opening chords of the next song, "Stevie Nix."

The events of "Stevie Nix" are hard to follow. It shifts more than once between a dialogical and narrative structure. It also seems to go back and forth between Holly's present, memories of the past, and flash-forwards to the future. Still, some things seem clear enough. Holly arrives at the party with the drugs she got from Charlemagne. She ends up in the emergency room "half dead," getting her stomach pumped.

At the beginning of the song, though, we meet an unnamed character in a "long black shawl." She reminds the people around her of Fleetwood Mac's Stevie Nicks, who often dresses in black and/or shawls. The party goers make jokes about the "white swan," which could be a reference to Nicks's song "Edge of Seventeen" which talks about a "white-winged dove." According to a The Hold Steady fan website, White Swan is also a brand of nursing scrubs, which leads to an interpretation of the Stevie Nix figure as someone who plays a key role in saving Holly's life after her overdose.[24] Important for our purposes is the fact that, in the Bible and in Christian art, the Holy Spirit is often portrayed as a dove. As such, the "Stevie Nix" title character would seem to be the figure of light, contributing to Holly's salvation, contrasted with the darkness of Charlemagne, who contributes only to Holly's ruin.

After Holly's "resurrection" in the emergency room, the song shifts into a narrative summary of Holly's backstory with foreshadowings of the future. It clarifies some pieces for the listener, and presumably for Holly herself. She is a Catholic girl

---

24. See the "Stevie Nix" entry on *Clicks and Hisses*, https://clicksandhisses.com/lyrics/stevie-nix/lost-lights.

with a strong religious imagination. "Screwed up by religion" and "confused about the truth," she sought transcendence and meaning through Charlemagne, who she mistook for a good person, for Christ. Charlemagne initiated her into a life of drugs and abusive sex: the false Christ gave her a false baptism.

The final four verses of "Stevie Nix" alternate endings between "Lord, to be seventeen forever" and "Lord, to be thirty-three forever." Seventeen, of course, is the age mentioned by Stevie Nicks in her song about the white-winged dove, and it is Holly's age when she began experimenting with drugs. Generally speaking, it is very much an adolescent age. At the edge of seventeen, innocence is lost. People seek a kind of transcendence at seventeen that is often a false transcendence, which was certainly the case with Holly. Thirty-three, on the other hand, is a very significant number in Christianity. Three is the number of the Trinity. Thirty-three is the age at which Christ is believed to have died. Thomas Aquinas suggested that thirty-three (or thereabouts) would be the age Christians would be in the kingdom of God since it represents the fullness of maturity before the onset of decay.[25] As such it is the age of the beatific vision, and the age we will indeed be "forever." Thus, by contrasting 17 and 33, Finn could be contrasting two transcendences: the transcendence offered by Charlemagne, which is really just an escape from reality and which ends in death, and a different transcendence, the true transcendence, which is spiritual rebirth and ends in the beatific vision.

## Act Four

Act Four consists of three songs, "Multitude of Casualties," "Don't Let Me Explode," and "Chicago Seemed Tired Last Night." They describe a road trip that takes the characters from Minnesota out west to Colorado and Arizona and then east to Chicago. This great American road trip is highly suggestive of the desert wanderings of the Israelites after their exodus from

---

25. *Summa Theologica* Suppl. Q 81.

Egypt. Indeed, in "Multitude of Casualties," we learn that Holly and her companions spend "a few months just wandering the Sonoma." This road trip is a time of choosing, just as the desert meanderings of the Israelites were a time of testing.[26] Holly spends part of the trip "high as hell and shivering and smashed." But she also seeks out "the 5:30 folk Mass," where the hymns make her cry and the "bloody cross" meets her in her "druggy little messed up teenage life."

The contrasting of paths continues in "Don't Let Me Explode." Lines like "fields of speed" and "[scoring] big in Denver" refer to drugs. Meanwhile, though, Holly is praying to St. Barbara, saying "don't let me explode."[27] In the context of the song, this invocation is a cry for help which provides a sense of just how desperate Holly feels as her life "corrodes." The fact that she is praying is a sign that grace is still operating in her life and that Holly still has a choice as to how her destiny will unfold.

The road trip trilogy concludes with "Chicago Seemed Tired Last Night," which describes an evening of live music in the Windy City. Sex, drugs, and rock and roll are linked in common parlance as an unholy triad. So far we've seen sex and drugs—especially drugs—thematized on *Separation Sunday* as gateways to the false transcendence. In "Chicago Seemed Tired Last Night," rock and roll finally comes under examination. Joseph Ratzinger wrote about how rock music, especially in a live format, can "assume a cultic character" and promise a transitory "redemption that can be tasted at least for a few moments." At its worst, says Ratzinger, rock becomes "a form of worship, in fact, in opposition to Christian worship."[28] Finn is attuned to the religious nature of the rock concert. He writes about how "mythologies" and "doxologies" are shared through "PA systems."

---

26. The story of the desert wanderings is told in the biblical books of Numbers and Deuteronomy.
27. St. Barbara is a patron saint of miners and is invoked to protect them from dying in explosions. Colorado, where the song takes place, has an important mining industry.
28. Joseph Ratzinger, *The Spirit of the Liturgy* (San Francisco: Ignatius, 2000), 148.

The band does not promise salvation but something close: "I'm not saying that we could save you / But we could put you in a place where you could save yourself." A contrast between two transcendences is again made: "If you don't get born again / at least you'll get high as hell."

The song title, however, indicates that the sex, drugs, and rock and roll scene is getting tiresome. Halfway through the song, we hear that something is changing for Holly. "St. Theresa came to Holly." Immediately after this line, we hear: "Yeah, when Judas went up and kissed him / I almost got sick." It is not clear that the "I" is Holly, but taken together with the line before it, the implication is a moment of conversion through the aid of St. Theresa. The world of sex, drugs, and rock and roll is feeling more and more like a dead end and a betrayal. The scene is tiring. The false transcendence is not satisfying.

It is intriguing that St. Theresa is chosen as the herald or instrument of this conversion. While there are several saints who could be the one referenced here, a likely candidate is Teresa of Ávila.[29] In the Roman church of Santa Maria della Vittoria there is a famous statue of her by Gian Lorenzo Bernini. Crafted in the seventeenth century and considered a masterpiece of Baroque sculpture, the statue is famous for blending erotic and spiritual themes. The statue depicts Teresa in the depths of mystical prayer. She is pierced by an arrow held by an angel, and she appears to be in ecstasy. The statue's theme is drawn from Teresa's own spiritual writings. Following the tradition of the biblical Song of Songs, she used spousal, even erotic, language to describe her mystical experiences.[30]

---

29. Teresa of Calcutta was not yet canonized at the time the story takes place or even at the time *Separation Sunday* was released. Besides her, the two most famous Theresas are St. Teresa of Ávila and St. Thérèse of Lisieux.

30. The statue was directly inspired by the following passage: "I saw in his hand a long spear of gold, and at the iron's point there seemed to be a little fire. He appeared to me to be thrusting it at times into my heart, and to pierce my very entrails; when he drew it out, he seemed to draw them out also, and to leave me

If the St. Theresa of *Separation Sunday* is St. Teresa of Ávila, then bringing her into the story at the point when Holly is ripe for conversion is an interesting choice. When we were first introduced to Holly, she appeared as a young woman driven by hunger and desire. She announced that a time would come when she would "have to go with whoever" would "get [her] the highest." St. Teresa was also a woman of strong desire but one who found true fulfillment through her relationship with God. Reflecting on her mystical experience, Teresa stated: "The soul is satisfied now with nothing less than God. . . . It is a caressing of love so sweet which now takes place between the soul and God."[31] St. Teresa's appearance heralds the possibility that if Holly encounters the true object of her desire, it will put the sex, drugs, and rock and roll in their place.

It is also possible, however, that the Theresa in question is St. Thérèse of Lisieux. Like Teresa of Ávila, Thérèse was a Carmelite nun. While Teresa of Ávila lived in Spain during the sixteenth century, Thérèse lived in France at the end of the nineteenth. Thérèse of Lisieux is known for her doctrine of the "little way," which teaches that the soul grows in sanctity through a path of humility and increased trust in God. Thérèse was also known for a statement she uttered on her death bed: that "everything is a grace."[32] She did not mean that all things and forces are benevolent. "Everything is a grace" reflects the truth that even when we are in dark places we can be confident

---

all on fire with a great love of God. The pain was so great, that it made me moan; and yet so surpassing was the sweetness of this excessive pain, that I could not wish to be rid of it. The soul is satisfied now with nothing less than God. The pain is not bodily, but spiritual; though the body has its share in it, even a large one. It is a caressing of love so sweet which now takes place between the soul and God, that I pray God of His goodness to make him experience it who may think that I am lying" (Teresa of Ávila, *The Life of Teresa of Jesus*, XIX.17).

31. Teresa of Ávila, *The Life of Teresa of Jesus*, XIX.17.
32. Thérèse of Lisieux, *Her Last Conversations*, trans. John Clark (Washington, DC: Institute of Carmelite Studies, 1977), 57.

that God remains connected to us, and even sin and suffering can be used by God to lead us back to him if they prompt us to reach out for his help. The fact that Finn does not specify which Theresa he means allows us to consider that the insights of both saints apply to Holly. The figure of Teresa of Ávila suggests the lesson that God is one's true end who satisfies one's hunger in a way the world never can. The figure of Thérèse of Lisieux recalls the truth that even when we stray from God, the sins we commit and the sufferings we endure in that separation can be used by God to draw us back to him. Indeed, it is returning to God that constitutes the theme of *Separation Sunday*'s final act.

## Act Five

Act Five is constituted by two songs, "Crucifixion Cruise" and "How a Resurrection Really Feels." The first thing we note is that these are the first two songs on the record that have explicitly Christian, as opposed to generic biblical, imagery in their titles. Coming at the very end of the album, they reinforce the sense we have of *Separation Sunday* as a salvation story which parallels the over-arching biblical narrative. When we open the Bible, we notice that the Old Testament is really much longer than the New Testament, that the story of Christ actually comes only at the very end, making up less than a fifth of the Bible as a whole. Similarly, these two songs, describing crucifixion and resurrection—the central events of the new covenant—come at the end of the record, completing the story and giving the album a biblical look. Also, if the first nine songs were the story of Holly's innocence followed by rebellion and separation from God, these final two songs articulate her reunion with God—which happens on a Sunday. This reunion with God will require a different kind of separation, this time from the world. The final two songs thus make sense of *Separation Sunday* as an album title.

The penultimate track describes Holly, nearly out of drugs and "infested with infection," going to confession, where she has a sort of "coming to"—"she climbed the cross" and "liked the view." She reflects on the resurrection and on her "old connection," a likely allusion to the God who scratched his covenant on her soul, tattooed his promise on her person, and tied the string of his love and grace around her finger. The piece concludes with her praying for the Lord's help to turn her life around. She says: "Lord, what do you recommend / To a real sweet girl who's made some not-sweet friends? / Lord, what would you prescribe / To a real soft girl who's having real hard times?"

Though "Crucifixion Cruise" is a short piece, it is packed with content and vitally important to the narrative. Holly is sick and sinful. She confesses to Christ who heals and forgives. Her concluding prayers indicate that a real encounter has taken place and a relationship has begun anew.

"How a Resurrection Really Feels" completes Holly's story. The scene takes place at an Easter Sunday Mass. Holly shows up, disheveled and limping. Her entrance interrupts the liturgy, and she asks the priest if she can tell the assembly "how a resurrection really feels." In addition to providing a happy and comical ending to Holly's legacy, the song provides more information about the protagonist. We learn that Holly has now been away from home for years: she had "been disappeared for years" but "today she finally came back." The church she enters on Easter Sunday appears to be the church she grew up in.

In ways explicit and subtle "Resurrection" continues the theme of reconciliation introduced in "Crucifixion." Her coming back to the church of her youth implies not just a new beginning but a return to key relationships. We are informed in the first verse that Holly's original name, the name her parents gave her, was Hallelujah. Bringing up this information suggests that she is returning to herself. It is evocative of Christ's parable of the prodigal son (Luke 15:11–32) which describes a boy who "squandered his property in dissolute living" (15:13) but who later "came to himself" (15:17) and returned to his father's house, where he was received with mercy. We then hear from Holly about what she has done and been through: "She's been stranded" at parties which started "lovely" but got "druggy" and turned "ugly" and "bloody"; she "laid beneath [her] lovers"; she mistook a bad man for her savior. Through all of this she nevertheless felt "protected," though at other times "afraid."

Most importantly, we are told "she's sorry." But the emphasis is on Holly's return, and this is achieved through the repetition of two lines: "Today she finally came back" and "Walk on back." Thus, *Separation Sunday* completes the creation-fall-redemption cycle with Holly's restoration to her God, church community, and family.

## Theological Analysis

We have so far seen how *Separation Sunday* is replete with biblical and Catholic imagery and that these symbols are used to support a creation-fall-redemption narrative. In what remains, I would like to highlight and evaluate some specific theological positions of *Separation Sunday* that pertain to these very topics of creation, fall, and redemption. First, I will look at two things *Separation Sunday* gets particularly right from a Catholic theological perspective. Then, I will look at some places where the album might lend itself to a problematic interpretation.

### Eros

A first thing *Separation Sunday* gets right is the way it portrays *eros*. *Eros* is a desire for ecstasy, a desire for transcendence. In the words of Benedict XVI, eros is a "searching" and "ascending" love in pursuit of "infinity, eternity—a reality far greater and totally other than our everyday existence."[33] Finn presents Holly as full of erotic desire: she seeks out and enjoys the feeling of connection she gets at rock concerts, and wants to reach the "highest" plane. Driven by eros, she is drawn to things that promise transcendence, be they spiritual or sensual. She has this hunger, this desire. It is powerful, but it can lead her either to God or to trouble.

---

33. Benedict XVI, *Deus Caritas Est* (On Christian Love), December 25, 2005, 6, 7, 5.

Eros is a good thing because it is instructive and, at least potentially, constructive. It is instructive because it reveals the human person as incomplete in himself or herself and only fulfilled in union with another.[34] Ultimately, it points to God. As the *Catechism of the Catholic Church* puts it, God "freely created man to make him share in his own blessed life."[35] Insofar as eros is a restless desire, hungry for more than what is offered in everyday life, it reminds us of that divine destiny. Along these lines, St. Augustine stated: "You have made us for yourself, O Lord, and our hearts are restless until they rest in you."[36] When eros does indeed lead us to seek God, it serves a healthy purpose—thus its constructive power.

On the other hand, eros can be destructive. As we see with Holly, while eros drives her to seek transcendence, it does not discern whether that transcendence is reached in truth or falsity, good or evil. Eros does not, by itself, have clarity about its true object or the right way to reach its object. It can therefore lead us astray. As Pope Benedict XVI explained, while eros promises a "foretaste of the pinnacle of our existence, of that beatitude for which our whole being yearns," it must be "disciplined and purified" through a path of renunciation and healing.[37] The

---

34. Man "cannot fully find himself except through a sincere gift of himself" (Second Vatican Council, *Gaudium et spes* (Pastoral Constitution on the Church in the Modern World), 24).
35. *CCC*, 1.
36. St. Augustine, *Confessions*, 1.1.
37. *Deus Caritas Est*, 4; see also 5. Benedict goes onto explain that an unredeemed eros is "insecure, indeterminate and searching" (6) and can even become "covetous" (7). Only through the power of graced conversion does eros become elevated to the sure guide of agapic love. Benedict describes *agape*, the true love to which we are called, as "love which involves a real discovery of the other, moving beyond the selfish character that prevailed earlier. Love now becomes concern and care for the other. No longer is it self-seeking, a sinking in the intoxication of happiness; instead it seeks the good of the beloved: it becomes renunciation and it is ready, and even willing, for sacrifice" (6).

reason is that eros has been affected by sin, so we experience eros as fallen creatures. We can, and often do, direct eros wrongly and/or find ourselves directed wrongly by it.

Thus, to frame eros correctly, we must avoid both Manichean and Pelagian errors about the status of creation. The Manichean heresy was strongly dualist in its metaphysics, portraying creation as intrinsically evil. While strictly speaking the Manicheans were not Christian, the same kind of evaluation of creation is present in the errors of those Christians who have portrayed creation, or more specifically, human nature, as "totally depraved" after the fall.[38] If this were true, then human desires could only be, and will only be, for evil things. The Pelagian heresy, on the other hand, was overly optimistic about human nature. Pelagius was an influential teacher in the early Church who minimized any lasting effects of the fall and thus failed to recognize human nature's profound woundedness and radical dependence on grace. In failing to recognize the brokenness of human nature, Pelagianism tends to overestimate desire, assuming it will point rightly.[39] St. Augustine battled both these heresies in his life. Against the Manicheans, he emphasized the goodness of creation. Against the Pelagians, he emphasized that creation, though good, had been damaged by the fall. As such, desire had become concupiscent, meaning that it had become disordered, wanting things in the wrong measure, in the wrong way, and at the wrong time. When the two strands of Augustine's thought are brought together, we have the basis of the Catholic anthropological vision and a way to measure eros. Insofar as eros is a created energy it is a good, because creation is good. It is not unambiguously good, however. It is affected by the evil

---

38. "Total depravity" of fallen humanity is one of the essential tenets espoused by strict five-point Calvinism. See Edward T. Oakes, *A Theology of Grace in Six Controversies* (Grand Rapids, MI: Eerdmans, 2016), 149.

39. See Pelagius, "Letter to Demetrias," in *Theological Anthropology*, ed. and trans. J. Patout Burns (Philadelphia: Fortress, 1981), 39–55.

of concupiscence, a result of the fall, and it needs the help of grace and reason in order to aim rightly.[40]

*Separation Sunday* seems on target in its portrayal of desire. Holly is driven by desire for transcendence. Insofar as that desire drives Holly to seek something elevated and beyond herself, it is good. However, Holly's eros is affected by concupiscence and leads her astray. Holly's redemption will not be the annihilation but rather the elevation of her eros. We see that transformation implied through her connection with St. Teresa, who models the right ordering of eros to the true transcendence. Inasmuch as *Separation Sunday* gets eros right, it also gets anthropology right more generally. By virtue of creation, we are good. By virtue of the fall, we are "bent," as C. S. Lewis would put it, and in need of grace.[41]

## Justification by Grace

A second thing *Separation Sunday* gets right is justification by grace. Justification is shorthand for the re-establishment of sinful humanity in right relationship with God. The *Catechism* defines justification variously as "the gracious action of God which frees us from sin and communicates 'the righteousness of God through faith in Jesus Christ' (Rom 3:22)"; as participation "in Christ's Passion by dying to sin, and in his Resurrection by being born to a new life"; as incorporation into "his Body which is the Church"; and as "the sanctification and renewal of the interior man."[42] We can see that if eros belongs to our creaturely status

---

40. For a discussion of how Augustine's responses to Manicheanism and Pelagianism are responses to how each thought about desire, see Christopher Roberts' section on Augustine in his *Creation and Covenant: The Significance of Sexual Difference in the Moral Theology of Marriage* (New York: T&T Clark, 2007), 39–77.
41. C. S. Lewis, *Out of the Silent Planet* (New York: Scribner, 2003), 68.
42. *CCC* glossary, cf. 1987; 1988; 1989 (Council of Trent [1547]: DS 1528); see also 1987–1992.

but points to our eschatological finality, justification is the key to reaching that finality.

Many readers will be familiar with justification as a point of contention in ecumenical settings where believers debate what it means to be "saved" and how one "gets saved." It sometimes happens that Protestants insist justification happens through faith, and Catholics feel they must counter by defending the importance of works. This debate can be traced back to the sixteenth century. Luther, Calvin, and other leaders of the Protestant Reformation saw the Catholic penitential system as promoting a false "works-righteousness" understanding of justification. In opposition, they emphasized that justification was by grace alone, and that the response that mattered for one's salvation was faith (not works).

Importantly, the Council of Trent, which was called to formulate a Catholic response to the Protestant Reformation, did not simply take the opposite position of the Protestants. Instead, it strongly centered its own theology of justification on grace,[43] and only after establishing grace's priority proceeded to talk about faith and works, which the Council framed as responses to grace which must in fact be enabled by grace.[44]

---

43. In scholastic fashion, Trent listed four causes of justification. It identified the final cause of justification as God's glory; the meritorious cause as Jesus Christ's saving work; the instrumental cause as baptism; and the formal cause as God's justice. Notably, human efforts did not make the list. See Council of Trent, *Decree Concerning Justification*, Ch. VII, https://www.ewtn.com/catholicism/library/decree-concerning-justification--decree-concerning-reform-1496.

44. Trent stated: "Now, they are disposed to that justice when, aroused and aided by divine grace, receiving faith by hearing, they are moved freely toward God, believing to be true what has been divinely revealed and promised, especially that the sinner is justified by God in his grace, through the redemption that is in Christ Jesus; and when, understanding themselves to be sinners, they, by turning themselves from the fear of divine justice, by which they are salutarily aroused, to consider the mercy of

Grace was won by Christ on the Cross and is extended to human beings as a pure gift through the sacraments.[45] Trent, therefore, in its own way, concurred with the Protestant prioritization of grace and critique of works-righteousness. But, instead of entering a contest of faith and works, the council argued for the importance of both while simultaneously insisting that both were secondary to and dependent on grace. Trent even cautioned against turning the act of faith into its own brand of works-righteousness such that it was the fact of one's belief rather than grace which justified a person.[46]

Unfortunately, Trent's articulation of a grace-first doctrine of justification was not enough to prevent the schisms of the Reformation. However, in more recent years significant ecumenical progress has been made on the question of justification precisely through prioritizing grace's role.[47] Recognizing grace as the key to justification is not only theologically accurate, it is also existentially essential. When works are isolated from and

---

God, are raised to hope, trusting that God will be propitious to them for Christ's sake; and they begin to love Him as the fountain of all justice, and on that account are moved against sin by a certain hatred and detestation . . ." (*Decree Concerning Justification*, Ch. VI).

45. See Council of Trent, *Decree Concerning Justification*, Ch. VII.
46. See Council of Trent, *Decree Concerning Justification*, Ch. IX.
47. In 1999, the *Joint Declaration on the Doctrine of Justification* was issued by the Catholic Church and the Lutheran World Federation. It has since also been signed by the World Methodist Council, the Anglican Communion, and the World Communion of Reformed Churches. It states: "We confess together that all persons depend completely on the saving grace of God for their salvation. The freedom they possess in relation to persons and the things of this world is no freedom in relation to salvation, for as sinners they stand under God's judgment and are incapable of turning by themselves to God to seek deliverance, of meriting their justification before God, or of attaining salvation by their own abilities" (*Joint Declaration on the Doctrine of Justification* (1999), 19, https://www.ewtn.com/catholicism/library/joint-declaration-on-the-doctrine-of-justification-2356).

prioritized over grace in discourse about justification, it leads to the dangerous position of thanking oneself for one's salvation.[48]

*Separation Sunday* gets right the priority of grace in Holly's justification journey. Holly is a fallen figure. However, even while Holly was in her darkest moments, she remained connected to God, a connection symbolized through the song etched on her soul, her tattoos, and the string tied around her finger. The latter image, insofar as it suggests Waugh's "twitch upon the thread," attributes Holly's return to a divine initiative. Holly wanders far but God pulls her back through a tie that he has never surrendered. Holly didn't merit God's work on her behalf by anything she did; she received it as a mercy. Similarly, the aid of St. Theresa, if it is understood as an allusion to St. Thérèse of Lisieux, is a reminder that "all is grace." God is present in the darkest valleys of Holly's life and can use even her trials to inspire her to return to him.

While we can say with St. Thérèse that "all is grace," Catholics understand that the ordinary and certain way grace is given by God is through the sacraments.[49] Sacraments are not only signs but causes of salvation.[50] For some Protestants, on the other hand, sacraments are signs but not truly causes. In my view, *Separation Sunday* has a particularly Catholic emphasis on the causal role of sacraments. Again, the song scratched on the soul, the tattoos, and the string are all evocative of the Catholic understanding of baptismal character. Baptismal character is an indelible mark on the soul which disposes one toward grace, thus maintaining one's connection to God.[51] Another important sacrament on *Separation Sunday* is reconciliation, also known as

---

48. See Otto H. Pesch, "Existential and Sapiential Theology: The Theological Confrontation between Luther and Thomas Aquinas," in Jared Wicks, ed., *Catholic Scholars Dialogue with Luther* (Chicago: Loyola University Press), 61–81, esp. 73.
49. See *CCC*, 1257.
50. Again, Trent calls baptism the "instrumental cause" of justification (*Decree Concerning Justification*, Ch. VII).
51. *CCC*, 1121. See also Council of Trent, *Decree Concerning the Sacraments*, Canon IX.

confession or penance. Holly "came to in the confession booth" on Holy Saturday, which immediately anticipates her Easter Sunday return to the worshipping assembly and her speech about "how a resurrection really feels."[52] The Council of Trent recognized the sacrament of penance as causal of justification for those who had sinned after baptism, stating:

> Those who through sin have forfeited the received grace of justification can again be justified when, moved by God, they exert themselves to obtain through the sacrament of penance the recovery, by the merits of Christ, of the grace lost.[53]

In the same section, Trent called this sacrament a "second plank" of salvation given by God for the remediation of post-baptismal sin. Holly's journey really is the story of a fallen-away Catholic who returns to communion through the doorway of confession.

A final way *Separation Sunday* gets justification right is that it shows Holly as free to accept or reject the grace of justification. Some Christians have upheld the idea of "irresistible grace."[54] The Council of Trent, to the contrary, affirmed that human beings possess free will, that free will cooperates with grace, and that free will could "refuse its assent if it wishes."[55] Three key moments on *Separation Sunday* reveal Holly's freedom. At the beginning, in "Hornets! Hornets!," Holly announces that she will follow "whoever" can get her "the highest." The language of "whoever" coupled with the Edenic setting implies a choice to be made. In the middle of the album, in "Stevie Nix," a contrast is made between being "seventeen forever" and "thirty-three forever," suggesting again that there is a choice to be made between destinies. Finally, at the end, in "How a

---

52. There is a long tradition of sacramental confession during Lent in anticipation of Easter when penitents as well as new Christians are received into full communion with the assembly.
53. Council of Trent, *Decree Concerning Justification*, Ch. XIV.
54. See Oakes, *A Theology of Grace*, 149.
55. Council of Trent, *Decree Concerning Justification*, Canon IV.

Resurrection Really Feels," Holly is overheard saying "I love you," which are the words Peter said to Christ when Jesus gave Peter a second chance to choose him after Peter's threefold denial (John 21:15–17).

On the question of freedom, some Christians emphasize the importance of living with "blessed assurance," an alleged grace of certitude about one's salvation. Trent, however, warned against presuming one's predestination or final perseverance. Looking at Christ and trusting in his promises, we should be hopeful and confident about our salvation. Looking at ourselves, however, we must recognize our capacity to lose our salvation.[56] Holly illustrates the right disposition pretty well. It is in looking at Christ that she has hope ("damn right, I'll rise again") and the courage to change. Looking at herself, though, she recognizes that she is capable of throwing it all away. In that final scene of "How a Resurrection Really Feels," Holly says, "Don't turn me on again / I'll probably just go and get myself all gone again." It's an indication she is aware of her own freedom to throw away the gift she has been given.

## Being Born Again and Rising Again

So far we've seen that *Separation Sunday* presents a Catholic vision of eros and the priority of grace in justification. *Separation Sunday*'s depictions of conversion and resurrection are, however, more ambiguous and have at least the potential for a problematic interpretation.

In Christian parlance, conversion is sometimes described as being "born again." One of the challenging things about *Separation Sunday* is that it applies the same language of being "born again" to drug-induced ecstasy ("Banging Camp"), to recovery from a near-death experience ("Cattle and the Creeping

---

56. Council of Trent, *Decree Concerning Justification*, Ch. XII and XIII; see also *Joint Declaration Concerning the Doctrine of Justification*, 36.

Things," "Stevie Nix"), and to spiritual awakening/conversion ("Chicago Seemed Tired Last Night"). On the one hand, this multivalent approach is a useful poetic device that allows Finn to link types of transcendence and ask his listeners to ponder how they differ. Rather than providing a deductive sermon about how one transcendence is superior to another, it allows the listener to arrive inductively at the conclusion that while multiple things might promise transcendence, only one (the spiritual conversion) is really satisfying. On the other hand, it should not be taken for granted that all listeners will arrive at this hoped-for conclusion. Unfortunately, the music does not always give the clearest cues. Sometimes guitars, drums, and voice crescendo triumphantly at the very moments when characters are talking about getting "high as hell" or something similar, which can give the impression that the false transcendence is being celebrated and should therefore be embraced rather than renounced.

The depiction of resurrection is also ambiguous in a way that could invite flawed understanding. Holly delivers her final speech in the context of the Easter Mass, saying, "Father, can I tell your congregation how a resurrection really feels?" The word "really" gives pause because it seems to put Holly's experience of spiritual resurrection in competition with something. What is that something? It seems that there are two possibilities. It could put Holly's personal and immediate conversion experience in competition with the historical resurrection of Christ that the community has gathered to celebrate, as if the former were more real than the latter. Sadly, there is a strand within Christianity that denies Christ's bodily resurrection, perceiving it as a mere symbol of a spiritual awakening or felt presence of God experienced in the hearts of Christians. The influential twentieth-century German biblical theologian Rudolf Bultmann, for example, taught along these lines.[57] In the words of Cardinal

---

57. See Rudolf Bultmann, *Interpreting Faith for the Modern Era*, ed. Roger A. Johnson (Minneapolis, MN: Fortress Press, 1987);

Kasper, "Easter, for Bultmann, is something that happens not to Jesus, but to the disciples."[58] If *Separation Sunday* is interpreted through a Bultmannian lens, Holly's spiritual awakening is the "real" resurrection and Christ's being raised from the dead is not a historical fact but just a useful symbol for "comeback stories." Holly's tale could then just as easily be told through appeal to the myth of the phoenix. If that were the case, then *Separation Sunday* would no longer be an expression of Catholic faith. It would just be a story told with Christian language. I don't think that's the right interpretation, but I can see how the album might be open to it.

There is another possibility, however. When Holly says "Can I tell your congregation how a resurrection really feels?," she could be contrasting her experience of survival and return—a dramatic grace-filled experience indeed—not with the historical resurrection of Christ (which it does recapitulate) but with the limp liturgy and stilted enthusiasm of the congregation that is all too often the case in Christian worship, even at Easter. I consider this more likely to be the intention, and if so then there is no problem, only a good joke. It is the irony of the wayward prodigal revealing the meaning of the gospel to those who were taking it for granted.

## Conclusion

*Separation Sunday* is a fascinating rock album. While listeners may easily pick up the biblical and Catholic images and themes present, it is more difficult to apprehend their full meaning. This chapter has been an attempt to offer a theological interpretation of *Separation Sunday* that will facilitate a more theologically aware listening experience. Hopefully, it has established that *Separation Sunday* can be understood as a creation-fall-

*New Testament and Mythology and Other Basic Writings*, trans. Schubert M. Ogden (Philadelphia: Fortress Press, 1984).

58. Walter Kasper, *Jesus the Christ*, rev. ed. (New York: T&T Clark, 2011), 121.

redemption story informed strongly by a biblical imagination and Catholic theology. It has argued that *Separation Sunday* juxtaposes two transcendences and makes a case for finding meaning and communion in faith. Along the way it presents an accurate picture of the human person in relation to God and the role of grace in justification. In those places where *Separation Sunday* is open to a problematic theological interpretation, it is due to vague lyrical and musical cues, which in my opinion are not at all enough to sabotage an otherwise Catholic vision.

# Dylan and the Donatists
## The Heresies of an Artist Born Again and Again

Robert E. Alvis

On his 1967 album *John Wesley Harding*, Bob Dylan included the song "I Dreamed I Saw St. Augustine." Like many dreams, it lacks a straightforward narrative, offering instead a series of arresting images that create an unsettling mood. Augustine is portrayed as a wandering prophet "in the utmost misery," crying "without restraint," lamenting the absence of martyrs "whom you can call your own." Upon awaking, the dreamer feels "alone and terrified" and is ultimately reduced to tears.

"I Dreamed I Saw St. Augustine" is a spare song that offers no obvious insights into the saint's life and thought. At the same time, the song is oddly relevant to Dylan's storied musical career. Its linking of Augustine and martyrdom calls to mind the Donatist controversy that roiled the Church in northern Africa in the fourth and fifth centuries AD and threatened to create a lasting schism. In his role as bishop of Hippo, Augustine fought hard against the Donatists and played an instrumental role in quelling the controversy. In this chapter, I argue that Dylan repeatedly had to contend with modern-day Donatists, who took umbrage at the "Augustinian" quality of his development as an artist. The chapter begins with a brief review of the Donatist controversy and Augustine's response to the same. It then considers three phases within Dylan's musical journey: his initial fame as a folk artist in the early 1960s, his life as a rock star from the mid-1960s to the late 1970s, and the Christian music he made in the late 1970s and early 1980s. As he transitioned between these phases, Dylan provoked reactions that echoed the ancient Donatists. The chapter concludes with a brief consideration of the Augustinian sensibility that seems to animate Dylan's 2020 album *Rough and Rowdy Ways*.

## The Donatists and Augustine

To understand Donatism, it is first essential to take stock of the Christian experience within the Roman Empire. At the time of Christ's death, the empire encompassed the territory surrounding the Mediterranean Sea, including the Holy Land. The Romans were relatively tolerant of the varied religious traditions of the peoples they ruled, but they remained ill-disposed toward Christianity, which they regarded as extreme. They were particularly incensed by its "atheism," that is, the refusal of Christians to show respect to the deities of other religious traditions. As a result, in the first three centuries of their existence within the empire, Christians repeatedly faced persecution. These attacks tended to be localized and episodic, often emerging in response to crises that Roman officials blamed on Christians. The early Church held in particularly high esteem the martyrs, those Christians who remained true to the faith even in the face of death.

The Christian population grew at an impressive clip in antiquity, and by the late third century it was impossible to ignore. This set the stage for the "Great Persecution" (303–311), the most sustained and systematic attempt ever by imperial officials to undermine the Christian faith. A great deal of pressure was applied against Christian leaders in particular, in an effort to decapitate the Church. The effort ultimately failed, and in 313 Emperor Constantine granted Christians formal toleration, but the persecution had exacted a heavy toll. This was especially true in northern Africa, the epicenter of the Donatist movement.

During the Great Persecution, some Christian priests and bishops surrendered copies of Scripture and other sacred objects to imperial agents in order to avoid harsh punishments. Afterward, their critics disparaged them as *traditores*—a Latin term meaning "handers over"—and some began to argue that such men, on account of their betrayal of the faith, had forfeited their rights to office and the capacity to celebrate the sacraments in a valid way. The issue first emerged in northern Africa around the year 308, when a man named Caecilianus was appointed to serve as the new bishop of Carthage. A rigorist faction accused him of being a *traditore* and of having been consecrated by a *traditore* bishop, thereby nullifying his claim to the office. They elected an alternate bishop named Maiorinus. Succeeding Maiorinus in 313 was Donatus (d. 355), whose name became synonymous with the faction he helped lead over the next three decades.

This turmoil within the Christian community of northern Africa came to the attention of Constantine, who was keen to promote unity in the Church, with which he increasingly identified. He helped organize two synods of bishops, both of which ruled in favor of Caecilianus, but the Donatist party remained unmoved. A subsequent show of military force failed to intimidate the Donatists, whose very identity was rooted in unwavering resistance to imperial threats.

Constantine eventually relented, and divisions in northern Africa hardened into a formal schism. In town after town throughout the region, Catholic and Donatist bishops oversaw parallel churches that coexisted uneasily and periodically came to blows. The Donatists were known to refer to themselves as the "church of the pure" or the "church of the martyrs," which reflected their belief that the true Church was exclusive, consisting of Christians of the highest caliber.[1] They sometimes dismissed their Catholic rivals, by contrast, as the "church of Judas."[2] In their writings, Donatists echoed Old Testament ideas of ritual purity, namely, that priests could lose their "spiritual potency" through impure actions.[3]

Throughout much of the fourth century, the Donatists appear to have been the larger of the two groups.[4] By the 390s,

---

1. Noel Lenski, *Constantine and the Cities: Imperial Authority and Civic Politics* (Philadelphia: University of Pennsylvania Press, 2016), 247.
2. Peter Brown, *Augustine of Hippo: A Biography* (Berkeley: University of California Press, 1967), 213.
3. Ibid., 218–19.
4. When church leaders based in northern Africa gathered in Carthage for a council in 411, representatives from 429 dioceses took part. Of these dioceses, 198 had both a Catholic and a Do-

however, their fortunes began to turn. They were weakened by internal divisions, which left them less capable of managing exterior threats, including growing pressure from Emperor Honorius (395–423) and a new generation of Catholic leaders, most notably Augustine. Born in the northern African settlement of Thagaste in 354, Augustine explored a variety of philosophical and religious traditions before accepting baptism in 387, during a formative five-year sojourn in Italy. He returned to Africa in 388, was ordained to the priesthood in 391, and was appointed bishop of Hippo in 395. His extended exposure to the Church and the world outside of Africa informed his staunch opposition to the Donatists. He waged a relentless campaign against them in his sermons, letters, and treatises, advancing arguments that undermined their credibility.

Integral to Augustine's case against the Donatists was his understanding of the essential nature of the Church. Christ intended it to be one body that extended throughout the world, Augustine believed. The Donatist claim that their modest corner of the Church was alone pure, while the rest was awash in darkness, was both deeply flawed and highly presumptuous. In a letter written in 405 to a Donatist bishop, Augustine casts doubt on the group's claims by highlighting their isolation from the broader Christian community:

> I grieve that you are severed and separated from the Catholic Church, which is spread through the whole world, as it was foretold by the Holy Spirit. I do not know why [you chose this separation]. For it is certain that a large part of the Roman world . . . knows nothing of the sect of Donatus.[5]

He drives home the same point in a commentary on Psalm 95. He begins by quoting verses 9–10: "Let the entire earth be moved before His face. . . . For He has corrected the whole

natist bishop; 149 had only a Donatist bishop; and 82 had only a Catholic bishop (Lenski, *Constantine and the Cities*, 256).

5.  William Harmless, *Augustine in His Own Words* (Washington, DC: Catholic University of America Press, 2010), 251–52.

world, which is not to be moved." He discerns in this passage evidence of the Church's universality: "What great testimonies for building up the house of God! Heavens' clouds thunder out throughout the whole world where God's house is being built up." He then offers a biting rebuke: "Meanwhile the [Donatist] frogs croak from their marsh, 'We alone are the Christians!' What testimonies can I bring forward? Psalms. . . . Look at the testimony of the whole world. 'Let the whole world be moved before His face.'"[6]

A truly universal Church is destined to be diverse, Augustine believed, encompassing both the virtuous and the wicked, the pure and the not-so-pure. Ultimately it is up to God, not church leaders, to distinguish between the two. He gives voice to this view in a letter from 396: "No one blots from the earth the Church of God. He promised the whole earth; [the Church] has filled the whole earth, and she includes both bad and good; but she loses none on earth but the bad, and admits to heaven none but the good."[7] In another letter, he points to the parable of the wheat and the chaff to argue that, by God's design, the Church on earth is a mixed body, containing both nourishing seeds and lifeless husks. "The Lord strengthened the patience of His servants by these and other parables," he notes, "to prevent them from thinking that their virtue would be defiled by contact with the wicked, and thus, through vain and human dissensions, they should lose the little ones, or they themselves should perish."[8] In a sermon from 407, Augustine illustrates the Church's diversity by comparing it to Noah's ark:

> Noah had the raven there; he also had the dove. That ark contained each kind. If the ark symbolized the Church, you see, of course, that it is necessary for the Church in this flood of the world to contain each kind, both the raven and the dove. Who are the ravens? They who seek

---

6. Ibid., 254.
7. Ibid., 249–50.
8. Ibid., 253.

the things that are their own. Who are the doves? They who seek the things that are Christ's.[9]

Augustine's arguments contributed to the gradual eclipse of the Donatist party in northern Africa. Indeed, the last-known traces of their existence date to the sixth century. That said, the principles for which they were best known, including the insistence that only morally upstanding priests could perform efficacious sacraments, have resurfaced from time to time among later figures and movements.[10] More generally, the term *Donatist* has come to describe an exclusivist understanding of the Church that encompasses only Christians of the highest caliber. In an address to the clergy of the Diocese of Rome on February 27, 2020, Pope Francis warned that "the evil one tempts us and pushes us towards a 'Donatist' vision of the Church: inside are the impeccable ones and outside are those who make mistakes!" He urged his audience to stand instead with Augustine: "The Bride of Christ is and remains the field on which the good seed and the weeds grow, until the *parousia*."[11]

## Bob Dylan (Un)plugged

Born in Duluth in 1941 and raised in the northern Minnesota town of Hibbing, Robert Zimmerman found his calling as a musician during adolescence. Tuning in to distant radio stations at night, he stumbled across a cornucopia of recorded music, including country, blues, and early rock and roll. He was mesmerized by artists such as Hank Williams, John Lee Hooker, Johnnie Ray, Chuck Berry, Little Richard, and Elvis Presley.

---

9.  Ibid., 258.
10. Peter Waldo (d. 1218) and John Wycliffe (d. 1384) both advanced similar arguments.
11. "Address prepared by Pope Francis, read by H. E. Cardinal Angelo de Donatis, His Holiness' Vicar General for the Diocese of Rome," https://www.vatican.va/content/francesco/en/speeches/2020/february/documents/papa-francesco_20200227_clero-roma.html.

Reflecting back on the impact of his discoveries, he observed: "It affected me at an early age in a very, very powerful way and it's all that affected me. It's all that ever remained true to me."[12] It could be said that his unfolding discovery had a religious dimension, lending meaning and direction to his life. In high school, he participated in a number of rock and roll bands, which opened his eyes to the excitement of performing before enthralled audiences. Drawn to the possibility of a musical career, he searched for a more compelling stage name, eventually settling on Bob Dylan.

After graduating from high school in 1959, Dylan briefly enrolled at the University of Minnesota in the Twin Cities, where he was captivated by the local folk music scene. That scene was part of a national phenomenon known as the American folk music revival. Starting in the 1930s, a number of mainly urban elites endeavored to collect, catalogue, and preserve an array of musical styles that had developed in regions across the country. They recognized these traditions as essential expressions of the nation's culture, which were in danger of being lost in the wake of rapid modernization. This "preservationist" effort coexisted uneasily with a left-wing "politicizing" impulse, a push to leverage folk music to oppose the exploitation of working-class Americans by the forces of business and industry.[13]

Folk music began attracting larger audiences as a new generation of performers like Woody Guthrie and Pete Seeger rose to prominence in the late 1930s and early 40s. Its leftist politics became something of a liability in the late 40s and much of the 50s, as fears of communism shaped the national discourse. What Dylan encountered in 1959 was an emerging second wave of the folk revival, which was animated in part by countercultural

---

12. Howard Sounes, *Down the Highway: The Life of Bob Dylan* (New York: Grove Press, 2001), 30.
13. Ron Eyerman and Scott Barretta, "From the 30s to the 60s: The Folk Music Revival in the United States," *Theory and Society* 25 (1996): 507–12.

forces stirring just below the surface of a decade often associated with conformity and conservative values.[14]

Dylan embraced the folk scene with the zeal of a new convert, studying the musical choices and techniques of local performers. He immersed himself in seminal recordings and devoured literature on the topic. As one of his acquaintances put it, Dylan "was a sponge. He was taking it all in."[15] He also began applying what he was learning in performances at local venues. A year or so into this musical catechism, Dylan decamped to New York City, the epicenter of the folk revival's second wave.

As in its earlier iteration, folk music in the late 1950s and early 60s was propelled forward by both preservationist and political impulses. Its leading practitioners carefully attended to the rubrics of established genres, playing traditional instruments in traditional ways and often covering songs from the folk canon. In many respects, faithful imitation was held in higher esteem than innovation. The politics of the second wave remained decidedly leftist but with new concerns rising to the fore, including the civil rights movements of the period, Cold War fears, and opposition to the country's deepening involvement in Vietnam. The most devoted followers of the new folk revival tended to be young adults, who found in the movement important values to anchor their lives. The authentic feel and high ideals of the music offered a welcome reprieve from a mainstream culture they despised for its commercialism, emphasis on conformity, and disregard for gross injustices at home and abroad. Folk music was typically performed in intimate venues that fostered a sense of connection between artist and audience. For many fans, experiencing a live performance by their favorite musicians was something approaching the sacred.[16]

After his arrival in January of 1961, Dylan embedded himself in the folk music scene, which was centered in Greenwich Village. Showing early flashes of his charisma and musical gifts,

---

14. Eyerman and Barretta, "From the 30s to the 60s," 513–23.
15. Sounes, *Down the Highway*, 56.
16. Eyerman and Barretta, "From the 30s to the 60s," 520–33.

he landed a recording deal with Columbia Records in October of that year. His first album, the self-titled *Bob Dylan* (1962), embodies the folk music conventions of the time. Eleven of the thirteen tracks are covers of folk standards, which he sang in a style reminiscent of Woody Guthrie to the accompaniment of an acoustic guitar and harmonica. His debut effort was politely received by a handful of critics and sold a modest 5,000 or so copies in the initial year of its release, offering little indication of the staggering success he was about to enjoy.

As Dylan embraced the songwriter's craft in earnest, lyrics of increasing power and sophistication began pouring forth from his pen. On his second album, *The Freewheelin' Bob Dylan* (1963), eleven of the thirteen songs are original compositions, which he structured around traditional melodies. Several of them tap deeply into the social concerns of the era, including "Blowin' in the Wind," which gives voice to mounting antiwar sentiment and rebukes those who remain complacent in the face of injustice. Dylan's third album, *The Times They Are a-Changin'* (1964), offers further evidence of his maturation as a songwriter. The title track reflects the perception that the world was on the cusp of transformation in the early 1960s, and summons his generation to rise to the occasion while their elders give ground.

Dylan's second and third albums transformed him almost overnight into the leading light of the folk scene. The spare, acoustic arrangements of his songs offered the intimacy and authenticity so esteemed by folk purists, while the arresting lyrics seemed to epitomize the zeitgeist of the decade. Peter Yarrow, of the trio Peter, Paul and Mary, pronounced Dylan "the most important folk artist in America today" at the 1963 Newport Folk Festival. Music critic Ralph J. Gleason anointed him as "one of the great warning voices of our time." Arlo Guthrie, son of Woody and soon to be a leading folk figure in his own right, discerned in Dylan's lyrics "the truth," not just for Guthrie as an individual listener, "but for an entire generation."[17] Folk music

---

17. Sounes, *Down the Highway*, 140, 155, 127.

itself evolved in his wake, with less emphasis on the established canon and more room for original compositions.

Despite his dizzying success, Dylan started losing patience with the unyielding dogmas of the folk world. "Folk Music was a strict and rigid establishment," he later recalled. "If you sang Southern Mountain Blues, you didn't sing Southern Mountain Ballads and you didn't sing City Blues. If you sang Texas cowboy songs, you didn't play English ballads. It was really pathetic. You just didn't."[18] Dylan had a more eclectic set of influences to draw from and a wider array of themes to explore than the genre allowed. He also took notice of the British Invasion: musical acts like the Beatles, the Rolling Stones, and others that were breathing new life into the American tradition of rock and roll, the music of his teenage years. The infectious rhythms and the absence of ponderous social commentary intrigued him.

Dylan began bucking folk conventions in terms of his appearance, his flippancy in interviews, and, most importantly, his music. Early evidence of his evolution can be discerned in his fourth album, *Another Side of Bob Dylan* (1964). The sound of the music is resolutely folk, but the serious-minded lyrics of his earlier albums are largely absent. Instead, most of the songs address romantic entanglements in some fashion. His fifth album, *Bringing It All Back Home* (1965), offered an even ruder shock to his established audience. On the first side of the album, Dylan is backed by an electric band. None of the songs are particularly political, and its biggest hit, "Subterranean Homesick Blues," delivers a flood of absurd, stream-of-consciousness imagery that entertains without conveying anything of substance.

In July 1965, in what has come to be seen as the defining moment of his break with the folk scene, Dylan performed at the Newport Folk Festival, an annual event that marked the high point in folk music's liturgical year. Dylan mounted the stage in a black leather jacket and plugged in an electric Fender guitar. He and his band launched their three-song set with an

---

18. Cameron Crowe, Liner notes to *Biograph* (New York: Columbia Records, 1985), 8.

aggressive rendition of "Maggie's Farm," contrasting sharply with the more dulcet music of other performers. This aural rupture was intensified by problems with the sound system, rendering Dylan's lyrics barely intelligible. The audience reacted with hostility. "They certainly booed, I'll tell you that," Dylan recalled later. "You could hear it all over the place."[19]

To purists, genuine folk music opened a window into vital social realities, gave voice to inspiring ideals, and forged a spiritual connection between artist and audience. From this perspective, Dylan's latest recordings and performances represented a kind of heresy. Like the Donatists of yore, they condemned him for compromising with the enemy, which in this case was the crassness of mainstream music and the apathetic majority that was not willing to stand up to injustice. One of the first to discern Dylan's "troubling" drift was Irwin Silber, editor of *Sing Out!*, a leading folk music publication. In November 1964 he published "An Open Letter to Bob Dylan" in response to *Another Side of Bob Dylan*. In the letter he expresses concern that Dylan "had somehow lost contact with the people," perhaps as a consequence of his growing fame. More troubling still was Dylan's abandonment of protest songs: "Any songwriter who tries to deal honestly with reality in this world is bound to write 'protest' songs. How can he help himself?"[20]

By 1965, many others had come to share Silber's concern, with that year's Newport Folk Festival serving as a crystallization point. Folk singer Oscar Brand summed up the significance of Dylan's performance there as follows: "It was the antithesis of what the festival was supposed to be doing. . . . The electric guitar represented capitalism . . . the people who were selling out."[21] Dylan repeatedly encountered the same anger while on tour with his backing band The Hawks (later known as The

---

19. Crowe, Liner notes to *Biograph*, 11.
20. Irwin Silber, "An Open Letter to Bob Dylan," *Sing Out!*, November 1964, http://www.edlis.org/twice/threads/open_letter_to_bob_dylan.html.
21. Sounes, *Down the Highway*, 185.

Band) in 1965–66. They performed loud, electric music before audiences yearning for a more traditional folk experience, a scenario primed for combustion. In the words of lead guitarist Robbie Robertson: "We set up, we played, they booed and threw things at us. Then we went to the next town, played, they booed, threw things, and we left again. I remember thinking, 'This is a strange way to make a buck.'"[22] During a performance at the Free Trade Hall in Manchester, England, in 1966, the deep sense of betrayal felt by fans was epitomized when one of them shouted the very insult the Donatists once hurled at their enemies: "Judas!"[23]

## Rock (of Ages)

Dylan's musical choices in 1964 and 1965 were not just a rejection of the folk music creed. They were also an embrace of the music that had meant so much to him as a teenager. When Robert Zimmerman first encountered rock and roll in the early 50s, it was still in its infancy. Its founding fathers—Chuck Berry, Elvis Presley, Little Richard, et al.—drew from gospel, rhythm and blues, country, and other musical styles to forge a fresh and compelling amalgam. Many of them had been shaped by exuberant worship experiences in Pentecostal churches, and, as Randall J. Stephens notes, "The leap from unbridled sanctified music to rock was not a great one."[24] The new sound was in some respects the antithesis of folk music. Folk relied on acoustic instruments that fostered intimacy between performer and audience, while rock was defined by the harder, up-tempo rhythms generated by electric guitars and drums that drove fans to their feet. Folk prized the preservation of musical traditions of various social groups, while rock was an evolving mash-up that celebrated

22. Crowe, Liner notes to *Biograph*, 12.
23. Sounes, *Down the Highway*, 215.
24. Randall J. Stephens, *The Devil's Music: How Christians Inspired, Condemned, and Embraced Rock 'n' Roll* (Cambridge, MA: Harvard University Press, 2018), 37.

innovation. Folk emphasized the value of addressing hard social realities and the quest for justice, while rock catered to the more elemental concerns of its mainly young fanbase, including sexual desire and freedom from traditional constraints.

By the mid-60s, rock music was undergoing a fundamental transformation. A variety of bands on both sides of the Atlantic were studying one another's music, experimenting with new sounds, and competing to achieve higher levels of sophistication. Dylan was captivated by the artistic ferment, and as he made his early forays into the genre, he exercised a powerful influence of his own. His lengthy, image-laden lyrics inspired a wide array of bands, including the Beatles, to move beyond banal rhymes and to pursue something deeper and truer. In these same years, rock music developed into an integral component of the emerging counterculture, a diffuse phenomenon that took root particularly among young adults in the developed world and that was animated by the quest for a more fulfilling, authentic, and just world, which usually entailed a rejection of the stultifying values of preceding generations. "At every turn, the creation and enjoyment of music was . . . the beating heart of a deep and broad process of cultural renewal and generational becoming," Brian Lloyd writes.[25] Sociologist Robert Putnam links the period with the erosion of social cohesion and a privileging of the individual, and he recognizes Dylan's musical evolution as emblematic of broader social change: "Dylan moved deliberately from inspiring community-building and social protest to expressing his individuality."[26]

*Bringing It All Back Home* was the first of three seminal records Dylan cut between January 1965 and March 1966, arguably the most fecund period of his remarkable career. They have come to be recognized widely as three of the greatest rock albums

---

25. Brian Lloyd, "The Form Is the Message: Bob Dylan and the 1960s," *Rock Music Studies* 1 (2014), https://www.tandfonline.com/doi/full/10.1080/19401159.2013.876756.
26. Robert D. Putnam with Shaylyn Romney Garrett, *The Upswing: How America Came Together a Century Ago and How We Can Do It Again* (New York: Simon and Schuster, 2020), 305.

of all time. The second of this trilogy is *Highway 61 Revisited* (1965), a critical and commercial success that cemented Dylan's status as a leading figure in the rock world. Critic Hank Kalet celebrates it as "one of a handful of albums . . . that gave literate rockers the green light to create a kind of intelligent, probing rock music that had not existed before."[27] Consistently excellent, the album opens with "Like a Rolling Stone," an angry account of a hypocrite's fall from grace that surely ranks as the most famous song in Dylan's vast catalogue. Less than a year later, Dylan released *Blonde on Blonde* (1966), a double album that many regard as his greatest work. One of the biggest hits from the collection is the raucous and somewhat ridiculous "Rainy Day Women # 12 & 35," with its notorious refrain "Everybody must get stoned," but the album overflows with multifaceted gems. Critic Rob Sheffield lauds it as Dylan's "most expansive music, with nothing that resembles a folk song—just the rock & roll laments of a vanishing American, the doomed outsider who's given up on ever belonging anywhere."[28]

This stunning period of creative ferment came to an end on July 29, 1966, when Dylan had a motorcycle accident, an experience that prompted him to step back from extensive touring and to extract himself from a blur of commitments that threatened to overwhelm him. For the next eight years, he maintained a lower public profile, focusing more on his marriage and raising a growing family. He receded as a force in the evolving rock scene of the late 60s and early 70s, but continued to make excellent music that reflected his eclectic tastes.[29]

---

27. Hank Kalet, "Bob Dylan's Highway 61 Revisited," *PopMatters*, February 6, 2004, https://www.popmatters.com/dylanbob-highway61mft-2495871353.html.
28. Rob Sheffield, "'Blonde on Blonde' at 50: Celebrating Bob Dylan's Greatest Masterpiece," *Rolling Stone*, May 16, 2016, https://www.rollingstone.com/music/music-news/blonde-on-blonde-at-50-celebrating-bob-dylans-greatest-masterpiece-158223/.
29. He issued a series of critically lauded, high-selling albums in these years, including *John Wesley Harding* (1967), *Nashville Skyline* (1969), and *New Morning* (1970).

In the mid-70s, Dylan reestablished his place in the upper echelons of the rock pantheon with a new series of recordings. He reunited with The Band to record *Planet Waves* (1974), his first album to reach the top of the US Billboard charts. This set the stage for a highly successful coast-to-coast tour that has been called the "first major stadium tour of the rock era."[30] His extended absences from home and the temptations of the road wreaked havoc on his marriage. Mounting emotional turmoil inspired some of the rawest, most powerful songwriting of his career, including "Simple Twist of Fate," "Idiot Wind," and "You're a Big Girl Now." These and other standouts found their way onto *Blood on the Tracks* (1975), a sonic triumph that topped the charts and was met with critical adulation. A year later he released *Desire* (1976), yet another critical and commercial success. Its strongest track is "Hurricane," a scorching indictment of the arrest, trial, and incarceration of boxer Rubin Carter.

For all his professional success, Dylan was growing increasingly disillusioned with the rock industry of the 1970s. As he later described it:

> It was just a big show, a big circus except there weren't any elephants, nothing really exceptional just Sound and Lights, Sound and Lights, more Sound and Lights.... The highest compliments were things like, "Wow, lotta energy, man." It had become absurd.... Actually it was just big industry moving in on the music. Like the armaments manufacturers selling weapons to both sides in a war, inventing bigger and better things to take your head off while behind your back, there's a few people laughing and getting rich off your vanity.[31]

Dylan's personal life was in shambles, culminating in the collapse of his marriage in 1977. In this difficult period, he was keeping company with a number of evangelical Christians, who influenced his thinking. He also had a powerful religious experience in a hotel room in Tucson, Arizona, in November

---

30. Sounes, *Down the Highway*, 275.
31. Crowe, Liner notes to *Biograph*, 22.

of 1978. "There was a presence in the room that couldn't have been anybody but Jesus," he recounted. "Jesus put his hand on me. . . . I felt my whole body tremble. . . . I truly had a born-again experience."[32]

Early in 1979, Dylan met with a pair of evangelical pastors affiliated with Vineyard Fellowship in Los Angeles, and he agreed to participate in an intensive Bible study at their church. Convinced by the teachings he encountered there, he accepted baptism. At the heart of his new faith were a few key principles: Christ was the Messiah prophesied in the Hebrew Bible who came to save souls from damnation; salvation entails having faith in Christ, which typically manifests in a moment of clarity (being "born again"); those not saved are destined to suffer in hell for all eternity. Like millions of other evangelical Christians in this period, Dylan was influenced by Hal Lindsey's *The Late Great Planet Earth* (1970), a best-selling book that discerned in contemporary events signs that the "end times" were near and that Christ would soon come again to preside over the last judgment.

Like many new converts, Dylan was eager to testify, which led to an outpouring of songs centered around Christian themes. The end result was *Slow Train Coming* (1979), a highly polished and thoroughly Christian album from start to finish. Its finest tracks include "I Believe in You," a stirring testament to the narrator's faith in God, and the title track, which spies Satan's hand in the problems of the world and uses the metaphor of a slow train to warn of impending judgment. *Slow Train Coming* sold well, bolstered by an enthusiastic reception among Christian listeners.[33] The reactions of rock critics, however, were decidedly mixed. Charles Shaar Murray of *New Musical Express* dismissed

---

32. Quoted in Jim Irvin and Colin McLear, eds., *The Mojo Collection: The Ultimate Music Companion*, 4th ed., (Edinburgh: Canongate Books, 2007), 427.
33. Christian listeners were quick to appreciate Dylan's new musical direction. The Gospel Music Association honored *Slow Train Coming* with a Dove Award in 1980 for best album by a secular artist.

it as "unpleasant and hate-filled."[34] Greil Marcus railed against Dylan's "arrogant, intolerant . . . and smug" lyrics and accused him of "offering a peculiarly eviscerated and degraded version of American fundamentalism."[35]

Criticism escalated as Dylan began sharing his newfound convictions from the stage, especially during a set of concerts in San Francisco later that year. He performed only Christian material and offered pious commentary between songs, including references to his eschatological beliefs. The audiences for these shows included many who had come to hear his older material, and they howled in disapproval, echoing the rough reception Dylan had experienced in 1965 and '66. Critic Philip Elwood described one of the concerts as follows: "Ninety minutes of poorly played, poorly presented and often poorly written sounds . . . is a pretty grueling experience."[36] The *San Francisco Chronicle*'s Joel Selvin savaged Dylan's latest offerings as "some of the most banal, uninspired, and inventionless songs of his career."[37]

Dylan was not deterred. After writing a new set of songs, he cut an album in Muscle Shoals, Alabama, utilizing local musicians (The Swampers) and a team of female backup singers to achieve a distinctly gospel sound. The result was *Saved* (1980), an album as explicitly Christian as its original cover art, which depicts the hand of God reaching down from the blood-red heavens to a cluster of smaller hands stretching upward. Its tracks

---

34. Charles Shaar Murray, "Bob Dylan: *Slow Train Coming* (CBS)," *New Musical Express*, August 25, 1979, https://www.rocksbackpag-es.com/Library/Article/bob-dylan-islow-train-comingi-cbs-2.

35. Greil Marcus, *Bob Dylan by Greil Marcus: Writings 1968–2010* (New York: PublicAffairs, 2013), 95–98.

36. Quoted in Randy Roark, "Creating a Social and Historical Context for Dylan's Christian Period," August 20, 2001, http://randyroark.com/august-20-2001-creating-a-social-and-histori-cal-context-for-dylans-christian-period-presented-at-the-mizel-center-denver/.

37. Joel Selvin, "Bob Dylan's God-Awful Gospel," *San Francisco Chronicle*, November 3, 1979, 34.

include "Saved," an expression of gratitude for being saved from damnation, and "Are You Ready?," which asks listeners whether they are prepared for the final judgment. The response of rock critics was withering. Kurt Loder acknowledged the album's musical quality but insisted that "it's nowhere near as good as it might have been were its star not hobbled by the received wisdom of his gospel-propagating cronies."[38] Dave Marsh piled on: "If the songs weren't so utterly devoid of Christian charity, the prospect might have succeeded; but with Dylan simply ranting ceaselessly about the perils of unbelief, the result is sterile and unsoulful."[39] Tepid sales offered a kind of collective judgment of the album's limited appeal.[40]

Dylan returned to the well of his newfound faith a third time with *Shot of Love* (1981). This effort contains just one overtly Christian song, "Property of Jesus." Six other tracks address religious themes like faith, morality, and death, but with considerable subtlety. They include "Every Grain of Sand"—arguably the most beautiful song Dylan has ever composed—in which he reflects upon the course of his life and discerns evidence of God's presence throughout it. The album also contains two purely secular tracks. Despite his efforts to bridle his evangelical zeal, the critics pounced. Paul Nelson approved of "Every Grain of Sand," but he lamented that one track "isn't enough to hide the hate that powers the majority of songs on *Shot of Love*. It doesn't make you forget the creepy conservatism, the chaos and the cancerous urge to lash out and get even for some unknown sin."[41] British critic Nick Kent dismissed it as "Dylan's worst

38. Kurt Loder, "Saved," *Rolling Stone*, September 18, 1980, https://web.archive.org/web/20070626070353/http://www.rollingstone.com/artists/bobdylan/albums/album/175580/review/5944002/saved.

39. Dave Marsh, *The New Rolling Stone Record Guide* (New York: Random House, 1983).

40. *Saved* only reached the 24th spot on the charts, making it Dylan's lowest-charting album since 1964 (Sounes, *Down the Highway*, 336).

41. Paul Nelson, "Bob Dylan: Shot of Love," *Rolling Stone*, Octo-

album to date."[42] The general public did not much care for it either, judging by its poor sales.[43]

Dylan's conversion to evangelical Christianity triggered a sustained burst of artistic inspiration, yet the returns on his investment were dispiriting. In the rock realm, which he had helped transform in the mid-60s and had dominated in the mid-70s, he was becoming increasingly irrelevant. How is one to make sense of this steep fall from grace? It turns out that the genre itself, having once liberated Dylan from the strict conventions of folk music, had its own firm limits. As noted earlier, rock music tended to privilege individual aspiration over communal obligation, with a particular emphasis on desire, freedom, and experience. It was certainly possible to articulate longings for the transcendent,[44] even in an explicitly Christian manner.[45] At the same time, artists had to avoid coming across as judgmental of the life choices of others—including the pursuit of corporeal pleasure, the subject of countless rock classics. Dylan's new gospel was rooted in a wholly different ethos. He condemned the indulgences of his era as sin and warned of collective judgment. He challenged people to clean up their acts while they still had the chance. For rock aficionados, his latest music was, in short, a huge downer. It ignited a Donatist reaction among the gatekeepers of the genre, who called him out for betraying the principles of good rock music. His most recent songs were deemed to be "hate-filled," "arrogant," "intolerant," and "devoid of . . . charity," charges that reflect anger at being

ber 15, 1981, https://web.archive.org/web/20071001195937/ http://www.rollingstone.com/artists/bobdylan/albums/album/301820/review/5940864/shot_of_love.

42. Quoted in Jon Bream, *Dylan: Disc by Disc* (Minneapolis, MN: Voyageur Press, 2015), 131.
43. *Shot of Love* reached only number 33 on the charts (Sounes, *Down the Highway*, 348).
44. Some noteworthy examples include George Harrison's "My Sweet Lord" (1970), Van Morrison's "Full Force Gale" (1979), and U2's "I Still Haven't Found What I'm Looking For" (1987).
45. The Doobie Brothers' recording of "Jesus Is Just Alright" rose to number 35 on the *Billboard* Hot 100 in 1973.

judged for having a good time. Ordinary fans seemed to agree. And so Bob Dylan, a demigod of the rock world for more than a decade, was unceremoniously toppled from his pedestal. Like the *traditore* priests of the fourth century, he was seen as having lost his powers on account of his sins.

## (In)fidel

The tempered Christian message in *Shot of Love* was an early sign of an enduring change in Dylan's music. Whatever his personal religious convictions may have been, he would no longer wear Christianity on his sleeve. By the fall of 1981, he resumed performing more of his classic repertoire in live shows. His new direction became clearer still on his next album, the suggestively titled *Infidels* (1983). Religious references surface here and there, but on the whole the album has a decidedly secular feel. There are a number of songs about current events, including environmental despoilment ("License to Kill") and economic globalization ("Union Sundown"). The songs "Sweetheart Like You" and "Don't Fall Apart on Me Tonight" explore relationships. The response of critics was generally positive; Christopher Connelly of *Rolling Stone* assessed it as "Bob Dylan's best album since the searing *Blood on the Tracks* nine years ago, a stunning recovery of the lyric and melodic powers that seemed to have all but deserted him."[46]

Connelly's review foreshadows the collective memory that has come to surround *Infidels*: It is widely seen as a "return to form" for Dylan after an embarrassing Christian interlude.[47] Such a reading obscures more than it clarifies. It suggests that there has been a stable core, or form, to Dylan's musical genius, and it does not fully appreciate the many turns and tangents

---

46. Christopher Connelly, "Infidels," *Rolling Stone*, November 24, 1983, https://www.rollingstone.com/music/music-album-reviews/infidels-247152/.
47. A Google search of "Infidels" and "return to form" offers many results in the vast commentary on Dylan available online.

that have defined his career. From an early age, he has had a capacious appreciation of music—folk, country, rural and urban blues, rhythm and blues, rock, gospel, soul, pop, etc.—and in over six decades of performing and recording he has drawn inspiration from these varied traditions.

Dylan's expansive appreciation of music can be seen as Augustinian in a certain sense. Recall that Augustine railed against the Donatists, a faction within the Church in northern Africa that held the clergy to rigid standards of purity and cast aside those who fell short. Augustine had a much broader experience of the Church and the world to draw upon, and this experience nurtured within him an appreciation of the Church's diversity. This diversity was not a flaw, he concluded, but a feature of God's design. And so he could compare the Church on earth to Noah's ark: "That ark contained each kind. If the ark symbolized the Church, you see, of course, that it is necessary for the Church in this flood of the world to contain each kind, both the raven and the dove."

Dylan's Augustinian breadth was essential to his genius. Time and again he defied the conventions that defined the various types of popular music he explored, and in the process he helped expand the scope of the possible. He upended the folk scene by setting aside faithful imitation in favor of strikingly original compositions of his own, and then by abandoning high-minded protest songs in favor of less weighty fare. As a rock musician, he challenged his peers to move beyond simple rhymes and the three-minute format most likely to receive airplay, and then challenged his audience by preaching hellfire and brimstone. Dylan's expansive vision often earned him critical praise and commercial success, but it also triggered fierce denunciations, particularly from musical purists. In a period marked by the decline of institutional religion in the industrialized world, popular music provided more than mere entertainment in the lives of many fans. It often served as a form of identity, a wellspring of values, an ultimate concern. For such devotees, Dylan's boundary violations felt like sacrilege, and they sometimes responded with Donatistic fury.

If there is an Augustinian quality to the arc of Dylan's career, can the same be said of his religious vision itself? This is difficult to ascertain. With the exception of his brief period as an outspoken evangelical Christian, Dylan has not addressed the topic publicly in any sustained way. His silence in the decades since the release of *Infidels* has led to speculation as to whether he remains a Christian, has returned to Judaism, or has abandoned religion all together.[48] What we are left with is his music, in which it can be difficult to untangle personal conviction from flights of artistry. Nowhere in his oeuvre is there evidence that he was a serious reader of Augustine. That said, in some of his lyrics it is possible to discern a sensibility that the saint would celebrate.

This is particularly true of his most recent album, the much lauded *Rough and Rowdy Ways* (2020). In "I've Made Up My Mind to Give Myself to You," he expresses a longing to "preach the gospel, the gospel of love." Several of the album's songs dwell on the topic of mortality, and the afterlife is viewed through a Christian lens. Dylan spies the "city of God" ("False Prophet") and anticipates "Judgment Day" ("My Own Version of You"). In "I Contain Multitudes," he identifies with the fighter, the artist, the partier, the painter, and the image-conscious dandy. He is "from Salt Lake City to Birmingham, from East L.A. to San Antone" ("I've Made Up My Mind"). He plays the "Gumbo Limbo spirituals" and knows "all the Hindu rituals" ("Key West (Philosopher Pirate)"). In other words, his "I" is not unlike the ecclesial "I" of Augustine's inclusive Church. And though he prefers "that old time religion" in a "straightforward puritanical tone," and wants someone to "thump on the Bible, proclaim a creed," he nonetheless lives "on a street / . . . where the Jews, and Catholics, and the Muslims all pray" ("Goodbye Jimmy Reed"). Judging from this latest album, Dylan's mature religious outlook seems to encompass the values of inclusion, solidarity, and catholicity, even while adhering to traditional Christian truth claims. If this is in fact the case, it is an Augustinian perspective indeed.

48. See Jeffrey Salkin, "What Religion is Dylan Now?," *Religion News Service*, June 23, 2020, https://religionnews.com/2020/06/23/dylan-album/.

# On the Good and its Counterfeits:
## Kurt Vile and Flannery O'Connor

William C. Hackett

*Mr. Vile is a philosopher in search of philosophy, happy to keep looking.*[1]

To name the good is to risk trivializing it. To avoid naming it is to fail to see it.

Thinkers through the ages have employed a family of strategies to make the good accessible while also preserving its integrity and freedom. Here's a representative sample: the "hymn of silence" (*sigē*) of ancient philosophers that witnesses to an unutterable, unknowable union beyond words and understanding; the "negative theology" of the theologians, the method of affirming what we can know, in our finite way, the divine is *not* (thereby making an all-the-greater affirmation about its transcendence); or the mystics' turn back to images when reason dissolves into abstraction (images of darkness with the properties of light, of sexual union, of giving birth, of mutual in-breathing, etc.).[2] Kurt Vile—of The War on Drugs (2003–2008) and since 2008 eponymous, performing with The Violators—you could

---

1. Rob Tannenbaum, "Kurt Vile, Indie Rock's Charming Riddle," *The New York Times*, September 26, 2018, https://www.nytimes.com/2018/09/26/arts/music/kurt-vile-bottle-it-in-interview.html.
2. If interested in these strategies, the reader would do no better than to consult the works of St. John of the Cross, who represents everything just named. He drew pictures, wrote poetry, and composed scholastic-style commentaries on the poems that altogether are meant to explicate, ever indirectly, the mystical experiences of the living God he enjoyed. See *The Collected Works of St. John of the Cross*, trans. Kieran Kavanaugh, OCD, and Otilio Rodrigues, OCD (Washington, DC: Carmelite Publications, 1991).

say, employs his own strategy: reconciliation with the banal. Like philosophers, theologians, and mystics, Vile's art witnesses to the "freedom of the good in being" (let's call it that), its ability to be found everywhere there is something, anything—just insofar as it is something, anything. Being is good; a condition for being is, first, goodness.

Let's also make a contrast with what it is not: Vile's art is *not*, on the one hand, proposing a celebration of opacity, a remainder-less reconciliation with the immanent, a foreclosure of the possibility of any transcendence before the game of being is played, as if the everyday were, on its own terms, an inexhaustible "opening" of itself, like an eternal circle or stream that is one with its own source, with no leftover, no excess, no beyond.[3] Neither, on the other hand, in Vile's artistic imaging does the ordinary become revelatory of something else (or rather Something else), a plane for the disclosure of what is absolute or eternal, suddenly manifested in the palimpsest of the real, leaping out at you as from a 3-D poster if you focus your eyes just right.[4]

---

3.  This point of view is promoted by the post-Heideggerian French thinker, Jean-Luc Nancy. See *Dis-Enclosure: The Deconstruction of Christianity*, trans. Bettina Bergo, Gabriel Malenfant, and Michael B. Smith (New York: Fordham University Press, 2010). For the author's criticism of this perspective the reader is welcome to see my brief review of the aforementioned text in *Modern Theology* 26:1 (2010), 163–165. The short of the critique is that Nancy misunderstands the divine kind of transcendence of which Christianity claims to be the bearer, ruling out *in advance* the possibility of a self-disclosure of the divine that in that very self-disclosure transcends the reductive grasp of finitude. In the end, his perspective—though not without some charm—is only an extension of the eighteenth-century concept of "religion within the bounds of reason alone."

4.  There are, of course, loosely religious themes that pepper his discography, albeit weighted a little toward the earlier albums. Check out songs like "And There Was Blood" (*10 Songs*, 2003), "Overnite Religion" (*Childish Prodigy*, 2009), and "Jesus Fever" (*Smoke Ring for My Halo*, 2011). But all this comes rather naturally in rock and roll territory.

Vile is not a theological thinker, or singer. Yet he is not caught up in a refusal of the theological either. That is, one does not directly perceive the theological conviction of his thinking and singing, as if it were expressed in a set of thetic statements, affirmations about what is there, *names* given to the excess of the good in being—even if they really are there in the oceanic depths of his human soul. That, for the moment, is neither here nor there. What we want to keep our intellectual-aesthetic eyes focused on is precisely what Vile is asking us to see. And what he points us to in his music is (to use another fancy phrase) *the mystery of the quotidian*, what philosophers in ages past have called "wonder," *thaumazein*—the "beginning," they used to say, of the search for wisdom.[5]

To be more specific—if we would permit ourselves the guilty pleasure of interpreting it in a wider cultural milieu—Vile's music is an expression of the *metaphysical* wonder "that there is." Weighty thinkers with fittingly weighty Germanic names like Heidegger and Schelling and Leibniz have asked the question in this way: "Why is there something rather than nothing?"[6]

To be sure, Vile is *not asking why* at all. That is the work of a philosopher. He is only doing the essential or characteristic human thing of being in awe that there *is* at all, and that it is, so remarkably is. In wondering that there is, that he is there, that being is something to be marveled at, Vile is singing, in a pre-philosophical way, in a universally human way, at the fact of his being, of his "being there." With that phrase introduced, let's wade into Vile's music.

---

5.　Plato, *Theaetetus*, 155d; Aristotle, *Metaphysics*, 982b.

6.　If you were to "duck duck go" (the "google" that does not track your information) the words "Why is there something rather than nothing?" you would find the Wikipedia entry for "Why is there anything at all?" which is another version of the question these philosophers ask. It references (as of November 3, 2020) the thinkers I have mentioned (minus Schelling) as well as a few others, and a few books related to the theme.

## The Vilean View

In Vile's discography (most recently, in fall 2020, the EP *Speed, Sound, Lonely KV*), the everyday, only the most banal and most free from all overthinking, is something to capture, to sing about.[7] There is the feeling, however fleeting, of getting by in life ("Loading Zones," on 2018's *Bottle It In*); and the startling recognition of one's own alienation from oneself through the progress of time that moves methodically on apart from our consciousness of it, and then, at a second step, the revelation of the startling ease with which one can reconcile oneself to that fact in the soft ecstasy of being alive ("Pretty Pimpin," on 2015's *b'lieve i'm goin down...*). There is also the astounding discovery that what you say and do can be painfully awkward at times, but this, remarkably, signifies that things are deeper than what you can reveal, especially of yourself, to you and others ("Bassackwards," *Bottle It In*). There is the simple wonder of being forgetful—forgetful both about the uncountable good things that flow over and through you every day and about the less numerable bad things that it is good to forget ("How Lucky," sung as a duet with John Prine a few months before he died of Covid-19 in early 2020).[8] "How lucky" one is for that forgetfulness.

"Pretty Pimpin" captures the Vile sensibility with almost unmatched poignancy. As I mentioned, it's a song about what it is like when something mundane reveals itself to you as more than that. That revelation, which could be difficult to swallow, is at the same time something you choose to accept, and which is not hard to accept at all in that moment of recognition that you are alive and that life's temporality is a part of its reality.

Let us approach a phenomenology of this experience in two steps. It is as if, once upon a time, you were stopped in your grammatical tracks by the strangeness of a word you have spelled

---

7.   I will expand on this concept of "overthinking" below.
8.   "How Lucky," written by John Prine, is originally from his album *Pink Cadillac* (1979).

all your life. *That* word, "and," is actually spelled a-n-d: what a weird-looking word. I haven't looked at that word in its own substantial presencing since I learned how to read. And it was only because I was typing so quickly that I accidentally misspelled it, and it stared at me "a-n-b," broken, without signification, lost. Before then, I've only seen it as absent, as absenting itself so that it can perform its grammatical conjunctive activity; I've only seen "a-n-d" as there *for* other words, specifically, to join other words or phrases together: "he *and* she;" "I would like a small daily roast with a drop of cream *and* one of those chocolate chip cookies over there"; I have not seen "and" in itself, for itself—until now, when I have been seen by it (as it were), when the directedness of my mind has been stopped cold in its hurry through "and" and has been turned back on itself by it.

Now replace the word a-n-d with yourself—not the word "yourself" but the experience of yourself in the third person, as when you look in the mirror. The look in the mirror must not be an act of self-perception for another purpose, not even the purpose of examining yourself in the third person, which is an end external to the *straight experience* of third-person viewing. Imagine you have locked yourself in the bathroom by accident; you can't get out. You were busy doing your bathroom thing, say, brushing your teeth. You are singing/humming a Vile tune, like "Loading Zones": Neil Young meets the next generation, "bum be da dum bum bum, bum": you know where to "park for free!" in this town that is your life. Ready for the day, you spit, sip some water out of your cupped hand, gargle, and expel. As you run some water to wash out the sink, you are already thinking about, say, the lecture you have to give in about an hour on St. Augustine's conception of *illuminatio*—wherein you are going to (brilliantly) demonstrate the proximity of the two "g" words, "Good" in Plato and "God" in Augustine, in order to contrast their shared radical vision of transcendence with the merely intra-cosmic good of Aristotle, showing your rapt students—rapt by the ideas, not by yourself, only captured by your, well, *brilliant* presentation that does the job of unveiling the profundity, the wonderful profundity of these ageless, ever new, human-defining *ideas*—when you reach for the door, hitting the switch—

The room is dark, but your eyes are already adjusting. The door handle does not turn. You shake it and stop. "Well, fudge" you say, not under your breath. (Although you don't say "fudge.") Suddenly, you recognize at your left a gray human form, bathed in soft natural light. You turn. You are looking at yourself. The *you* in the mirror is looking at *you*. That's me, you realize. *That*, that face in the mirror, that's me. That's me? *I* am the "a-n-d": how strange I am. "I woke up this morning, / Didn't recognize the man in the mirror," Vile sings ("Pretty Pimpin"). But he's reconciled to himself. The stranger that is himself is indeed wearing his clothes: "I gotta say, pretty pimpin," he says in approval. Life is *alive*, and nothing about *it* is boring. When it jumps out at me, I will embrace it, and sing about it.

Above, I used the term "overthinking" to explain what Vile avoids or gets behind to reach the epiphany of the everyday. Instead of "overthinking" one could say "idolatry," by which I mean the confusion of the Good with any particular good of direct experience. At the level of immediacy that I have called the banal, "overthinking" is to lose the flow of freedom that lets things be what they are, bathed in their own freedom as things that are, presencing their own irreducible goodness. Vile, covering '70s country singer Charlie Rich, calls this "Rollin' with the Flow."

## Vile Style

The perspective I have taken on the music of Kurt Vile stands at a remove from all the music magazine articles I have seen online about his work.[9] If I were to ape those presentations, it would go like this:

---

9. A near exception is the rather serious and insightful review of *b'lieve i'm goin down...* by Mark Richardson in 2015 for *Pitchfork*: Vile's "tossed-off musings . . . remind you that every sage worth a damn knew that life was absurdly funny and tragic si-

Kurt Vile's style—understated guitar virtuoso drifter rock located somewhere in the city limits of Philadelphia on a late autumn weekend after dark sitting in a folding chair on the porch of a not-so-busy street with a beer in hand—is marked by a care-less-ness, a dirty foot-stompin' freedom that is as authentic as the kid who knows too much but is happy not caring beyond being sure to be free not to care. My mother-in-law calls my hair—which has not received the caress of a plastic comb or brush in nearly two decades—"calculated indifference": Vile's songs are my hair on uppers and downers that meet in the middle and say to each other in gravelly unison, "yeah man . . . *yeah*."

This all, clearly, abides on the surface. And it is true, as far as it goes—if music or a human being were merely a surface. Kurt Vile is "just looking for a good time and a calm mind," or so says the leading pull quote in a 2018 *Rolling Stone* piece.[10] I am too—and I am a philosophy professor! But as a human being there is more to me than that. And to art—to rock and roll—there is more than that.

This possibility of double perspective, the surface and the depth, is captured in Vile's response in an interview in the *New York Times*. The interviewer comments that Vile's music "[echoes] the cosmic musings of 60s psychedelic rock," which could lead to conceiving Vile as a "spaced out stoner." Referring to the line in "Bassackwards," "I was on the moon, but more so, I was in the grass, / So I was chilling out, but with a very drifting mind," Vile says, "That's not drugs, that lyric. That's more being in space from, you know, the weight of the world. Stress is often a part of it. Being in a fog because of all the things I've got to

---

multaneously" (https://pitchfork.com/reviews/albums/20840-kurt-vile-blieve-im-goin-down/).

10. Simon Vozick-Levinson, "Kurt Vile Abides," *Rolling Stone*, October 8, 2018, https://www.rollingstone.com/music/music-features/kurt-vile-bottle-it-in-interview-733191/.

do."[11] Kurt Vile plays rock and roll. Capturing an experience that sometimes marks all of us—"weight" and "stress" and "fog"—and making it appear in its strangeness that can be mistaken for drug-induced vision: this is the Vilean view. Vile, in this way, can remind me of the surplus of my being by his appeal to the freedom of the good in being.

I gain access to that "+" dimension, that excess of being over itself, when I allow myself to conceive that there is more to what is possible than the secularized self-erasure of being as potential for my projects or the other merely finite horizon of a reenchanted earth where I may mingle with semi-transcendent powers that pervade the shared order of sky and earth. I can find myself dissatisfied with either of these options, and I can find an excess to my being, on the farthest edge of earth and world, before the Absolute, the Origin or Source that gives being to itself in a redundant gesture of excess so complete that the only adequate response is the total gift of the being that one is in return. Searching for and finding the Name of this Origin and End sets the human wonderment onto the plane of an adventure that eclipses the horizon of finitude, even if only in the deferred form of a promise and of the disclosure of a new field of possibility.[12]

Vile sings about the freedom of being, its sheer gratuity, its goodness. The world is intelligible and significant: the world is given to me *that way*, as meaningful, before and beyond my manipulation of it, before and beyond the use to which I will put it as I bend its potentialities toward my aims and ambitions. As I hear it, Vile's music exemplifies this wonder (of self, of world, of inexhaustible meaningfulness), and that is why, I suggest, it

---

11. Tannenbaum, "Indie Rock's Charming Riddle."

12. I am indebted here to a line of articulation made by French philosopher Fr. Jean-Yves Lacoste, who proposes a third possibility, beyond an atheist "World" and a pagan "Earth," an inhabitation on their margins, called the "Kingdom," a way of being that he calls a "liturgical existence," a choosing to be-before-God. See Jean-Yves Lacoste, *Experience and the Absolute*, trans. Mark Raftery-Skehan (New York: Fordham University Press, 2008).

is good art: the artist and the philosopher, each in their own way, magnify or concentrate the universally human awareness, ultimately, of—if we can try to gather the entire sensibility within the boundaries of a single phrase—*the gratuity of being.* Vile wonders at his life; he receives it for what it is. He keeps an open hand to what is given.

Art would probably suffer to the point of kitsch if it were just an allegorization of any philosophical conceptuality. The best a theorist can do, it seems to me, is give us an interpretive matrix in which the Vile phenomenon can be set free to alert us to the epiphany of being that we have forgotten how to see. The charm and force of Vile's music is found in its innocence, an innocence that, whether willed or not, is brilliant and not forced but free. It is common to mistake this artist's freedom for a Gen-X-to-Z carelessness that says of anything that disturbs his self-made frothy bliss: "This is f---ing bull---t, man," like the vacationing American teen whose parents require him to participate in a walking tour of the fountains of Rome before they pay for gelato and a restaurant dinner. That attitude, one of a refusal of disturbance, and hence a refusal of the *contingency* of meaningfulness, is, at heart, a refusal or avoidance of the gratuity of being.[13] And it is, I would like to say, utterly opposed to the Vilean view. Vile does not sing out of a child-of-hippies, "It's all good bro!" sensibility (in which no one knows, including the one saying it, what "it" or "good" means) either. Vile does not want to be left alone so that he does not have to care: rather, he is sharing his epiphany through the craft of his art. He knows

---

13. By "disturbance" I mean the refusal of what Aristotle calls "pain," which is, along with education, a condition for the realization of virtue. Pain, along with pleasure, is the first teacher, inasmuch as, by these, we learn what to avoid and what to be drawn to. We have to learn, says Aristotle, how to take pleasure in higher things and to be pained by things that make access to those things difficult or impossible. To take pleasure in the good for its own sake, as in true friendship, is the epitome of virtue. It makes happiness accessible. See Aristotle, *Nicomachean Ethics*, Books 7 (on pleasure and pain) and 8 (on friendship).

he has found something good, the gratuity of being, and wants to create an opportunity for you to share in it as well.

Vile, of course (and I will say it again), sings nothing of the new horizon of the Absolute, of an opening of the fabric of world and earth by the disclosure of a surplus to finitude, of the revelation of a Music that sings to us beyond or behind the order ruled by death, and one that, with the eyes of faith, *sees*, with the new eyes of Easter, sees with eyes that, blinking, bewildered, can see just only the first intimations of the "life to come," eyes like those of a newborn child wholly incapable of comprehending the new world into which it has just, terrifyingly, been born, but comforted nonetheless by its mother's warm skin. . . . Yet his authentic wonder at being is the beginning—*thaumazein!*—of entry into such an unfathomable newness, like Dorothy's open door from the greyscale world of Kansas to the technicolor Land of Oz.

## He's Good People

To find the kind of theological radicality of which I have been writing, one would have to situate Vile's "gratuitous freedom" in the wider setting of the drama in which "human" and "being" find their ultimate and defining place, the drama of good and evil.[14] This more than intimates that the possibility of "being-before-death" suffering an *eclipse* by "being-before-God," found hidden in the mysterious surplus of being that humans enjoy, is not marginal, but central to what we most secretly are. Human life, as a relentless aspiration for what the ancients called *eudaimonia*

---

14. I have a rockabilly Anglo-Catholic priest friend who argues, convincingly, that the heart of rock and roll is not satanism (neither literally nor metaphorically, i.e., as the celebration of self-destructive freedom based in anarchic rejection of all rules, fundamentally those of the Creator), but is, in actuality, gospel, the love and praise of the liberating God. The genealogy he provides—from slave spirituals to African American gospel music to rock—is like that of folk music: think Elvis and Johnny Cash as archetypes. Rev. Dr. Jeffrey Hanson, please write your book.

("happiness"), is played out in a high stakes game of absolute risk between good and evil. And this game is played out nowhere else but in the field of the banal, the realm of daily life.

We would do worse than to take as our wider setting the religious commonplace, the "southern gothic," of Flannery O'Connor. Take "Good Country People" (1955), for example.[15] This is the story of a girl—a single, aging PhD in philosophy who has an artificial leg from a hunting accident, lives with her divorced mother, and has embraced a pseudo-enlightened "nihilist" point of view (love it!)—who gets pulled into a tryst with a traveling Bible salesman, Manley Pointer.

Hulga is crushed by the banality and purposelessness of her place in life, her suffering, her existence, and only finds solace in interpreting life itself, and being as such, *as meaningless*. This is so much the case that she legally changed her name from Joy to Hulga after graduation, which she imagines as an echo of the name for the Roman god of fire, Vulcan ("ugly sweating Vulcan"), who represented her "highest creative act," the power of self-transformation to which her philosophical embrace of the nothingness of everything has liberated her (and who also, according to myth, fell from heaven and broke his leg on impact). Pointer is apparently one of those "good country people" Hulga's mother, Mrs. Hopewell, always talks about, much like Mrs. Freeman and her two daughters, their hired help. The fact that Mrs. Freeman is a gossip—an annoying and, on balance, overwhelmingly burdensome personality to all around her—should warn the reader that "good country people" are not always what they seem. Pointer appears at the front door and charms his way into staying for dinner and then to a date with Hulga the following day.

---

15. In Flannery O'Connor, *A Good Man Is Hard to Find* (New York: Harcourt Brace, 1955). Vile, whose wife has a higher degree in literature, has a passion for O'Connor. The first line of "Dead Alive" (*Childish Prodigy*, 2009) references O'Connor's famous short story and the title of the collection in which "Good Country People" is found.

Hulga dreams of seducing Pointer, and of disabusing this good country boy of his innocence, his religion, his shortsighted faith in the goodness of things. In actuality, Pointer is in total control, forcing a kiss as they walk through the woods, before guiding her up, without a protest, to the hayloft of the barn. In the loft he forces her to tell him that she loves him before asking her to show him where the prosthesis meets her leg. She allows him this deep intrusion of her privacy, even teaching him to put it on and take it off, not because she wanted to but because she, despite herself, has become a completely passive instrument to him. Pointer opens one of his Bibles, which is really a hollow container filled with vulgar items: a pack of dirty cards, a flask of whiskey, and a box of condoms. At the climax of the story, Pointer removes Hulga's prosthetic leg, kicking it out of reach. She protests and is roughly pushed down to the hay. Bewildered, Hulga mutters, "Aren't you . . . aren't you just good country people?"

Hulga's name is an anagram of l-a-u-g-h: she laughs at the world and she laughs at being and she laughs at those who do not, like her, see through being—not to goodness, but to nothingness—just as she laughs at those beneath her who are not witted enough to understand her name. Ironically, the last laugh is on her: true nihilism is as far beyond her shortsighted intellectualism as her prosthesis is out of the reach of her hand. It is with this recognition dawning (at least on the reader) that, in the last lines of the story, Hulga sees Pointer through the loft opening, her prosthesis stuffed in his salesman's valise: a "blue figure struggling successfully over the green speckled lake."

Fire, when it burns hot, shows green flashes and especially blue. Manley Pointer, walking over the lake, deceptive imitator of the divine, is the true god of fire, the real nihilist, the devil. He is the true believer in nothing. The reader begins to see the truth in all this when Pointer removes Hulga's glasses and places them in *his* pocket. Here her pseudo-intellectual prosthesis—her glasses—is taken away. And this is also the moment of the great revelation to Hulga of the meaning of true belief in nothing as much as of her own utterly un-sophisticated erudite imitation.

She is merely the "goddess" who "had to come [to Vulcan] when called." Hulga, in her self-serious, condescending "nihilism," is actually a silly pseudo-intellectual, manipulated by the birthday party magician wearing the ridiculous mask of her "philosophy" that could only ever deceive a child. At some point, however, the child who plays with fire, fascinated by the flame, gets burned. And that is, precisely, the moment of grace in O'Connor's story. Only when Hulga becomes blind—becomes reconciled to her blindness—can she begin to see. The fact that Pointer removes and runs away with her fake leg suggests that Hulga may have also just had her nihilism amputated from her mind. In the end, I think, Pointer should be seen as an ambiguous figure. His devious actions that strip Hulga of her fake leg and her glasses are conditions for her enlightenment. Even the devil's actions can bring about divine grace. Sometimes, as in the Cross, that is the supreme way.

The ordinary is always more than that; being is more than itself and that is why, and indeed how, *it is*. Perception of the goodness of being is not enough unless that goodness is recognized in its fragile freedom, as implicated in the music of unimaginably great proportions, as, ultimately, an apocalyptic vortex of wills in combat, as challenged and counter-challenged at every point in a drama that runs through the center of the order of things and of the human soul. I have emphasized throughout this chapter that Vile is neither a nihilist nor a theologian but an artist who sees and celebrates the freedom of goodness in the everyday. And that is a remarkable event of artistic accomplishment. But to practice the art of listening to, and perhaps even daring to sing a few full-throated chords of, the Deeper Music that only echoes, like a rumor, or a glimpse, in the mystery of the quotidian: that, man, *that* is rock and roll.

# Have You Seen Him Whom My Soul Loves?:
## Taylor Swift and Pope Benedict XVI on the Search for Love

Brian Pedraza

There are few things—or none, in the opinion of this writer—that move a person more than love. In the Christian tradition, this thought is captured by Augustine in vivid color when he claims, "My weight is my love, and wherever I am carried it is this weight that carries me."[1] In the midst of a discussion on creation and the Spirit hovering above the primordial waters, the saintly North African bishop seemingly makes a quick aside to ponder aloud the tendency of weight to move downward. Weight, however, is not simply subject to gravity. In a jot of late fourth-century physics he tells us that fire tends upward, a stone downward. Oil, when poured below water, will find its way up. Thus, things do not always move to a lower place; rather, they seek their *quies*, their rest. And to not find the place of ultimate rest is to be subject to ultimate restlessness.

Love is, then, in the Augustinian view, the weight of a human being, and it is both the source of our restlessness and the path to our repose. Considering that the subject of this book is song, I think it is fair to say that even a lazy thumbing through the pages of music history will prove Augustine right. This goes for both so-called secular and Christian music. I dare not patronize the reader, who can surely think of a few love songs that demonstrate intense longing or promise fulfillment. But, in terms of Christianity, it seems appropriate to draw our attention to the Song of Songs, the love poetry of the wise Solomon,[2] a canticle that brings ecstasy to

---

1.   Confessions 13.9.10, in St. Augustine, *Confessions*, trans. Maria Boulding, OSB (Hyde Park, NY: New City Press, 1997), 348.
2.   There are few scholars who actually think Solomon is the author of the text, though most acknowledge it is associated with him in some way, as the text itself suggests.

the mystics and blushing redness to the cheeks of youth. Here, if I may speak anachronistically, Augustinian love is on full display. A young woman, madly in love with her beloved, rises from bed at night to seek him but finds him not. She calls out for him and, hearing nothing, leaves her home and wanders the city streets in search of him. When she comes upon the city watchmen, she asks, "Have you seen him whom my soul loves?" (Song 3:1–3). This longing is, in both Jewish and Christian tradition, symbolic of the love shared by the people of God and their Lord, and yet its power surely lies not only in the symbolic meaning but also in the visible symbol of passionate and restless love.

This, I hope, provides a good starting place for the work of this chapter, since in it, I compare the thought of two persons who share an Augustinian attentiveness to human love and the restlessness that accompanies it: Taylor Swift and Pope Benedict XVI. A hallmark of Swift's impressive and ongoing musical career is the exceptionally relatable way she describes the search for love. Combined with her characteristic confessional style—such that those who hear her songs actually "read my diary," as she puts it[3]—this search acts as a lens by which to view the arc of her entire musical oeuvre while simultaneously shedding light on the enduring appeal of her music. Benedict's attentiveness to love is most clearly seen in the first major work of his pontificate, the encyclical *Deus Caritas Est*, in which he confronts the

---

3.   In a 2014 interview with NPR, Swift says, "The formula has never changed, in that I try to make an album that best represents the last two years of my life. People have essentially gotten to read my diary for the last 10 years. I still write personal songs, and sometimes people like to put a very irritating, negative, spin on that—as if I'm oversharing, as if it's too much information—when this has been the way I've lived my life and run my career the entire time. So I do think it's really important that I continue to give people an insight into what my life is actually like, even though it comes at a higher cost now" (Melissa Block, "'Anything That Connects': A Conversation with Taylor Swift," https://www.npr.org/2014/10/31/359827368/anything-that-connects-a-conversation-with-taylor-swift).

Nietzschean critique that Christianity wrongly rejects *eros*, or desiring love, in favor of *agape*, or sacrificial love. Through his own examination of these two Greek terms, Benedict argues that eros, while often marred by disordered passion, is nevertheless genuinely human and thus can and should be taken up by the self-giving and characteristically divine agape. In comparing Swift and Benedict, I argue that Swift's descriptions of love help confirm Benedict's analysis that a searching love is essential to human experience; yet, even at its heights, Swift's version of love only begins to show a distinctive agapic character that would point the way for her listeners to ultimate human fulfillment.

In the following I proceed by outlining what I consider to be the eros-driven progression of Swift's albums before turning to a synopsis of Benedict's contemplation of love, though, in this second movement, it will be important to take up Nietzsche's challenge to the way love is often conceived in Christianity. Finally, after championing Benedict's vision in the face of this challenge, I return to Swift's music in hopes that the German pontiff has a genuine contribution to make to the understanding of love found there.

## Love According to Swift

Born in 1989 in Reading, Pennsylvania, Taylor Swift recorded her first top-40 song, "Tim McGraw," at the age of 16. Since then, and in a matter of about fifteen years, she has transformed from a squeaky-clean country singer—lauded by daughters and their mothers alike—into a best-selling crossover pop and rock mogul, garnering three Grammy awards for Album of the Year (tied for first among artists) and outselling all musicians in yearly album sales numerous times, including in 2018, 2019, 2020, and 2021.[4]

---

4. See Recording Academy, "Taylor Swift," https://www.grammy.com/grammys/artists/taylor-swift/15450; and Billboard's "Year-End Charts: Top Album Sales," https://www.billboard.com/

Her success is easily yoked to her genius-level ability to write good melodies and diary-like lyrics, and her tireless efforts in recording, advertising, and performing. So, too, is she lauded by more than just casual fans. Even the likes of Paul McCartney have found inspiration in her, and rock 'n' roll hall-of-famer Dave Grohl has admitted that he is "obsessed" with her work.[5] Such achievement and recognition make her music and persona a lightning rod of sorts for commentators, suggesting that critics and fans alike should tread carefully with their prose.

My own review of her oeuvre concentrates on her professionally recorded albums, as well as the most popular songs from them. For other artists, this may not be the best path for analysis, but it seems warranted for someone like Swift who both creates music and, admittedly, has drawn a large part of her identity from such factors as popularity, recognition by fans, and awards earned. In this sense, she has often been more reactionary than self-defining, a person driven by a relentless search for acceptance or perfection (or perhaps it is better to say that she holds her perfection to be ultimate acceptance). In fact, I believe this restless search is the thread that unifies her entire body of work. It is the most prominent leitmotif even when it is seemingly absent from her lyrics and despite the transitions that have occurred in her career.[6]

---

charts/year-end/2018/top-album-title-sales/ (with the year changed accordingly). Because of Swift's ability to sell hard copies of albums in the era of streaming music, Mary Fogarty and Gina Arnold call her "the last great rock star" ("Are You Ready for It? Re-Evaluating Taylor Swift," *Contemporary Music Review*, 40/1 (2020): 3).

5.  For McCartney's inspiration, see Mark Savage, "Paul McCartney on handling crowds, and why he calls Donald Trump 'the mad captain,'" *BBC News*, September 13, 2018, https://www.bbc.com/news/entertainment-arts-45482360. For Grohl's remarks, see Madeline Roth, "Dave Grohl Dedicated a Bunch of Songs to Taylor Swift after Admitting He's 'Obsessed' with Her," *MTV*, May 25, 2015, http://www.mtv.com/news/2168779/dave-grohl-dedicates-songs-taylor-swift/.

6.  Swift expresses her preoccupation with acceptance in Lana Wil-

Swift's first three albums establish the hallmarks of her songwriting: unsurpassably relatable lyrics wedded to a pop sensibility. That these albums are clearly country in genre, tied to the experience of white middle-class Americana, and filled with the experiences of desire and hurt in young love is important for contextualizing their content, but the universal (and, therefore, cross-cultural and cross-socioeconomic) experience of love gained and lost are of most interest here.[7] In her 2006 self-titled album debut, we find Swift pining for the unaware Drew, the cause of the "teardrops on her guitar." This pent-up desire is re-presented on 2008's *Fearless*: In "Love Story," the artist casts herself as the lonely Juliet, whose father refuses the courting of Romeo. The album's other most notable song, "You Belong with Me," returns us to the high school halls of her first album, the narrator once again befriending a boy whose interest lies elsewhere. "She wears high heels, I wear sneakers," Swift sings, painting herself as the underdog to the cheer captain she watches from the bleachers. The song marvelously conjures the vibe of smalltown America and welcomes all similarly overlooked listeners to sing from their forlorn bedroom windows, "Why can't you see? / You belong with me."

The songs of 2010's *Speak Now* complete the artist's country trilogy and repeat the themes of the earlier albums. In "Mine," Swift sings of the ups and downs of a relationship that begins in fear but, through vulnerability and trials, retains the hope that love can last. New on this album is a song of remorse—in "Back to December" Swift is apologetic about a broken relationship

---

son's documentary *Miss Americana* (Los Angeles, CA: Tremolo Productions, 2020).

7. At the time of this chapter's writing, Swift had begun the work of re-recording her first six albums after a controversy in which she struggled to secure the master tracks from Scott Borchetta and Big Machine Records and the ensuing sale of them to Scooter Braun. Since the original popularity of the songs released in these albums is important to my argument, I will stick to the lyrics that were published under the Big Machine label while, nevertheless, lauding the ingenuity of Swift's latest efforts.

that, in hindsight, she wishes could be changed. Also new is an important theme that will burgeon in the future: the remarks of critics and the effect they have on the songwriter. In "Ours," Swift clings to love despite the contempt of onlookers, encouraging her beloved with the words, "This love is ours," even though "people throw rocks at things that shine." In "Mean" she more directly confronts a critic from her position as the youthful underdog: "Someday, I'll be big enough so you can't hit me / And all you're ever gonna be is mean."

The next two albums of Swift's career mark an important shift. *Red* (2012) and *1989* (2014) usher in a change of image from the "girl next door" to the mega pop star performing in front of sold-out arenas. The earlier album signals the transformation gently, straddling the line between country and pop in such songs as "Red" and "22," the first leaning more toward her country roots and the second toward pop experimentation. Still, the two most popular songs of the album represent her unabashed entry into the world of pop music. "I Knew You Were Trouble" and "We Are Never Ever Getting Back Together" appear to trade the identity of the pining youngster for that of the carefree woman who no longer desires but, rather, willingly regrets past love. For example, in the latter, Swift is entirely in control of the fate of a relationship. Seemingly no longer a prisoner to desire, she tells her on-again, off-again lover with confidence that they are "never, ever, ever, getting back together."

*1989*, named after the year of her birth, reaffirms this new-found blasé persona emphatically. In "Shake It Off," a pop song almost engineered for large dance group concert performances, Swift dismisses critics who say she goes "on too many dates" but "can't make 'em stay." "Blank Space" borders on flippancy in continuing this theme, as she claims that her "long list of ex-lovers" would "tell you I'm insane," yet "I've got a blank space, baby / And I'll write your name." Finally, in "Bad Blood," Swift confronts a fellow artist after a well-publicized spat;[8] the official

---

8. Swift's 2013 rift with Katy Perry apparently started when dancers from the *Red* tour jumped mid-tour to Perry's *Prismatic* tour.

music video employs numerous Hollywood, music, and fashion stars in an over-the-top action movie reproduction designed to prove that Swift is no fragile personality or damsel always destined to be in distress, whether from broken relationships or the pressures that come from extraordinary success.

Still, if one were tempted to think of the genre change of these two albums as a symbol of Swift's transformation from restless lover to thick-skinned warrior, then the subsequent era of her career should lay such thoughts to rest. The period from 2014–2017, years of relative silence spurred by a public spectacle involving none other than Kanye West and Kim Kardashian, can be considered a period of darkness or even metaphorical death for Swift. In her own words, "When you're living for the approval of strangers and that is where you derive all your joy and fulfillment, one bad thing can cause everything to crumble."[9] Indeed, everything seemed to crumble during this time.

She emerged from this "darkness" in 2017, signaling her rebirth by wiping clean her social media accounts (surely the symbol of a millennial's re-creation) and posting a glitching image of a snake.[10] This was the precursor to 2017's *Reputation*, a stunning departure from her earliest albums, one that still builds on the previous pop transition but this time laces its tracks with heavy urban, industrial, and R&B loops and hooks. In the album's most-played track, "Look What You Made Me Do," in a musical interlude following the bridge, Swift overdubs a pretend conversation in which she answers the phone. "I'm sorry," she says, "but the old Taylor can't come to the phone right now / Why? Oh, 'cause she's dead." Along with the recognition of her own death, Swift casually remarks, "Honey, I rose up from the dead, I do it all the time." Nevertheless, it is more accurate, I believe, to say that her resurrection only *begins* to show itself in this album.

---

9. Wilson, *Miss Americana*.
10. The snake imagery, presumably an ironic reclaiming of a derogatory term, ended up playing a significant role on her *Reputation* tour, forming the massive backdrop for much of the set.

In the opening track, "…Ready for It?," Swift revamps her desire for love, no longer in the role of the one wanting to be pursued but as the pursuer. She ironically describes herself as a "robber" who steals hearts, runs off, and never says sorry, while noting about her prey, "But if I'm a thief, then he can join the heist." Despite her appearing to adopt a snake-like façade in the song and, indeed, throughout the album, Swift's post-album reflections on *Reputation* belie her apparent transformation into a callous half-stoic, half-epicurean superwoman. In an interview with *Rolling Stone*, Swift noted that the album embodied the confrontation with criticism witnessed in songs like "Blank Space," but writ large. In other words, by fully embracing the role of the disparaged, she produced an album that borders on parody and is almost entirely a reaction to being unloved.[11] Thus, within the narrative of the album she is the hardened huntress; in the narrative beyond the album she is still the one aching for acceptance.

Even so, moments of genuine resurrection peek through the cracks in the hardened exterior of her music. One is seen in a secondary but perhaps more genuine theme woven into the album, and the other stems from Swift's experience of performing the songs on tour. Regarding the first, Swifties—the given name for the artist's superfans—unhesitatingly point to her relationship with Joe Alwyn, one kindled in the period of darkness, as unique and superior to all others. In "Delicate," Swift sings of this relationship: "My reputation's never been worse, so / You must

---

11. See Brian Hiatt's "9 Taylor Swift Moments That Didn't Fit in Our Cover Story," *Rolling Stone*, September 30, 2019, https://www. rollingstone.com/music/music-features/taylor-swift-moments-that-couldnt-fit-in-our-cover-story-890700/: "That album was a real process of catharsis . . . because it was creating this strange defense mechanism. And, I'd never really done that in that exact way before. The only way I'd done it in the past, was with 'Blank Space,' which I wrote specifically about criticisms I had received for supposedly dating too many people in my twenties. I took that template of, OK, this is what you're all saying about me. Let me just write from this character for a second."

like me for me." That this experience of a love with no ulterior motives had a powerful effect on her is also evident in "King of My Heart," in which she describes finding "the one I have been waiting for," a love embracing her "body and soul" that could be the "end of all the endings," and in which her "broken bones are mending." These descriptions are furthered in "Call It What You Want," in which someone Swift trusts "like a brother" loves her like she is "brand new." The final song of the album, "New Year's Day," is a surprisingly soft ballad. Swift imagines the end of a New Year's Eve party with girls leaving, carrying their high heels, though "candle wax and Polaroids on the hardwood floor" remain. Yet, she promises her lover that "I'll be cleaning up bottles with you on New Year's Day," a symbol of a willingness to work through hardships and of persistence when the fleeting joys have passed. That the setting for the song is a time of new beginnings also seems to fit a genuine re-creation that lies behind the more reactionary tone of the rest of the album.

The second note of true resurrection stems from Swift's experience on the *Reputation* tour. Approaching it, she described her confrontation with criticism as one of dehumanization; but during performances, her encounter with fans changed something in her:

> So often with our takedown culture, talking s— [*sic*] about a celebrity is basically the same as talking s— about the new iPhone. So when I go and I meet fans, I see that they actually see me as a flesh-and-blood human being. That— as contrived as it may sound—changed [me] completely, assigning humanity to my life.[12]

---

12. Alex Suskind, "New Reputation: Taylor Swift shares intel on TS7, fan theories, and her next era," *Entertainment Weekly*, May 5, 2019, https://ew.com/music/2019/05/09/taylor-swift-cover-story/. Swift's experience is yet another example of what Pope Francis has called the "throwaway culture" in which humans are commodified as consumer goods.

It seems that the experience of genuine love in her self-described worst times—whether from a lover or from fans—was transformational.

Despite the claims of *Reputation*, 2019's *Lover* is Swift's album of true resurrection. This time, the interior and the meta narratives correspond. As Swift's first album apart from her earliest label, *Lover* is a testament to newfound creative freedom. Additionally, songs like "You Need to Calm Down" and "The Man" reveal her willingness to openly take political and social stances, even at the risk of alienating previous fans.[13] So, too, does the joyful, even airy tone of much of the album seem to confirm Swift's embrace of an identity apart from the approval of critics. The opening track, "I Forgot That You Existed," whimsically speaks to the critics who had claimed "free rent" in her mind and proclaims: "Something happened one magical night / I forgot that you existed."

The other popular tracks on the album are an indication that the experience was genuine. The lead single, "ME!," is an ode to self-worth. Swift tells her lover, "You're the only one of you" while she is "the only one of me." The album's title track keeps a steady and swaying 12/8 rhythm and conjures images of contentment. Swift sings of a "forever and ever" kind of love, one in which she and her lover have established a home together. With a nod to marriage vows, she announces, "I take this magnetic force of a man to be my lover."

Swift's re-creation is expressed throughout the album, but it is the last song, "Daylight," that captures it most powerfully. After the darkness of the *Reputation*-era experience, she speaks

---

13. Though the first clearly departs from biblical and traditional sexual ethics, Christians and others holding to orthodox Christian mores can learn from the way they are described in the song: People holding signs and screaming condemnation are hardly the witnesses to the joy of the gospel that can effectively transform the world. The second is a powerful expression of the unjust inequalities present in American culture. Swift is correct that many critics of her life have a double standard when it comes to the actions of men and women.

of a "morning" in which love is "golden." Still, the outro of the song provides the most direct declaration: "I wanna be defined by the things that I love / Not the things I hate / Not the things I'm afraid of / . . . I just think that / You are what you love." By ending with this Augustinian dictum, Swift fittingly closes an album that showcases the effects of true resurrection: previous natures are not discarded but are taken up and transformed, bringing something surpassingly new while remaining in continuity with what was before.

Swift's final two albums to date are creations that emerged from the global isolation of the Covid-19 pandemic. With the *Lover Fest* tour cancelled, and living through lockdown, she created what are arguably her most lauded albums yet, 2020's *Folklore* and *Evermore*. She released the first album in July and then surprised the music world with the follow-up in December of the same year, showcasing the talent as well as the resources and power few artists could. Both manifest a pared-down, folk, alternative rock style, though the first is more whimsical and the second more somber in tone.

One of the most intriguing aspects of these sister albums is the artist's venture into telling stories unrelated to her own life. In a primer for *Folklore* released on social media, Swift explained:

> Stars drawn around scars. A cardigan that still bears the scent of loss twenty years later. . . . Pretty soon these images in my head grew faces or names and became characters. I found myself not only writing my own stories, but also writing about or from the perspective of people I've never met, people I've known, or those I wish I hadn't.[14]

Does this break from autobiography signal a shift from the restlessness of the majority of Swift's oeuvre, or is it merely a result of the escapism needed to psychologically weather a global pandemic? Without denying the second, there are, I

---

14. The message is found on Swift's social media accounts, e.g. https://www.instagram.com/p/CDAsU8BDzLt/.

believe, hints in these albums that the genuine resurrection she expressed in *Lover* has solidified further. Even the largely mythical character of most of the songs is representative of this development, something I will take up in the final section of this chapter. But for now, it is fitting to end this brief tour through Swift's body of work by calling our attention to one of the few autobiographical songs from the pandemic albums, *Folklore's* "peace." Expressive, once again, of her relationship with Alwyn, Swift opines that her beloved will always be faced with the pressure of onlookers while being involved with her—"I could never give you peace" is the repeated theme of the song. Despite the "danger" that follows her, Swift treasures her beloved, describing him as a man of integrity and honor. In her strongest profession of love yet, she expresses that she will be with him during the times of his greatest hopes ("I'd swing with you for the fences") and worst trials ("Sit with you in the trenches"). Even more, she is willing to create a family with him and give him the "silence that only comes when two people understand each other." Lastly, she chooses his family for her own. From these lines, it is fair to say that all of Swift's post-*Reputation* work is marked by a new experience of love, one that has brought about, at the very least, the beginning of a significant transformation to the way she approaches the subject.

## Love According to Benedict XVI

It may seem surprising to move from the musings of an American country-pop-rock megastar to those of a nonagenarian German pope, but Pope Benedict XVI was no stranger to surprises. As the previous head of the Congregation (now Dicastery) for the Doctrine of the Faith, he was rudely labeled "God's Rottweiler" and, worse, the "Panzer Cardinal" by critics who disdained his upholding of traditional teaching. Thus, his first papal document must have been a stunning, if not bewildering, surprise for such observers given its message: God is love.

For those more familiar with the entirety of his career, *Deus Caritas Est* is familiarly Ratzingerian—erudite and contemplative, concerned with the experiences and challenges of the modern world but seeking answers in Christian tradition, biblical and Christ-focused.[15] It is, in his words, the fruit of his desire "to speak of the love which God lavishes upon us and which we in turn must share with others."[16] Its first half concerns the interpersonal experience of love, its second the Church's vocation to love in society. My own reflections pertain to the first half.

*Deus Caritas Est* is a bold manifestation of what the pope calls elsewhere a "pedagogy of desire."[17] The unstated goal of the encyclical is to show that all earthly and human loves, if they are to reach the end of their yearnings, must encounter and be taken up by divine love.

Benedict illustrates this claim by recalling the various words used by the Greeks which are captured inadequately and without distinction by the English word "love." Readers may be familiar with these words from the work of C. S. Lewis.[18] Lewis speaks of *storge* (affection), *philia* (friendship), *eros* (need-love), and

15. We should put to rest the old trope that the young Ratzinger was daring and creative, unafraid to challenge orthodoxy, while the old Ratzinger was a stuffy conservative. Certainly, no one would deny that the publications of the CDF or the pope should be more chastened than those of an academic. But a genuine reader of his early and later works will find a fundamental continuity in them, and Ratzinger's self-interpretation rejects the aforementioned dichotomy. See, for instance, his comments in Richard N. Ostling's "Keeper of the Straight and Narrow: Joseph Cardinal Ratzinger," *Time*, December 6, 1993: "I see no break in my views as a theologian."

16. *Deus Caritas Est*, 1. I have taken all selections from this document from Pope Benedict XVI, *Deus Caritas Est*, Vatican translation (San Francisco: Ignatius Press, 2006).

17. Pope Benedict XVI, "General Audience," November 7, 2012, Vatican, https://www.vatican.va/content/benedict-xvi/en/audiences/2012/documents/hf_ben-xvi_aud_20121107.html.

18. See C. S. Lewis, *The Four Loves* (San Francisco: HarperOne, 1960). While never mentioning Lewis, Benedict draws some of the same conclusions.

*agape* (gift-love).[19] Benedict, while mentioning John's use of philia in his Gospel, is mainly concerned with the final two. *Eros* is a desiring love, *agape* a self-giving love. Furthermore, eros is the epitome of earthly love, agape the embodiment of divine love. Thus, to restate his intentions: Benedict wishes to show that eros's search can only be completed by agape, and agape can integrate and purify eros, allowing it to become a path to the divine. That the pope sees no essential conflict between the two is controversial, as we will see below.

Before engaging with his thought on the two terms, it is worth asking why the Greek words are even significant at all to the discussion. A general reason is certainly that the terms are part of the foundational heritage of what has come to be known as Western classical thought. But a second reason holds greater import for this chapter. The Church emerged amid a Roman Empire that was fascinated and influenced by Greek thought. As one of the common languages of the empire at the time of Christianity's birth, Greek became the language of the New Testament. Thus, when Jesus' earliest followers wrote about love, they used Greek words to do so.[20]

---

19. In actuality, Lewis breaks from the Greek words with the fourth and calls it "charity," a cognate of the Latin *caritas*. Nevertheless, in other correspondence, he makes it clear that agape is what he has in mind. See, for instance, his "Letter to Mrs. Johnson," dated February 19, 1954, part of which is quoted in Zach Kincaid, "Lewis on Love," *C. S. Lewis: The Official Website of C. S. Lewis*, February 13, 2019, https://www.cslewis.com/lewis-on-love/.

20. Already, the Church's commitment to harnessing the complementarity of faith and reason is glimpsed here. In incarnational fashion, the language and thought of humanity became the pathway by which the faith could be expressed. Still, the adoption of human philosophy as a means to understand and hand on the faith was never wholesale—such thought had to be purified by the light of divine revelation, and in the first few centuries, various Christian figures were hesitant to harness the "spoils of the Egyptians" because of the inherent risk of diminishing or tainting the faith. But it was only in the Protestant Reformation that

This provides an important segue to Benedict's thoughts, because they are set within the context of the unprecedented uniqueness of the New Testament. As Benedict explains, at the time, the predominant term in extrabiblical Greek literature was *eros*. The New Testament writers, however, in sharp contrast to their surroundings, avoided the word altogether, instead opting for the rarer agape.[21] What could account for this choice, and should it be lauded?

Benedict addresses the first question by returning us to the origins of eros. Associated with the god of the same name, eros was, for the Greeks, a "kind of intoxication, the overpowering of reason by a 'divine madness' which tears man away from his finite existence and enables him, in the very process of being overwhelmed by divine power, to experience supreme happiness."[22] In this sense, though divine in origin, eros is the epitome of human love. It is an arresting desire, one so powerful that it imbues the yearning lovers have for one another with the promise of contact with the divine. As such, Benedict also refers to eros as an "ascending love," that is, a love by which one can climb to the heights of ecstasy.[23]

---

the complementarity of faith and reason was challenged in such a way that their supposed opposition became characteristic for large swaths of Christians.

21. *Deus Caritas Est*, 3. The Old Testament is largely written in Hebrew, with small portions in Aramaic and Greek. The New Testament is written in Greek, with infrequent small phrases (e.g., some sayings of Jesus) in Aramaic. A Greek translation of the entire Old Testament, known as the Septuagint, was known and available to the New Testament writers. In fact, the majority of Old Testament quotations found in the New Testament are from the Septuagint.
22. *Deus Caritas Est*, 4.
23. See, for instance, Socrates' speech in the *Symposium* 201d–212c, in which he speaks of eros as an intermediary between the gods and mortals, the latter being able to ascend by eros from a vision of beautiful bodies, to the beauty of knowledge, to the contemplation of the Beautiful itself.

Though holding such promise in theory, in practice, eros was associated with fertility cults in which people could bring their desire and unleash it upon temple prostitutes in an attempt to reach this ecstasy.[24] This "use" of women for sacred purposes, Benedict remarks, was nothing less than exploitation. They were "not treated as human beings and persons, but simply used as a means of arousing 'divine madness.'"[25]

It now becomes clear why biblical religion opposed eros as such. Not only was "erotic" worship of this type an affront to monotheism, but it also reduced human love to lust. The New Testament authors, harnessing the struggle for monotheism of the Old Testament and wishing to relay their experience of the love of God found in Jesus Christ, turned to the word *agape* to express what they meant by love. Agape, which characterizes God's self-gift in Jesus Christ, is a "descending" love, representing God's willingness to empty himself for his people. It is a love that "seeks the good of the beloved," even to the point of sacrifice.[26] With this emphasis, agape became intertwined with the faith such that Christianity came to be characterized by it. "By this everyone will know that you are my disciples, if you have love [*agapen*] for one another" (John 13:35). "No one has greater love [*agapen*] than this, to lay down one's life for one's friends" (John 15:13).

Though spurred by noble intentions, this move by the earliest Christian authors can easily give the impression that, by avoiding the word *eros*, Christianity has rejected eros outright. If true, the faith is then subject to the critique of prudishness, harboring a rejection of desire, sexuality, and even the human hope for loving fulfillment. Such was the claim of Nietzsche,

---

24. The existence of temple prostitution in Greek culture is debated by scholars, though the existence of ritual sex is not. The issue is merely one of compensation. Regardless, Benedict's reflections stand whether the women were paid or not.
25. *Deus Caritas Est*, 4.
26. Ibid., 6.

who wrote, "Christianity gave Eros poison to drink; he did not die of it, certainly, but degenerated to Vice."[27]

What are we to make of this claim, one that echoes today wherever Christianity is associated with a rejection of the body, sex, desire, and the like? Does the Church, "with all her commandments and prohibitions, turn to bitterness the most precious thing in life"? Does she "blow the whistle just when the joy which is the Creator's gift offers us a happiness which is itself a foretaste of the Divine"?[28]

Benedict gives a resounding "no" to these charges.[29] To him, the blame for the poisoning of eros does not fall to the Church. Rather, it falls to those cultures that adopt a "warped and destructive form" of eros, to those who endorse a "counterfeit divinization" of it that "actually strips it of its dignity and dehumanizes it." On the contrary, Benedict claims, Christianity must and should embrace eros, even as a path to the divine, but it must be "disciplined and purified" to become so.[30]

In the pope's view, desire belongs to human nature and is not the result of sin. Our sinfulness can pollute desire such that it seeks to approach earthly goods as mere objects for consumption and to treat humans as such objects, but desire in itself, when

---

27. Friedrich Nietzsche, *Beyond Good and Evil: Prelude to a Philosophy of the Future*, trans. Helen Zimmern (New York: MacMillan, 1907), 99. The work was first published in German as *Jenseits von Gut und Böse*.

28. *Deus Caritas Est*, 3. It is not non-Christian figures alone who claim Christianity rejects eros. In fact, the Lutheran Swede Anders Nygren wrote what was, until Benedict XVI, the most important study of eros and agape, in which he claims eros and agape are opposed. In his view, eros is a counterfeit divine love, taken up wrongly by Augustine in his "caritas synthesis," an ill-fated move that was only corrected by the Reformation. See Nygren's *Agape and Eros*, trans. Philip S. Watson (New York: Harper & Row, 1969).

29. Even so, Benedict does not shy away from the fact that, in certain corners and periods of Christianity, "tendencies of this sort have always existed" (*Deus Caritas Est*, 5).

30. *Deus Caritas Est*, 4.

shed of this darkness, is an essential and good part of human experience. Is it sinful for a wife to long for the affection of her husband, or evil when a person senses that first flutter of attraction when meeting another? Or more important still, why would the Scriptures use the image of the eros-driven young lover, running through the streets looking for her beloved, as an image of the love between God and his people, if this love was not to be lauded?

In this last image we see not only that eros is genuinely human, but also that this desire is a capacity implanted in us by God as a means to seek him. "You have made us and drawn us to yourself," Augustine wrote, "and our heart is unquiet until it rests in you."[31] It is precisely on this "pilgrimage" of desire that one can be opened to encounter the divine love of agape. When a human love, a romantic love, matures through a path of purification into the kind of love that seeks to stand the test of time, it will find a new path opening before it:

> The initial ecstasy becomes a pilgrimage. . . . Through this journey one will be able to deepen gradually one's knowledge of that love, initially experienced. And the mystery that it represents will become more and more defined: in fact, not even the beloved is capable of satisfying the desire that dwells in the human heart. In fact, the more authentic one's love for the other is, the more it reveals the question of its origin and its destiny, of the possibility that it may endure for ever. Therefore, the human experience of love

---

31. *Confessions* 1.1.1, 40. As Benedict says, "Man is the seeker of the Absolute, seeking with small and hesitant steps. And yet, already the experience of desire, of a 'restless heart' as St Augustine called it, is very meaningful. It tells us that man is, deep down, a religious being, a 'beggar of God.' We can say with the words of Pascal: 'Man infinitely surpasses man.' Eyes recognize things when they are illuminated. From this comes a desire to know the light itself, what makes the things of the world shine and with them ignites the sense of beauty" ("General Audience," November 7, 2012).

has in itself a dynamism that refers beyond the self. It is the experience of a good that leads to being drawn out and finding oneself before the mystery that encompasses the whole of existence.[32]

It is important to stress that eros's ascent will ultimately not be possible without agape. With its maturation, the lover's desire for the beloved will begin to seek the good of the beloved. Desire will be transformed to self-gift, which itself can draw out an even more purified form of desire: I desire you, and I desire what is good for you. Thus, for Benedict, eros and agape are not opposed but form a continuum in which eros can become agape, and agape can take up and transform eros and its path of ascent.

Still, the pilgrimage is only complete when eros finds its rest in a love that completely satisfies. This, for Benedict, is the love that is God. In fact, he claims, the descent of God's love and the ascent of human love meet in the person of Jesus Christ, fully God and fully human.[33] In Christ, humanity's eros becomes divine, searching for the lost sheep. In Christ, divinity's agape becomes human, giving itself on the Cross. The "I thirst" (John 19:28) of Jesus, spoken from the apex of the blood-soaked wood, is a manifestation of God's erotic love encompassed in the agapic love of total self-gift. From the pierced side of Christ, Benedict tells us, is where any true contemplation of love must begin. In this we find the "path along which [our] love and life must move."[34]

## Him Whom My Soul Loves

In Solomon's love song, the young bride first speaks of a desiring and searching love: "Let him kiss me with the kisses of his mouth! / For your love [*dodeka*] is better than wine" (Song 1:2). Later, however, this variation of the Hebrew *dodim* is replaced

---

32. Benedict XVI, "General Audience," November 7, 2012.
33. See *Deus Caritas Est*, 12.
34. Ibid.

by the word *ahabà*, a word that will come to be translated into Greek as *agape*: "I adjure you, O daughters of Jerusalem, / by the gazelles or the wild does: / do not stir up nor awaken love [*ha'ahabah*] / until it is ready!" (Song 2:7). In Benedict's words:

> By contrast with an indeterminate, "searching" love, this [new] word expresses the experience of a love which involves a real discovery of the other. . . . Love now becomes concern and care for the other. No longer is it self-seeking, a sinking in the intoxication of happiness; instead it seeks the good of the beloved: it becomes renunciation, and it is ready, and even willing, for sacrifice.[35]

Is this the same transition Swift makes in her songs? We have seen how, through most of her career, Swift's lyrics are a modern embodiment of the early, searching desire of the young woman in the Song of Songs. Not only in her music but also in her life, she has been driven by the need for acceptance, more reactionary than self-defining—a quality garnering both the empathy of fans and the antipathy of certain critics. She is, perhaps, our era's most skilled musical exegete of the human longing to be loved.

But we have also seen how her last few albums speak of love in new ways, hinting at resurrection, a desire for the good of the beloved, and a willingness to sacrifice. From this at least three conclusions can be drawn.

First, it seems clear that, amid the darkness of the *Reputation*-era, Swift experienced something of a genuine transformation. It is not our place to judge the extent or permanence of this change, but it is undoubtable that the secondary motif of *Reputation*, in which she sings of a newfound love experienced "at her worst," is more prominent in the albums that follow it. I consider the fictional storytelling embraced in *Folklore* and *Evermore* to be evidence of this fact. Before self-seeking desire matures into self-gift, the transitional stage of appreciation must

---

35. Ibid., 6.

occur. Goods can present themselves to our senses in ways that befuddle our tendency to consumerism, evoking appreciation within us. These goods can be as monumental as the birth of a child or as mundane and hidden as a perfectly blooming rose encountered upon a stroll, but, in either case, the object, without yet calling forth our own self-sacrifice, elicits our appreciation. It strikes us first not as a thing to be possessed but as something to behold in wonder.[36] Swift, in telling stories that are not her own, reflects this ability to encounter and to wonder. Thus, at the very least, she has moved past a persona that is purely desirous of others' acceptance.

Second, if this transformation (or at least its beginning) is true, then the arc of Swift's songwriting confirms Benedict XVI's claim that eros and agape are not opposed but form a continuum. The pope dispels Nietzsche's claim that Christianity rejects eros outright, but not without arguing that this love must mature, transformed by agape, if it is to reach the object of its desire. Judging by the way she speaks of receiving love from her newfound lover and from her fans, Swift, I imagine, would agree. Her previous longings were not quenched by desire alone—a strange claim to be sure—but by receiving love detached from ulterior motives. It is the experience of agapic love, in other words, that breeds agapic love.

A third and final conclusion stems from Swift's confirmation of Benedict's thesis. And here I simply wish to point out why this confirmation is so important for Christianity. Eros needs agape to reach its end. Christians should see, then, avenues for bringing the Gospel wherever desire is found. Even when mired and muddied by consumerism and lust, the spark of desire can open the human heart to the search for God. As Benedict puts it:

---

36. Lewis offers a similar theory, distinguishing between "need-pleasures" and "pleasures of appreciation." After experiencing the first, we tend to speak of ourselves: "I needed that." When experiencing the second, we tend to speak of the object: "That is wonderful." See *The Four Loves*, 16.

We must not forget that the dynamism of desire is always open to redemption. . . . Even in the abyss of sin, that ember is never fully extinguished in man. It allows him to recognize the true good, to savour it, and thus to start out again on a path of ascent.[37]

Conversely, if divine love can take up and redeem eros, then Christians should not fear what is genuinely human but rather welcome it in ways that affirm what is good in humanity. A Christianity that denies genuine human experience would be a Christianity that rejects the Incarnation, the taking on of our humanity by the Son of God. As Benedict illuminates for us, this does not mean the Church should accept what is sinful in this experience, but that the gospel can and should be a purifying and transforming force in every culture in which it is planted.

*Contra* Nietzsche, then, eros, with the full force of its desire, is welcome in Christianity. Surely, Taylor Swift's ability to speak so powerfully to the hearts of her listeners is evidence that the longing to be loved is essential to humanity and, thus, an essential aspect of redemption. And just as surely, Christians should hope that the pilgrimage of Swift and all those who long for love progresses to the only place one can find true rest, in the *quies* of God.

---

37. Benedict XVI, "General Audience," November 7, 2012.

# Standing for Truth:
## Sara Bareilles' "Brave" and Matthew 10

Elizabeth Woodard

Sara Bareilles' hit song "Brave" arguably enjoys such popularity because it verbalizes the mantra of a generation fed up with various forms of toxic secret-keeping. It is an anthem of radical honesty. It celebrates and encourages a person in embracing the totality of their story, overcoming fear of negative reactions or repercussions. Contemporaneous with the #MeToo movement, "Brave" is an artifact of the time during which an entire segment of society seems to cry, "I am done being silent for others' comfort! I am done keeping secrets because others might find the truth uncomfortable!" Bareilles' song proclaims that speaking the truth of one's story is the brave thing to do.

Such a mantra is solidly scriptural. Warning against the fear of negative responses to acknowledging him in public, Jesus encourages his disciples, "What I say to you in the dark, tell in the light; and what you hear whispered, proclaim from the housetops" (Matt 10:27). For "everyone . . . who acknowledges me before others, I also will acknowledge before my Father in heaven; but whoever denies me before others, I also will deny before my Father in heaven" (10:32–33). Known as the Missionary Discourse, this section of Matthew chapter 10 demonstrates the age of the problem of toxic secret-keeping. Our current generation may need a reminder just as Jesus' own disciples did, but we did not invent the concept of speaking truth to power or of speaking truth in the face of potentially dire consequences. The Missionary Discourse indicates that the need for encouragement to do so is at least as old as Christianity itself.

It would seem, then, that Sara Bareilles' "Brave" is a fitting anthem for the Christian needing courage to follow Christ *out loud*, so to speak, in an increasingly secular age. However, it would be rash to promote this song as congruent with the Christian message without first considering whether there is latent heresy hidden within its seemingly orthodox message. The heresy "Brave" is most likely to fall prey to is relativism. The undiscerning listener runs the risk of being trapped by the very secularization and relativism that Jesus' followers seek to thwart. Hiding within Bareilles' challenge to speak up—"Say what you wanna say"—is an insidious suggestion that truth is relative and subject to one's own subjective opinion or experience.

The call to speak up is only helpful insofar as it encourages the speaking of truth. If the song encourages every sort of speaking up, including even the propagation of beliefs that have no basis in reality, the song loses its strength as a mantra for Christians seeking to live truth in today's world. So we must ask, what sort of definition of truth is operative in "Brave"? The answer will indicate whether the song leads people toward the kind of unabashed commitment to speaking truth evident in Matthew 10 or away from it. An examination of the song's lyrics is necessary in order to parse out the degree to which it leads toward, or away from, orthodoxy.

## The Power of Words

Discerning orthodoxy and heresy in rock music is possible through an honest textual analysis. The main chorus of "Brave" is simple enough: It encourages the listener to "say what you wanna say." A repetition of this and other key phrases, along with the value judgment that such behavior would indeed be "brave" and "amazing" makes up the whole. The nonchalance of saying what one might "wanna say" with words that "fall out" is balanced by the repetition of these phrases, which makes it sound more like an urgent pleading. The singer almost begs the listener to be brave in this way. Bravery consists in speaking the words that are the most tempting to withhold, words that risk the greatest repercussions, words of substance.

The bridge further articulates this point. Bareilles indicates that words can be empty, but encourages listeners to speak words that are "anything but." She encourages words that speak "the truth." She does not explain what this "truth" is, and this line will take up a great deal of focus in our discussion of the song's orthodoxy or potential pitfalls.

Elsewhere, the verses emphasize the power of such words of truth. They can be weapons. They can be drugs. They have the power to make someone an outcast. Conversely, they have the power to hurt like nothing else can when they "settle 'neath your skin." Bareilles points out that such "disappearing" before potential hearers is a result of being defeated by "the enemy," a falling for, and even bowing down to, "mighty" "fear."

The message of the song is: Don't suffer such defeat. Boldly speak your words of truth, of substance, the words with the greatest risk if they see the light of day. While it is tempting to bow to the mighty adversary of fear of what may happen if you speak words of substance, playing it safe in this way "Won't do you any good / Did you think it would?" She beckons her listener out of the shadows of silence, out of the misery of using only words that are empty, out of the "cage" of holding back important truths. She encourages the listener not to run in fear by "disappearing" and by holding their tongue, but to release their words. The extent to which the listener can do this will indicate "how big [their] brave is."

## The Missionary Discourse

Matthew 10 begins with Jesus' summoning the Twelve and giving them authority over unclean spirits and authority to cure diseases. He sends them "to the lost sheep of the house of Israel" (10:6) rather than to Gentiles. He instructs them that their main message is none other than "the good news, 'The kingdom of heaven has come near'" (10:7). They should heal, as they have been given authority to do, and not receive payment or take extra supplies for the journey, surviving instead on the hospitality of those who receive them. "See, I am sending you out like sheep into the midst of wolves," Jesus warns (10:16). "They will hand you over to councils and flog you in their synagogues; and you will be dragged before governors and kings because of me" (10:17–18). However, he reassures the disciples not to worry "about how you are to speak or what you are to say; for what you are to say will be given to you at that time; for it is not you who speak, but the Spirit of your Father speaking through you" (10:19–20). Jesus does not promise that the words that the Holy Spirit will give them will make everything pretty; indeed, "you will be hated by all because of my name. But the one who endures to the end will be saved" (10:22). It is in this light that Jesus encourages:

> So have no fear of them; for nothing is covered up that will not be uncovered, and nothing secret that will not become known. What I say to you in the dark, tell in the light; and what you hear whispered, proclaim from the housetops. Do not fear those who kill the body but cannot kill the soul; rather fear him who can destroy both soul and body in hell. Are not two sparrows sold for a penny? Yet not one of them will fall to the ground apart from your Father. And even the hairs of your head are all counted. So do not be afraid; you are of more value than many sparrows.
>
> Everyone therefore who acknowledges me before others, I also will acknowledge before my Father in heaven; but whoever denies me before others, I also will deny before my Father in heaven. (Matt 10:26–33)

It should be obvious at this point just how much thematic crossover there is between "Brave" and the Missionary Discourse of Matthew 10. Both plead with the listener to overcome the fear of holding back a significant truth, words of real substance, even though the outcome may be burdensome. Both indicate that the results of withholding the truth are worse than whatever ill may find the person for speaking out. This thematic crossover, of course, is not sufficient cause to conclude that the theology of "Brave" is orthodox and without error.

Is it possible, instead, to read into the theme of the song other, more insidious theological positions? Namely, whereas Matthew 10 specifically instructs to proclaim that "the kingdom of heaven has come near" (10:7) in the person and work of Jesus

Christ, and to testify to this truth by healing miracles performed through God's own power bestowed upon the disciples, "Brave" instructs the listener to proclaim the much more ambiguous message, "what you wanna say." What if what I "wanna say" is outside of, even contrary to, the revelation given in Christ? What if what I "wanna say" is a convincing lie built upon a complex series of defense mechanisms designed to exculpate me from any real moral responsibility? What if what I "wanna say" is simply that, and no more? What if what I "wanna say" frees me but enslaves others? What if what I "wanna say" is in direct conflict with what I *oughta* say? Herein lies the greatest risk with "Brave." It does not adequately define what should be said—what the truth is.

If "Brave" is encouraging the listener to overcome the same fear that Jesus is empowering the disciples to overcome in Matthew 10, that is, a fear of speaking truth to power, then it is a powerful Christian anthem indeed. If it is simply encouraging the listener to overcome the fear of saying what one wants, whatever that may be, then it is simply propagating the myth that truth is in the eye of the beholder, and that each person has a unique "truth" that can be changed at will. If, in other words, "Brave" proclaims that truth is relative to one's opinion, and that bravery consists in simply asserting one's opinion as truth, then it falls prey to the folly named in Matthew 15, just a few chapters later: "This people honors me with their lips, / but their hearts are far from me; / in vain do they worship me, / teaching human precepts as doctrines" (Matt 15:8–9).

## St. Augustine as a Reference Point

As we dissect any source, be it a spiritual text or a rock song, it is useful to reference a theological authority to represent orthodoxy. Such a theological reference point keeps us from reading into the text simply what we want to hear, as it would be easy to do in this case. We have seen that "Brave" indeed encourages the kind of bravery called for in the Missionary Discourse, and we have also seen that it can be read as encouraging the kind of relativism that this discourse is decidedly against. What would a touchstone such as that great bastion of orthodoxy, St. Augustine of Hippo, have to say to inform our inquiry about objective Christian identity?

One of the most poignant lines in "Brave" encourages the listener to speak words that are "anything but empty," letting their words tell the truth. While Bareilles does not define truth in this or in any line of the song, if we take it at face value, it finds support in the work of St. Augustine. He was well acquainted with people who used empty words to speak much pomp and no substance. He refers to "many loquacious people, whom I have had to endure, who attempted to instruct me and had nothing to say."[1] He mentions also a great rhetorician, and "trap of the devil," Faustus, "by which many were captured as a result of his smooth talk."[2] He himself "used to teach the art of rhetoric. Overcome by greed myself, I used to sell the eloquence that would overcome an opponent."[3] He condemns this skill as a vain misuse of word, explaining, "Publicly I was a teacher of the arts which they call liberal; privately I professed a false religion—in the former role arrogant, in the latter superstitious, in everything vain."[4] It would, therefore, seem that Augustinian theology supports this line in "Brave." He seems to agree that words should be "anything but empty"; indeed, he criticizes himself and others for the practice of empty words for worldly gains.

If we do not take the word "truth" in Bareilles' song at face value, though, we again face the difficult question, is "Brave" simply an embodiment of the modern relativistic belief that each person possesses his or her own unique truth? If that interpretation is inherent to "Brave," does it discount the song's power as a catchy version of Matthew 10?

St. Augustine was not a stranger to the concept of searching within oneself for truth. Indeed, Augustine seems to be more

---

1. St. Augustine, *Confessions*, trans. Henry Chadwick (Oxford University Press, 1998), Book V, article vii, 79.
2. *Confessions*, Book V, article ii, 73.
3. *Confessions*, Book IV, article ii, 53.
4. *Confessions*, Book IV, article i, 52.

than willing to consider the self as revelatory: "By the Platonic books I was admonished to return into myself. With you as my guide I entered into my innermost citadel, and was given power to do so because you had become my helper."[5] He gives us pause as we ask how harmful it would really be for one to conceptualize one's own individual story as a unique claim to truth. Sound Christian doctrine is predicated on the reality of objective truth, asserting that our modern temptation to relativize everything into "your truth" and "my truth" undermines the very nature of the existence of truth. If two people each possess conflicting beliefs as truth, and we assert that they can each be true for the respective person, then we've abolished any sense of truth at all, have we not?

Perhaps. What if, however, the terms "my truth" and "your truth" were not as insidious as believing that truth is relative, but rather as simple as believing that truth is *personal*? If my truth, for example, is that Jesus Christ is both human and divine, but your truth is that he is only human, then one of us must be wrong. The Holy Spirit has guided the Church in articulating the latter as the heresy of Arianism. However, if my truth is that I connect to Jesus most profoundly in a specific way—for example, through thoughts and feelings that I encounter in the Eucharist—and your truth is that you connect to Jesus most profoundly in a different, also specific, way—for example, through an encounter with the "least of these"—both experiences of Jesus would be true, even though they are different, even conflicting (meaning, two different things cannot both be *most* profound in an objective sense).

Or, to consider an example not overtly pertaining to theology, think about how people often use the phrase "my truth" today. Perhaps someone was sexually assaulted. The truth of that assault is their truth to tell. They, uniquely, know what that experience was like. The assaulter or a bystander may also know what it was like, but they know it from the point of view of a bystander or the aggressor. The truth of the survivor's experience

---

5.   *Confessions*, Book VII, article x, 123.

is uniquely their personal truth, their unique story, and it is a true one. It is a facet of reality given uniquely to them, one that is theirs to share with whomever they choose, and not for others to explain to them. In this sense "my truth" is not to say that each person can decide for themselves what is true, relativizing God away. Rather, each person is given—gifted, even—a piece of the whole truth of God's story in creation, and the piece and its application to them are unique and personal.

St. Augustine has room for such relative, though not relativistic, views of truth and of God. He prays, "Truth, when did you ever fail to walk with me, teaching me what to avoid and what to seek after when I reported to you what, in my inferior position, I could see and asked your counsel?"[6] What one should avoid is at once personal (what each person needs instruction to avoid is dependent on the individual's struggle) and universal (some things ought to be universally avoided).

St. Augustine is sure, of course, not to allow the reader to think that the truth comes *from* the individual, but rather, that each one's truth is revelation of God alone, even when it is personal: "Without you [God], what am I to myself but a guide to my own self-destruction? When all is well with me, what am I but an infant sucking your milk and feeding on you, 'the food that is incorruptible' (John 6:27)?"[7] The inmost self is none other than a chapter in the story of God. We are not God, and we are not even pieces *of* God, but wholly distinct creations of his, receptive of his revelation. Indeed, Augustine goes so far as to state that "there is something of the human person which is unknown even to the 'spirit of man which is in him.' But you, Lord, know everything about the human person."[8] Indeed, humans "have a beginning and an end in time, and rise and a fall, a start and a finish, beauty and the loss of it. . . . They are made out of matter by you, not from you."[9]

---

6. *Confessions*, Book X, article xl, 217.
7. *Confessions*, Book IV, article i, 52.
8. *Confessions*, Book X, article vii, 182.
9. *Confessions*, Book XIII, article xxxii, 302.

This is to say that, while "God grant[s] to human minds to discern in a small thing universal truths valid for both small and great matters,"[10] these individual, personal truths that are revealed through small and personal things are none other than God's universal truth. If a person shares a "truth" that originates from herself and not from God, then the word "truth" is not appropriate for it.

Further, our knowledge is not complete. We "see the things you [God] have made because they are. But they are because you see them. We see outwardly that they are, and inwardly that they are good. But you saw them made when you saw that it was right to make them."[11] In short, when you grasp truth, and you share "your" personal truth, you are not simply saying "what you wanna say." To speak of something as true simply because one desires it to be true is tantamount to lying; to say something because one feels it strongly does not make it true. When you speak a personal truth, rather, it only makes sense to call it truth if it is indeed your honest rendering of the impression God has given you. Such an honest impression requires honest inquiry into the self.

It is not even possible for a human to properly discern and report on these things without a virtuous and honest soul. If we make of ourselves an end, concerned with appearance and taking it upon ourselves to craft a version of ourselves that fits our narrative, we are directed away from God, and, as St. Augustine would put it, are enjoying something that should rather be used:

> To enjoy something is to hold fast to it in love for its own sake. To use something is to apply whatever it may be to the purpose of obtaining what you love—if indeed it is something that ought to be loved. (The improper use of something should be termed abuse).[12]

10. *Confessions*, Book XI, article xxiii, 237.
11. *Confessions*, Book XIII, article xxxviii, 304.
12. St. Augustine, *On Christian Teaching*, trans R. P. H. Green (Oxford University Press, 2008), Book I, article 8, 9.

Further, "if we choose to enjoy things that are to be used, our advance is impeded and sometimes even diverted, and we are held back, or even put off, from attaining things which are to be enjoyed, because we are hamstrung by our love of lower things."[13]

And what is to be enjoyed? "The things which are to be enjoyed, then, are the Father and the Son and the Holy Spirit, and the Trinity that consists of them, which is a kind of single, supreme thing, shared by all who enjoy it."[14] God and God alone should be enjoyed. To be sure:

> Neither should a person enjoy himself, if you think closely about this, because he should not love himself on his own account, but only on account of the one who is to be enjoyed. A person is at his best when in his whole life he strives towards the unchangeable form of life and holds fast to it wholeheartedly. But if he loves himself on his own account, he does not relate himself to God, but turns to himself and not to something unchangeable. And for this reason it is with a certain insufficiency that he enjoys himself.[15]

## Conclusion

It seems, then, that "Brave" is indeed a fitting mantra for those already disposed to the proper sense of the concept of truth, but not a song that will encourage this understanding if it is not already possessed. If one comes to the song already disposed to the Augustinian theology offered here, then the play on words regarding light and shadows is a comforting and encouraging anthem for the weary Christian needing support. Just as Matthew 10:27 calls, "What I say to you in the dark, tell in the light," "Brave" sings with a beat: simply, "Let the light in." In

---

13. *On Christian Teaching*, Book I, article 7, 9.
14. *On Christian Teaching*, Book I, article 9, 10.
15. *On Christian Teaching*, Book I, article 40, 17.

both cases, the listener is encouraged to cast light on what may be ostensibly easier to keep in the shadows. And what may, ostensibly, be easier to keep in the shadows? One's personal experience and lived relationship with Christ. It is that light which directs away from the earthly city and toward the heavenly city, away from that which ultimately is not "redeemed from all evil and filled with every good thing; constant in its enjoyment of the happiness of eternal rejoicing, forgetting offences and forgetting punishments."[16]

"Brave" is not going to be the source of discernment about what truths should see the light of day. *What* we must be brave enough to share depends wholly on the objective reality of God and not on our subjective preferences, on what we "wanna say." As an illustration, St. Augustine recalls a story about a friend who, on the brink of death, was baptized while unconscious. During his reckless youth, Augustine found this mockable:

> He recovered and was restored to health, and at once, as soon as I could speak with him (and I was able to do so as soon as he could speak, since I never left his side, and we were deeply dependent on one another), I attempted to joke with him, imagining that he too would laugh with me about the baptism which he had received when far away in mind and sense. But he had already learnt that he had received the sacrament. He was horrified at me as if I were an enemy, and with amazing and immediate frankness advised me that, if I wished to be his friend, I must stop saying this kind of thing to him.[17]

To an undiscerning listener, the "brave" person in this story may be the young Augustine himself, insofar as he was unafraid to share how he truly felt about the absurdity of baptizing his unconscious friend. His sharing his thoughts despite what his friend might think might be considered, in today's age, the brave

---

16. St. Augustine, *The City of God Against the Pagans*, ed. R. W. Dyson (Cambridge University Press, 1998), Book XXII, chapter 30, 1180.
17. *Confessions*, Book IV, article iv, 57.

thing to do. Orthodox theology, however, would note that it is the friend who is truly brave. It was the friend who forwent the easy laugh and cheap connection with his friend for the sake of standing up for the gospel newly active in his heart. This is truly revolutionary. This is truly brave. This is what St. Augustine wants us to take from his story, his *Confession* of the event.

Thus, we conclude that "Brave" is not a tool for evangelization, but nonetheless a fitting mantra for the already evangelized. If the listener's identity is already rooted in being a redeemed child of Christ who is practiced in spirituality, honesty, and virtue, the song has more promise than peril. This listener is already disposed to understanding their unique truth as none other than their personal experience of Christ's objective, universal truth. If their identity is adrift, however, then this song could lead them further astray into the zone of relativism. If they are looking to the song—or to secular culture in general—for their identity, they are vulnerable to falling prey to the same comforting lies that befell Adam and Eve, lies with dire consequences indeed. But if a person is safeguarded by the armor of Christ, one's hope and prayer is that they will be strengthened against falling prey to the falsehoods of a world that wants to relativize God away. If a person lives according to a relationship, an intimacy, with the Lord, if they find their identity in being a redeemed child of the King of Kings, then even a secular song such as this, played on the instrument of their lips, can express and inspire holy truth.

# "Sinnerman":
## Nina Simone Hopes for Judgment Day

Nathaniel Marx

## Where You Gonna Run To?

"Do you believe in rock 'n' roll?" Christians who answer affirmatively should consider Don McLean's follow-up question: "Can music save your mortal soul?" Properly speaking, Christian orthodoxy insists on the *immortality* of the soul, but that only emphasizes the question's importance. Your soul's eternal destiny will be at stake when Christ comes again "to judge the living and the dead." Music won't save you then, but right now it might provide a crucial opportunity to examine how things stand with your soul. Following Jewish tradition and the parables of Jesus, Christians have long focused their self-examination by imagining the Day of Judgment. "That day" is coming, but even Jesus couldn't say when it will be: "No one knows, neither the angels of heaven, nor the Son, but only the Father" (Matt 24:36, cf. Mark 13:32).

Music has a way of transporting your mind and soul to "that day" instantly, before a reasoned argument or a fiery sermon is out of the gate.[1] Take the 1965 studio recording of Nina Simone's "Sinnerman."[2] The High Priestess of Soul has your attention before she has sung a word. Her opening vamp is just two chords on the piano, B-minor alternating with A-major in a steady, syncopated rhythm, sounding like a desperate scamper. Bobby Hamilton enters with high-hat sixteenths that heighten

---

1. For another example of music evoking the end times, see chapter 12 of this volume: "From Genesis to Revelation: The Eschatology of 'Supper's Ready'" by Lawrence J. King.
2. "Sinnerman," track 9 on Nina Simone, *Pastel Blues*, Philips – PHS 600-187, 1965.

the effect. In the seventh measure—as if coming to the last day of the week—Nina puts the question to her audience in her singular alto, precisely controlled and impossible to ignore: "Oh, Sinnerman, where you gonna run to? / Sinnerman, where you gonna run to? / Where you gonna run to? / All on that day?"

"Sinner Man," as it is elsewhere titled, is a Black spiritual with many variants. Eunice Waymon likely learned it as a young girl playing piano and organ at church services and revivals.[3] Later, after taking the stage name "Nina Simone," she incorporated this and other African American songs into genre-defying performances that joined her classically honed technique to the spontaneity of jazz, blues, and folk. From early in her career, Simone resisted dismissal of her artistry as the untutored entertainment of a "jazz singer."[4] She defied expectations of how a Black woman should present herself and her music, especially to white audiences. By the time she recorded "Sinnerman," Simone also had to contend with assumptions about the goals and tactics that a woman and a famous entertainer ought to embrace as a prominent participant in the civil rights movement.

---

3.  Eunice's mother, an ordained Methodist preacher, took her daughter to congregations all over the counties surrounding their first home in Tryon, North Carolina. Her mother also kept house for a white woman who recognized the child's talent and arranged for a piano teacher. Eunice trained to become "the first black classical concert pianist," eventually earning a summer at Juilliard after her high school graduation. The dream of her childhood was crushed when the Curtis Institute in Philadelphia rejected her application. The woman who became world-famous as "Nina Simone" had no way to know whether she was "just no good" or whether the school wasn't about to admit "a very poor unknown black girl" (Nina Simone, *I Put a Spell on You: The Autobiography of Nina Simone*, with Stephen Cleary [New York: Pantheon, 1991], 14–43). The Curtis Institute belatedly recognized Simone's contributions to music by awarding her an honorary degree one month after her death (Nadine Cohodas, *Princess Noire: The Tumultuous Reign of Nina Simone* [Chapel Hill: The University of North Carolina Press, 2010], 374).
4.  Simone, *I Put a Spell on You*, 68–69.

This chapter argues that Nina Simone's "Sinnerman" is part of her contribution to the struggle of Black Americans for freedom, justice, and equality. As in the medieval *Dies irae* chant, the images of divine judgment in "Sinnerman" are terrifying. Yet the song's primary purpose is not to frighten or threaten but to inspire hope in the vindication of God's justice, both as a spur to present action and as an assurance of final victory. The Last Judgment, according to Pope Benedict XVI, is "a setting for learning and practicing hope."[5] Simone's rendition of "Sinnerman" shows why Christian doctrine teaches us to look forward to Judgment Day. God's righteous judgment against slavery and oppression is the foundation of hope in God's merciful forgiveness of sin. When Simone shouts "Power!" in the refrain she adds to "Sinnerman," sinners may hear it as a plea for mercy. But on Nina's lips it is a demand for justice, uttered before God on behalf of her people. Sinners can confidently call on divine power in hope of redemption only if we faithfully respond to the cry for justice that God never fails to hear.

What does my interpretation of Nina Simone's "Sinnerman" have to do with discerning orthodoxy from heresy? I do not intend to examine the orthodoxy of the song or the singer. I am a white theologian listening to a song that originated in Black people's experience of suffering at the hands of white people. I am also a male theologian listening to a woman whose control over her life, career, and artistic work was frequently usurped by men. I cannot say what Simone or her ancestors ought or ought not to have meant by this song; I can only try to receive it as given. "Sinnerman" is an urgent plea for listeners to examine *themselves* before it is too late. It is a spur to discern orthodoxy from heresy, not in the song, but in yourself.

---

5. Benedict XVI, *Spe Salvi* (Encyclical Letter on Christian Hope), November 30, 2007, section III heading (see also the paragraphs of that section).

## The High Priestess of Soul

Nina Simone went from being acclaimed for her virtuosity to being shunned by the mavens of popular culture as she spoke out about racial injustice in ways deemed too controversial— even heretical. In music as in theology, some contributions fail to be appreciated until later generations return for another listen. Two decades after her death in 2003, the reassessment of Simone's legacy is in full swing. In 2018, she was inducted into the Rock & Roll Hall of Fame by Mary J. Blige, who praised her for being "bold, strong, feisty, and fearless."[6] That same year, the Library of Congress added Simone's 1964 single, "Mississippi Goddam," to the National Recording Registry, recognizing it as "one of the most vital songs to emerge from the Civil Rights era."[7] Every year, record companies release multiple compilations, remasters, and remixes of Simone's songs. Millions follow her on music streaming services. In 2015, Nina's daughter, Lisa, premiered *What Happened, Miss Simone?* at the Sundance Film Festival. It received an Academy Award nomination for Best Documentary Feature and continues to stream on Netflix. John Legend, who performed a tribute at the film's premiere, is one of many superstars on a long and diverse list of artists who cite Simone as a musical and spiritual influence.

There is a troubling side to this renewed enthusiasm, however, exemplified by the frequent use of Simone's music to conjure

---

6.  "Nina Simone," Rock and Roll Hall of Fame, 2018, https://www. rockhall.com/inductees/nina-simone.
7.  "'Mississippi Goddam' (single). Nina Simone. (1964)," *Recording Registry: Registry Titles with Descriptions and Expanded Essays*, National Recording Preservation Board, Library of Congress, https://www.loc.gov/programs/national-recording-preserva-tion-board/recording-registry/descriptions-and-essays/. See also the guest essay posted with the song's listing in the registry: Nadine Cohodas, "'Mississippi Goddam'—Nina Simone (1964)," Library of Congress, 2018, https://www.loc.gov/static/programs/national-recording-preservation-board/documents/MississippiGoddam.pdf.

a certain mood in entertainment pitched at white audiences. No item in her catalog has been appropriated for this purpose more often than "Sinnerman." It made Pierce Brosnan's heist scene sexy in the 1999 remake of *The Thomas Crown Affair*.[8] It has since been used over thirty times to score movies and TV shows, ranging from *Scrubs* to *Sherlock* to *So You Think You Can Dance*. One cultural critic finds it "bewildering if not offensive" that this "black gospel tour-de-force" has become a soundtrack for such diversions.[9] This usage exemplifies white appropriation of Black feminine "soul," whereby audiences experience a thrill of defiant and erotic power without threatening the supremacy of white males. "Nina Simone has become a watered-down symbol of Black Power. Instead of militancy and revolution, transgression is her appeal."[10]

Nina's song about the Last Judgment has long been supremely appealing. It's easy to imagine that the Sinner Man is somebody else and that his sins are harmless mischief. Listeners who casually enjoy the apocalyptic mood, however, lose any opportunity for spiritual benefit. This music can't help save your soul unless it first frightens you nearly to death.

## That Day of Wrath

"Sinnerman" shares scriptural roots with the *Dies irae*. For centuries, this iconic chant of the Roman Catholic funeral liturgy described the dire consequences of delaying repentance until "that day" catches a sinner unawares. The attribution of the medieval poem is uncertain, but it takes its famous first line from the prophet Zephaniah, who foretold the destruction of Jerusalem and the subsequent enslavement of its people in Babylon. Zephaniah

---

8. Except for a hapless black detective played by Frankie Faison, the movie is an overwhelmingly white affair onscreen.
9. A. Loudermilk, "Nina Simone & the Civil Rights Movement: Protest at Her Piano, Audience at Her Feet," *Journal of International Women's Studies* 14, no. 3 (July 2013): 129.
10. Ibid.

warned his unrepentant nation that an offended God was about to punish Judah and "cut off humanity / from the face of the earth," for none had been found innocent. "The great day of the LORD is near," he announced. "That day will be a day of wrath" (Zeph 1:3, 14, 15). In the Latin Vulgate, the prophet's warning reads, "*Dies irae, dies illa.*"[11]

The "day of the LORD," according to Jesus, is a day of judgment for "all the nations." On that day, "when the Son of Man comes in his glory," he will be enthroned as king over all people, and he will judge each person according to his or her deeds, disregarding tribe and nation. Those with power and wealth in this life will have neither on that day. Unswayed by earthly privilege, the king will deem "righteous" those who fed him when he was hungry, gave him drink when he was thirsty, welcomed him when he was a stranger, clothed him when he was naked, cared for him when he was sick, and visited him when he was in prison. He will assure them, "Just as you did it to one of the least of these who are members of my family, you did it to me." The righteous will "inherit the kingdom," while those who did none of these things "will go away into eternal punishment" (Matt 25:31–46).

"That day" is a day of mercy and salvation for the righteous. Still, it is no wonder that Christians of every generation have focused on the wrath, knowing our failures of mercy and charity toward "the least of these." But unlike a great deal of visual art depicting the Day of Wrath, the *Dies irae* and "Sinnerman" do not brandish the pains of punishment so much as they emphasize the folly of hiding from God's judgment. The *Dies irae* imagines the return of Christ with foreboding:

> What a trembling, what a fear,
> When the dread Judge shall appear,
> Strictly searching far and near! . . .
> Death shall shiver, nature quake,

---

11. Terence Bailey, "A Syllabic and Metrical Dies Irae? Variations on This Most-Famous Text and Melody," *Sacred Music* 143, no. 2 (2016): 25.

When the creatures shall awake,
Answer to their Judge to make.
Lo, the Book of ages spread,
From which all the deeds are read
Of the living and the dead.
Now before the Judge severe,
All things hidden must appear,
Naught shall pass unpublished here.
Wretched man, what shall I plead,
Who for me will intercede,
When the righteous mercy need?[12]

Although the chant transitions into a plea for mercy, the Lord remains the "Judge of righteousness severe." He forgave Mary Magdalene and "the dying thief," but that is no reason to expect that the "cursed" will not be "cast into devouring flame." The "lake of fire" into which the damned are thrown is described in the Book of Revelation, along with the "book of ages," in which the deeds of the living and the dead are recorded (Rev 20:11–15).

"Sinnerman" also uses the apocalyptic imagery of Revelation to imagine the Day of Judgment. In John's vision, the coming of the victorious Lamb of God causes "everyone"—but especially "the rich and the powerful"—to run and hide:

Then the kings of the earth and the magnates and the generals and the rich and the powerful, and everyone, slave and free, hid in the caves and among the rocks of the mountains, calling to the mountains and rocks, "Fall on us and hide us from the face of the one seated on the throne and from the wrath of the Lamb; for the great day of their wrath has come, and who is able to stand?" (Rev 6:15–17)

The verses of "Sinnerman" narrate this hopeless scramble from a first-person perspective. "Well I run to the rock, 'Please hide me,'" the Sinner Man begs. "But the rock cried out, 'I can't

---

12. Trans. in *Hours at Home*, ed. J. M. Sherwood, vol. 2, no. 1 (1868), 39–40.

hide you!'" After rebuking the rock, the Sinner Man runs to the river and to the sea, which are "bleedin'" and "boilin'." All too late, he tries running to the Lord: "Please hide me, Lord! Don't you see me prayin'?" But the Lord doesn't see in the Sinner Man one of his "sheep," who fed him when he was hungry or visited him in prison. He tells this evildoer to depart, in words that fit the "severe Judge" more than the Good Shepherd: "Go to the devil!" With nowhere else to hide, that is exactly where the Sinner Man runs at last, only to find the devil waiting for him at the gates of hell.[13]

At this point in the story, Simone's version of the song takes an unusual turn—but more about that later. So far, her lyrics echo the words her enslaved ancestors once sang.[14] There is no "original" or "definitive" version of "Sinner Man" to isolate. The spirituals began as an oral tradition, and the boundaries between one song and another were fluid. They mixed musical

---

13. Although I have told the story in third person, Simone sings the verses of "Sinnerman" in the first person. This shows how "the sense of immediacy, personal involvement, and the dramatic appeal are heightened in the Afro-American form" of spirituals that share some lyrics with Euro-American hymns (Erskine Peters, *Lyrics of the Afro-American Spiritual: A Documentary Collection*, The Greenwood Encyclopedia of Black Music [Westport, CT: Greenwood Press, 1993], xxviii).

14. There are virtually no written records of lyrics as sung by enslaved persons prior to emancipation. Erskine Peters has assembled the most complete compendium of lyrics to the spirituals as they appear in a variety of printed collections beginning in 1867. Not surprisingly, no single entry matches Simone's "Sinnerman" lyrics exactly. Similar lyrical elements are found in songs entitled "Heaven Bell A-Ring" (271–72), "In That Day" (277), "Oh, Sinner" (288), "There's No Hiding Place Down There" (296), "You Can't Find a New Hidin' Place" (301), and "Oh! Sinner Man" (367). Songs with "lyrics of judgment and reckoning" constitute one of nine broad categories in Peters' collection (263–303). See Peters, *Lyrics of the Afro-American Spiritual*.

and lyrical elements that can be traced back to African and European sources. Above all:

> Improvisation, or the African tradition of spontaneous creation, was a crucial element in the development of the spiritual, since spirituals were fashioned by combining verses from the Bible, the Psalms, and hymns with portions of sermons and prayers offered during worship.[15]

By the time white folklorists began collecting examples of "Sinner Man," they heard similar lyrics from both white and Black singers all over the southern Appalachians.[16] White writers variously described it as a "plantation song,"[17] a "holiness hymn,"[18]

---

15. Angela M. Nelson, "Spirituals," in *Encyclopedia of African American History, 1619–1895: From the Colonial Period to the Age of Frederick Douglass* (Oxford: Oxford University Press, 2006), https://www.oxfordreference.com/view/10.1093/acref/9780195167771.001.0001/acref-9780195167771-e-0535.
16. In 1917, the British folklorist Cecil Sharp was collecting folk songs in Eastern Kentucky when he heard a white woman singing something that sounded like a variant of "What Shall We Do with the Drunken Sailor?" Though he was an atheist on a mission to discover English ballads preserved in the southern Appalachians, Sharp enjoyed Mrs. Samples's singing and sense of humor enough to transcribe the hymn. She teased that it was about him, the "Sinner Man." Some time later—knowing that African American voices must have handed on this amalgam of sea shanty, ballad, Bible, and revivalist preaching—Sharp sang "The Sinner Man" for a formerly enslaved woman in Virginia, "which delighted her beyond anything." See Brian Peters, "Myths of 'Merrie Olde England'? Cecil Sharp's Collecting Practice in the Southern Appalachians," *Folk Music Journal* 11, no. 3 (2018): 23; and Brian Peters, "Cecil Sharp: A View from England," CDSS News, Fall 2021.
17. Howard Washington Odum and Guy Benton Johnson, *The Negro and His Songs: A Study of Typical Negro Songs in the South*, (Chapel Hill: The University of North Carolina press, 1925), 76–79.
18. Cecil J. Sharp, Olive D. Campbell, and Maud Karpeles, *English Folk Songs from the Southern Appalachians* (London: Oxford University Press, 1932), vol. 2, 289–91, 396.

and even "an ancient English song."[19] An influential British collector identified its melody as "a variant of a well-known English tune, commonly associated with 'The Drunken Sailor.'"[20]

Melody, lyrics, and poetic form do not define the spirituals, however. "Although numerous phrases and lines are borrowed from established Christian hymns, these phrases and lines, when molded and crafted into a new historical time and space, become a new chronicle, a new music and a new poetry."[21] Theologian James Cone therefore turns our attention from the history of music to the history of the people who sang the spirituals: "The spirituals are historical songs which speak about the rupture of black lives; they tell us about a people in the land of bondage, and what they did to hold themselves together and to fight back."[22] Cone's assessment echoes that of W. E. B. DuBois, who declared over a century ago that the spirituals are "the most original and beautiful expression of human life and longing yet born on American soil," for they are "the one true expression of a people's sorrow, despair, and hope."[23]

We can't faithfully interpret "Sinnerman" apart from that specific history of sorrow, despair, and hope. Simone's version belongs to the unbroken musical tradition of the spirituals because she shares in "the spirit of the people struggling to be free." If we don't try to understand how this song relates to that struggle, we risk misinterpreting it. The meaning of a spiritual, Cone insists, "is not contained in the bare words but in the black history that created it." The spiritual is the people's

19. "The Beggar's Rôle," *The Nation*, September 2, 1922. Reprinted in *The Nation & The Athenaeum*, vol. 31 (London: Loxley Brothers Limited, n.d.), 735–36, https://www.google.com/books/edition/The_Nation_and_the_Athenaeum/ellDAQAAMAAJ.
20. Sharp et. al., *English Folk Songs*, vol. 2, 396.
21. Peters, *Lyrics of the Afro-American Spiritual*, xvi.
22. James H. Cone, *The Spirituals and the Blues: An Interpretation* (New York: Orbis, 1972), 30.
23. W. E. B. DuBois, *The Souls of Black Folk* (New York: Dover, 1994), 116. This collection of DuBois's essays was originally published in Chicago by A. C. McClurg in 1903.

"religion, their source of strength in a time of trouble. And if one does not know what trouble is, then the spiritual cannot be understood."[24] Let us turn then to the trouble.

## The Conquest of a New World

The *Dies irae* is a general confession of sinfulness that has no particular sin in view. "Sinnerman," by contrast, is a prophetic oracle condemning the specific sin of opposing God's will that his Black children should live and be free. Because we haven't overcome this opposition in our society or in ourselves, it's tempting for white audiences to avoid the song's specificity and misinterpret it as a general reminder of death and judgment. Peter Tosh's 1970 reggae version prevents easy generalization of the song's subject matter by changing "Sinner Man" to "Oppressor Man" (or "Downpressor Man" in later recordings).[25] This lyrical change is in harmony with Simone's version, but it sounds like a correction or even a rebuke of white performers like Les Baxter, who was the first to sell a recording of "Sinner Man" and who often gets credit for "writing" the song. White people are free to perform and enjoy Black spirituals, but it heaps injustice upon injustice when they remain oblivious to the song's particular claim on their consciences. For Tosh, Simone, and generations of Black singers, "Sinner Man" is about liberation from white power.

There is poetic justice in turning the apocalyptic imagery of the Book of Revelation into an anthem of Black liberation. The abduction of people from Africa for enslavement in America is historically entangled with beliefs about the Last Judgment. When European Christians colonized the Americas, their eschatological understanding of divine judgment was central to how

---

24. Cone, *The Spirituals and the Blues*, 30, 31.
25. See Fred Clark, "Where You Gonna Run To? Tim LaHaye and Billy Graham vs. Peter Tosh and Nina Simone," *Slacktivist* (blog), on *Patheos*, August 24, 2015, https://www.patheos.com/blogs/slacktivist/2015/08/24/where-you-gonna-run-to-tim-lahaye-and-billy-graham-vs-peter-tosh-and-nina-simone/.

they interpreted both the evangelization and the exploitation of this "New World." Franciscan and Dominican friars were the first to seek the conversion of the native Caribbean and Mesoamerican peoples, and they understood their mission to be unlike any that had come before. As historian Jaime Lara explains:

> They appear to have had millennial expectations, believing that the discovery and evangelization of the "New World"—itself an eschatological term—was a sign of an approaching golden age of the Holy Spirit when the universal Church would be renewed in holy poverty and a way of life similar to that shared by the nascent church in the apostolic period.[26]

From the start, the reality of conquest fell far short of this paradisiacal vision, appearing instead to be a living hell for Amerindians, who were killed and enslaved by the thousands while untold millions died of smallpox and other European diseases.

No European colonist was more vocal in his disillusionment with *la conquista* than Bartolomé de Las Casas (1484–1566). The Dominican priest and eventual bishop of Chiapas is a complicated figure, lionized by some as "Protector of the Indians" but despised by others for proposing the importation of enslaved Africans to ease the suffering of America's natives. In recent years, Catholic theologians have retrieved Las Casas as a

---

26. Jaime Lara, "Roman Catholics in Hispanic America," in Geoffrey Wainwright and Karen B. Westerfield Tucker, eds., *The Oxford History of Christian Worship* (Oxford: Oxford University Press, 2006), 633–50, at 633. The missionaries' "millennial expectations" were based in the Book of Revelation, which describes a period of "a thousand years" between the initial defeat of Satan and the Last Judgment. In this interim period of peace before the final battle with Satan, the martyrs will come to life to be "priests of God and of Christ, and they will reign with him a thousand years" (Rev 20:1–6). The friars were not the first Christians to believe the predicted millennium was at hand, nor would they be the last.

resource for articulating an anti-racist Christian anthropology in continuity with the Church's natural law tradition. Opposing the conquistadors' logic of religious coercion as a justification for war and enslavement, Las Casas and some of his Dominican contemporaries "developed the scholastic natural law tradition by their commitment to the equality of natural rights for all human beings made in the image of God."[27] Las Casas was tragically limited in his practical application of this principle, however, by his simultaneous commitment to the millenarian dream of turning the "New World" into a new Eden. If it was wrong to force Amerindians to work the lucrative but dangerous sugar plantations, the ambitious cleric thought their labor could be replaced by that of enslaved Africans. He accepted the claim of Portuguese slave traders that these men, women, and children were captives "legitimately" taken in crusades against enemies of the faith.[28] Las Casas' later admission that he had been "woefully misguided" in recommending the importation of Africans was "too little too late" to reverse the beginning of the transatlantic slave trade—a historical horror that his own apocalyptic imaginings scarcely could have foreseen.[29]

Divine judgment played a central role in Las Casas' voluminous histories, treatises, and letters. As a young cleric with the ear of the crown, he described calamities that befell Spaniards

---

27. David M. Lantigua, "The Freedom of the Gospel: Aquinas, Subversive Natural Law, and the Spanish Wars of Religion," *Modern Theology* 31, no. 2 (April 2015): 317.
28. "The Portuguese on the ground knew perfectly well" that the Africans they kidnapped or bought from other Africans were not Muslims. It's true, however, that Catholic popes, rulers, and theologians in the early sixteenth century held that it was just to enslave Muslims captured in crusading war. "It was the ongoing conflicts with various Muslims that produced, by any canonical measure of the day, legitimate slaves" (Andrew Wilson, "Black Slaves and Messianic Dreams in Las Casas's Plans for an Abundant Indies," *Zeitschrift Für Missionswissenschaft Und Religionswissenschaft* 97, no. 1–2 [2013]: 113).
29. Lantigua, "Freedom of the Gospel," 336.

as God's righteous punishment of his nation for their cruel treatment of the Amerindians. As an old man, Las Casas faced the impending judgment of his own deeds with trepidation about the sentence the divine Judge could rightfully impose. He had spent half his life trying to reform or abolish the *encomienda* system by which he had formerly profited from the forced labor of Amerindians. Yet he remained troubled by his naïve and hypocritical endorsement of African enslavement as an alternative. David Lantigua describes Las Casas at the end of his life:

> His conscience remained deeply unsettled by his earlier prejudice towards black slaves as he painfully pondered the extent of God's mercy: "I am not certain that my ignorance and good-will shall excuse me before divine judgment." His final days were spent working out his salvation in fear and trembling.[30]

Lantigua may be right to consider Las Casas "the first European theological opponent of both Amerindian slavery and African slavery in the West,"[31] but he merits that distinction only if we take the bishop at his word and picture him trembling at the prospect of divine judgment.[32] Like him, we

---

30. Ibid. The internal quotation is from Bartolomé de Las Casas, *Historia de Las Indias* III, c. 129, 275: *"No estuvo cierto que la ignorancia que en ésto tuvo y buena voluntad lo excusase delante el juicio divino."* An English translation of the whole chapter is available in Bartolomé de Las Casas, *History of the Indies*, trans. Andrée Collard (New York: Harper & Row, 1971). Unfortunately, this abridged translation of Las Casas' monumental *Historia* lacks other relevant chapters and a scholarly apparatus.

31. Lantigua, "Freedom of the Gospel," 336.

32. Luis Rivera-Pagán's excellent analysis of the final letters Las Casas sent to the Spanish king and to the pope imagines the bishop hoping that his *History of the Indies* "will one day be read, by future generations or even maybe at the eschatological moment of reckoning in which his nation, Spain, might hear, with fear and trembling, the fateful hymn—*dies irae, dies illa, solvet saeculum in favilla*" (Luis N. Rivera-Pagán, "A Prophetic Challenge to the Church: The Last Words of Bartolomé de Las Casas," *Princeton*

must not count on "ignorance" or "good-will" to excuse our complicity—however small it may seem to us—in denying the New World descendants of enslaved Africans the full equality in justice that their creation in the image of God demands. Instead of protesting our innocence, we should be working out our salvation before we are called on "that day" to give an account of what we have done and what we have failed to do.

## The Creation of a New Society

"Sinnerman"—the condensed title of Nina Simone's take on the traditional spiritual—fits the urgency and intensity of her performance in the May 1965 recording.[33] That January, she had performed for a mostly white audience at Carnegie Hall. Simone sang "Mississippi Goddam," which she had written in September 1963 after the bombing of a Black church in Alabama left four young girls dead. She sarcastically set her words of fury and frustration to a jaunty "show tune" melody: "Everybody knows about Alabama / Everybody knows about Mississippi, goddam!"[34] At the Carnegie Hall concert, she optimistically commented that the song was "not quite as urgent as it used to be."[35] But progress in obtaining justice for murdered civil rights workers was soon overshadowed by new losses.

Less than a day after the Carnegie Hall concert, Nina sang at the funeral of her dear friend, Lorraine Hansberry. The activist and playwright best known for *A Raisin in the Sun* had succumbed to cancer at age 34. "Lorraine started off my political education," Simone wrote, "and through her I started thinking about myself as a black person in a country run by white people and a woman in a world run by men."[36] Hansberry's death in January was followed by the assassination of Malcolm X in

---

*Seminary Bulletin* 24, no. 2 [2003]: 218).

33. Cohodas, *Princess Noire*, 174.
34. Simone, *I Put a Spell on You*, 88–90.
35. Cohodas, *Princess Noire*, 166.
36. Simone, *I Put a Spell on You*, 87.

February. This too was a personal loss for Simone, who became "Aunt Nina" to Malcolm's daughters when his widow, Betty Shabazz, moved into a house two blocks away from Simone's in Mount Vernon, New York.[37]

Then, on March 7, 525 nonviolent demonstrators, including John Lewis and Martin Luther King, Jr., attempted to cross the Edmund Pettus Bridge in Selma, Alabama. It was the first stage in a march to Montgomery to demand that Black people be able to register to vote without discrimination or fear. Alabama state troopers ordered the peaceful demonstration to disperse, then fired tear gas and charged the crowd on horseback, aiming blow after blow at the heads of the retreating marchers. Eight days after "Bloody Sunday," President Johnson used a nationally televised joint address to Congress to declare his support for legislation that would become the Voting Rights Act of 1965. The protesters' march to the state capital resumed with federal protection on March 21.

Simone flew to Montgomery to perform at a star-studded concert for the marchers on the grounds of the City of St. Jude, a Roman Catholic campus that included the first integrated hospital in the southeast. A stage hastily built from plywood and empty coffins hosted such luminaries as Harry Belafonte; Leonard Bernstein; Sammy Davis, Jr.; Tony Bennett; Mahalia Jackson; Joan Baez; and Peter, Paul and Mary. Through the rain, Simone saw thousands squeezing into a muddy field, having been warned by the police that armed gangs of white supremacists were lurking in the surrounding woods. "Somehow, despite being wet, footsore and frightened, people kept their spirits together by singing and praying," Nina later reflected, "Performers use tired old phrases all the time and usually don't mean a word of them, but that night we all felt privileged to be playing in front of that audience."[38] This is high praise from a performer who

37. Alan Light, *What Happened, Miss Simone? A Biography* (New York: Crown Archetype, 2016), 110.
38. Simone, *I Put a Spell on You*, 101–103. Simone's autobiography, co-written with Stephen Cleary in 1991, describes some events

didn't hesitate to make her audiences, white or Black, feel "good and guilty" if they were "doing nothing" for "the struggle for black justice, freedom, and equality under the law."[39]

Nina knew she had power to move people the way Lorraine Hansberry had moved her. For those who had marched from Selma, she chose to perform "Mississippi Goddam," with its opening line, "Alabama's gotten me so upset." She had written it—her "first civil rights song"—at a moment when she had it in mind "to go out and kill someone" in retaliation for murdered children and civil rights workers.[40] Instead of improvising a zip gun, she loaded "Mississippi Goddam" with images of the violent apocalypse already gripping the country. In the Carnegie Hall recording, you can hear nervous laughter from the audience change to tense silence as the list of outrages and indignities suffered by Black people climaxes in a warning:

> Oh, but this whole country is full of lies
> You're all gonna die and die like flies
> I don't trust you anymore
> You keep on sayin', "Go slow"

Like Nina, the marchers in Montgomery were out of patience. They cheered loudest when she improvised a new line: "Selma made me lose my rest."[41]

"I'm not nonviolent," Simon had said when she was first introduced to Dr. King.[42] Even before King's assassination, the civil rights movement "had already pivoted from King-style nonviolence toward a more aggressive push for Black Power,

---

in her career out of sequence and "with considerable embroidery." Nevertheless, it offers "a window into her feelings about all that had transpired" (Cohodas, *Princess Noire*, 344).

39. Simone, *I Put a Spell on You*, 90.
40. Simone, *I Put a Spell on You*, 89–90.
41. Cohodas, *Princess Noire*, 173.
42. Light, *What Happened, Miss Simone?*, 96. This exchange between Simone and King was reported by her guitarist, Al Schackman, in 2009. No information about the date of their first introduction is given.

complicating its relationship to the white liberals who made up much of Simone's audience."[43] Fear of losing that audience didn't keep Nina from making her songs and performances more confrontational. She "loved Dr. King for his goodness and compassion," as she said in her autobiography, but she agreed with advocates of Black self-defense and self-reliance. Long before Stokely Carmichael ever shouted "Black Power" as a slogan, "Mississippi Goddam" had anticipated that movement's less conciliatory message to white America: "You don't have to live next to me / Just give me my equality." If full equality could not be won through nonviolent protest, then Nina believed "it was time for some Old Testament justice."[44]

Still, Simone would not condemn anyone simply for being white. The story of human society, from the murder of Abel to the slaying of Medgar Evers, is one in which domination infects human relationships and institutions. The desire to make slaves of other people enslaves all who grasp at power. Submission to God can liberate us from the "lust for domination,"[45] but from a worldly point of view, power is a zero-sum game. Simone saw it this way:

> I didn't believe that there was any basic difference between the races—whoever is on top uses whatever means they can to keep the other down, and if black America was on top, they'd use race as a way of oppressing whites in exactly the way they themselves were oppressed. Anyone who has power only has it at the expense of someone else

---

43. Ibid., 131.
44. Simone, *I Put a Spell on You*, 110.
45. The "lust for domination" (*libido dominandi*) is a central theme of St. Augustine's massive historical, political, and theological treatise, *The City of God*. Augustine contrasts the redeemed society of the Church—"the most glorious city of God"—with "the earthly city—the city which, when it seeks dominion, even though whole peoples are its slaves, is itself under the dominion of its very lust for domination" (Augustine, *City of God*, trans. William Babcock [Hyde Park, NY: New City Press, 2013], Preface).

and to take that power away from them you have to use force, because they'll never give it up from choice.[46]

To Simone, the realization that white power was built on Black disempowerment marked a "big step forward" in her political thinking: "I realized that what we were really fighting for was the creation of a new society." Constitutional rights were only the beginning. "True equality" meant a society in which no race has power at the expense of another, and that could only happen "if America changed completely, top to bottom."[47]

Nina Simone's language of rebellion against American society is not anti-Christian, but it opposes what Cone calls "the heresy of white Christianity": the belief that centuries of white power over the lives, labor, and legacy of Black Americans is consonant with God's will, even divinely ordained.[48] In opposition to this heresy, "the basic idea of the spirituals is that slavery contradicts God; it is a denial of God's will. To be enslaved is to be declared *nobody*, and that form of existence contradicts God's creation of people to be God's children."[49] It is tempting for white audiences and white theologians to argue that the heresy of white Christianity was suppressed with the emancipation of enslaved people. This claim culpably ignores the myriad ways—from lynching and terror to political exclusion and institutional racism—in which white Christians have continued, to the present day, to deny that every Black person is *somebody* whose life matters to God.[50]

---

46. Simone, *I Put a Spell on You*, 100.
47. Ibid.
48. Cone, *The Spirituals and the Blues*, 23.
49. Ibid., 33, emphasis in original.
50. In their 2018 pastoral letter against racism, the Catholic bishops of the United States acknowledge that slavery is not the only serious sin against the human dignity of African Americans for which white Christians bear responsibility. Because racism violates "the dignity inherent in each person," the bishops "unequivocally state that racism is a life issue." They reject as mistaken the belief "that racism is no longer a major affliction of our society," and they name specific examples that show how "the evil of rac-

It is also an evasion for white audiences to denounce Simone's threatening lyrics and her support for Black Power as too "militant" and "violent." Simone, like her ancestors before and after the end of slavery, understood "the present hopelessness of physical defence," which had not changed since W. E. B. DuBois described the situation that way at the turn of the century.[51] If the majority of enslaved persons "chose other forms of resistance" to white power, it wasn't because they believed violent resistance was unjustified. The spirituals, with their undeniably violent images of Judgment Day, were one important form of resistance to white power. White people, argues Cone, need to realize that "Black rebellion in America did not begin with the Civil Rights movement and Martin Luther King, nor with Black Power and Stokely Carmichael."[52] Then they might begin to understand why someone like Nina Simone would

---

ism festers." These include "racial profiling" of African Americans "for suspected criminal activity"; interactions with police that are "fraught with fear and even danger"; racial "discrimination in hiring, housing, educational opportunities, and incarceration"; and perceptions that African Americans—who have been historically denied "access to numerous wealth-building opportunities reserved for others"—are themselves to blame for poverty in their communities, are "unable to contribute to society," and are "unworthy" of social benefits. "Too often," the bishops add, "racism comes in the form of the sin of omission, when individuals, communities, and even churches remain silent and fail to act against racial injustice when it is encountered." Racist acts and omissions "are sinful because they violate justice." They ignore "the fundamental truth that, because all humans share a common origin, they are all brothers and sisters, all equally made in the image of God" (United States Conference of Catholic Bishops, *Open Wide Our Hearts: The Enduring Call to Love – A Pastoral Letter Against Racism*, November 2018, https://www.usccb.org/issues-and-action/human-life-and-dignity/racism/upload/open-wide-our-hearts.pdf).

51. DuBois, *The Souls of Black Folk*, 123.
52. Cone, *The Spirituals and the Blues*, 24.

hope for "black revolution" despite the hopelessness of victory through armed rebellion.[53]

For Simone, the justice of overturning white power was abundantly clear. The only question was whether there was another power that could overcome injustice and create the "new society" she was fighting for. In truth, it was the same fight Black people had been waging from the time they were first stolen from Africa and brought to a place where their captors declared that a slave is *nobody*. In that place, however, Simone's ancestors met a God who declares that every person is created in the image of God and is *somebody*. And this God has no equal in power or in justice.

## Nina cried, "Power!"

Simone's 1965 recording of "Sinnerman" follows traditional lyrics for the first two of its ten minutes. At about two minutes and ten seconds, Nina launches straight from the Sinner Man's hopeless search for a hiding place into the refrain that occupies much of the recording:

*Nina*: I cried, "Power!"
*Band*: Power!
*Nina*: Power!
*Band*: Power, Lord!

This call-and-response between Nina and the band continues for more than a minute, and it returns for two minutes at the end of the song. Nothing like this refrain exists in other recordings of "Sinner Man," and it holds the key to Simone's purpose in performing this spiritual and giving it her own stamp. What power is she calling upon? Where does it come from? And, most important, what does she hope this power will do?

To answer these questions, we need to look beyond the lyrics as they appear on a page. Although the cry for power seems to emerge from the Sinner Man's hopeless situation, it quickly

---

53. Simone, *I Put a Spell on You*, 100.

becomes clear that Simone is not simply imagining how that lost soul will feel on Judgment Day. As Nina cries "Power!" the song shifts from storytelling into something more like a ring shout.[54] Nina closes the first call-and-response section with a fierce piano chord and a descending run to the lowest note on the keyboard. The piano drops out, and Nina's longtime guitarist, Al Schackman, plays a solo. Eventually the guitar, drum, and bass give way to hand claps. For twelve seconds, only clapping, breathing, and stomping keep the rhythm going until Nina starts building the piano back into the mix. Nina sings "oh, yeah" three times, the high-hat sixteenths return, and the story resumes. The Sinner Man is still trapped with nowhere to hide, but the singer sounds like she has found hope in a power that can liberate her. Despite the frightening message of the song's verses, Nina Simone is *looking forward* to Judgment Day.

This eager anticipation of divine judgment is the key to understanding Simone's "Sinnerman" in continuity with the spirituals sung by her ancestors. White enslavers mistakenly assumed that the prominence of eschatology in the spirituals meant that Blacks were content to accept slavery in this life and patiently await heaven as a reward for obedience to white masters.[55] James Cone dispels this myth:

---

54. The ring shout was an ecstatic ritual of singing, dancing, and clapping with roots in West Africa. Dwight Andrews—a contemporary scholar, musician, and pastor—describes the ring shout as "the cornerstone for understanding the nexus between African religion and emerging African American religion." Historian Gates, Jr., elaborates: "Those enslaved persons who accepted Christianity found ways to make the new religion their own, infusing the religion of their captors with their own African spirituality. There is no Black Church without music and dancing—never was, never will be—and the drum and dance would be unifying forces of Black forms of worship, expressing adulation and exaltation, signifying inheritance and belonging" (Henry Louis Gates, Jr., *The Black Church: This Is Our Story, This Is Our Song* [New York: Penguin, 2021], 32–34).
55. According to W. E. B. DuBois, "passive submission" was precisely the goal of white enslavers in distorting Christian doctrines

What is actually at stake in the image of heaven is the righteousness of God. The central theme of biblical religion is the justice of God. Yahweh is known by what God does in history, and what God does is always identical with the liberation of the poor from the injustice of the strong.[56]

Far from being a justification for white power over Black lives, the promise of heaven meant that no earthly power—not even the power to enslave and kill—could ultimately overcome God's power to liberate his people.

The righteousness of God is the power of God to achieve victory for the oppressed. . . . The event of the resurrection is the disclosure of the power of God's righteousness unto salvation, God's will to make plain that there is a future for the weak which is not made with human

---

into tools for turning Africans into "valuable chattel." DuBois is therefore one of the first Black intellectuals to criticize the promise of a "Great Day," when God would "lead His dark children home," as nothing more than a "comforting dream" that contributed to "a religion of resignation and submission" inimical to the struggle for freedom. Yet he credits Black abolitionists with changing the "dream" of freedom into a "real thing," so that "the 'Coming of the Lord' swept this side of Death, and came to be a thing to be hoped for in this day" (*The Souls of Black Folk*, 120–21). Today, theologians like James Cone and historians like Henry Louis Gates, Jr., agree with DuBois about the self-serving goals of white enslavers, but they argue that the Black church effectively thwarted white efforts to make Christianity into an instrument of oppression. Instead, Christianity in the hands of African Americans has remained faithful to the gospel of Jesus Christ, who proclaims freedom, not bondage, for all who believe in him. "As wisdom texts," writes Erskine Peters, the spirituals "are instructional agents that functioned to controvert the distorted Christian catechesis that was created to indoctrinate the enslaved Africans into submission" (Peters, *Lyrics of the Afro-American Spiritual*, xv).

56. Cone, *The Spirituals and the Blues*, 92.

hands. Heaven, in the black spirituals, was an affirmation of this hope in the absolute power of God's righteousness as revealed in God's future.[57]

The spirituals take hell as seriously as they take heaven. "Sinner Man" is not exceptional in its frightening description of the consequences of sin. But in the spirituals, the images of judgment that made Christians tremble to hear the *Dies irae* are a source of encouragement to downtrodden people. Cone explains:

> Black slaves accepted the biblical concept of judgment. For them judgment will be the time when Christ comes to judge the living and the dead. The righteous will be received into the heavenly kingdom amid rejoicing and shouting. The wicked will be punished in hell. . . . Judgment was understood as an inevitable element in God's fulfillment of the divine promise. No one will be able to avoid it because "My Lord says He's gwinter rain down fire."[58]

Cone cites another spiritual closely related to "Sinner Man" that emphasizes the impossibility of escaping judgment: "Oh I went to de rock to hide my face, / De rock cried out, 'No hidin' place,' / 'Dere's no hidin' place down dere."[59]

The spirituals hold that Christ will judge *all* nations and all people, but "because black slaves believed that they had been faithful to God's righteousness, they did not fear God's coming judgment."[60] The spirituals testify that enslaved Black people welcomed judgment as the fulfillment of God's promise to set them free. In 1871, the Jubilee Singers of Fisk University toured the northern states and then Europe, raising enough money from white audiences to keep their new school in Nashville open.[61]

---

57. Ibid., 92–93.
58. Ibid., 93–94.
59. Ibid., 94.
60. Ibid., 95.
61. The moving story of the Fisk Jubilee Singers is told by many authors, but perhaps most powerfully by W. E. B. DuBois in his classic essay, "The Sorrow Songs." See DuBois, *The Souls of Black*

Their early repertoire of spirituals included a version of "Sinner Man,"[62] but it was not the only one of their songs to look forward eagerly to "that day." For example: "Judgment, Judgment, Judgment day is rolling around; / Judgment, Judgment, O how I long to go" and "Oh! Hallelujah to the Lamb, / Judgment will find you so; / The Lord is on the giving hand, / Judgment will find you so."[63]

The hope expressed in the spirituals is not eagerness to see sinners punished, but confidence that "just as you live, just so you die, / And after death, Judgment will find you so."[64] Both testaments of Christian Scripture depict the oppressed celebrating the downfall of their oppressors.[65] The most famous example,

---

*Folk*, 155–64. For more on the 150th anniversary of the Fisk Jubilee Singers' founding, see Margaret Renkl, "They Didn't Want to Sing Spirituals, but They Did — and Changed American Music," *The New York Times*, October 4, 2021, https://www.nytimes.com/2021/10/04/opinion/fisk-jubilee-singers-black-spirituals-anniversary.html. The Fisk Jubilee Singers continue to perform and record. Their 2021 album *Celebrating Fisk!* won a Grammy in Roots Gospel. Listen to Audie Cornish, "The Jubilee Singers, HBCU Fisk University's A Cappella Ensemble, Celebrate 150 Years," *All Things Considered* (National Public Radio, October 22, 2021), https://www.npr.org/2021/10/22/1048492641/the-jubilee-singers-hbcu-fisk-universitys-a-cappella-ensemble-celebrate-150-year.

62. Theodore F. Seward, George L. White, and E. M. Cravath, eds., *Jubilee Songs as Sung by the Jubilee Singers of Fisk University*, Complete Edition (New York: Biglow & Main, 1872), http://digital.library.wisc.edu/1711.dl/MillsSpColl.JubileeSongs, 61.

63. Ibid., 34, 47.

64. Ibid., 47.

65. The examples in the Old Testament are too many to list, but the one that figures most prominently in the spirituals is the celebration that follows God's destruction of Pharaoh's army in the Red Sea (Exod 15:1–21). In the New Testament, the cry of the martyrs described in the Book of Revelation is closely related to the lyrics of "Sinnerman." Immediately before John sees "the rich and the powerful" running for cover, he sees "the souls of those who had been slaughtered for the word of God and for the testimony they had given." These martyrs cry to God,

Mary's *Magnificat*, doesn't revel in the suffering of the powerful. But the unavoidable counterpart to God having "lifted up the lowly" and "filled the hungry" is that the strong arm of God has "brought down the powerful from their thrones" and "sent the rich away empty" (Luke 1:46–55). The spirituals are similarly unambiguous about the fate of sinners who rely on their own power instead of God's. "All have sinned" (Rom 3:23, 5:12), but sinners who call on the powerful mercy of God are both forgiven and freed from every other power, including death:

> Children, we all shall be free,
> When the Lord shall appear. . . .
> Give ease to the sick, give sight to the blind,
> Enable the cripple to walk;
> He'll raise the dead from under the earth,
> And give them permission to fly.[66]

"All have sinned," but only those who persist in opposing God's justice have anything to fear from God's judgment.

Simone's shouted refrain in "Sinnerman" is evidently the inspiration for Hozier's 2018 track "Nina Cried Power." The young Irish songwriter asked Mavis Staples, another iconic voice of the civil rights movement, to sing the bridge:

> And I could cry power
> Power has been cried by those stronger than me
> Straight into the face that tells you to
> Rattle your chains if you love bein' free

While a gospel choir repeats "Power!" Hozier names his heroes who dared to challenge the powers of the present world. These include James Brown, Pete Seeger, Marvin Gaye, Etta James, and

---

"Sovereign Lord, holy and true, how long will it be before you judge and avenge our blood on the inhabitants of the earth?" (Rev 6:9–10).

66. Seward et al., *Jubilee Songs*, 13.

more: "Lennon cried power / Patti cried power / Billie, power / Dylan, power / Woody, power / Nina cried power."[67]

Like Peter Tosh's "Downpressor Man," Hozier's anthem amplifies Simone's demand for justice in "Sinnerman." He hears Nina's cry for what it is: a claim that the righteous power of God is on the side of Black liberation. But awareness is just the beginning of a response to Simone's music. "It's not the waking, it's the rising," Hozier sings. Nina didn't perform "Sinnerman" to inform white consciences or correct white prejudices. Like a prophet of old, she was compelled to proclaim what God has said will be. "That day" is surely coming when God will lift up the lowly, and no amount of running will keep the Sinner Man on top. Will you fall with the powerful on that day? Or will you rise with the weak today?

## That Day of Hope

It may seem, especially to white audiences, that "Sinnerman" inspires more fear than hope in divine justice. But Christian hope only becomes more than wishful thinking when we trust the righteousness and power of God. Divine justice is the basic premise of Christian hope, and "justice," Augustine says, "is only present when the person is obedient to God's rule."[68] Obedience to God's rule is the antithesis of slavery and the epitome of freedom, for it is a fully reasonable and righteous obedience of faith and love. "Just as a single person lives by the faith that works through love, so does the whole company and people of the just. This is the love by which a person loves God as God ought to be loved, and his neighbor as himself."[69] The orthodox Christian teaching about hope is that "a single person lives" by a radical commitment to justice—a commitment to being part

---

67. "Nina Cried Power," featuring Mavis Staples, track 1 on Hozier, *Wasteland, Baby!*, Rubyworks, 2019.
68. Augustine, *City of God*, 19.26.
69. Ibid., 19.23.

of the "whole company and people of the just" who love God and neighbor as they ought to be loved. The only saving faith is a faith that "works through love" on behalf of God's justice. Hope without a burning desire for justice is false hope.

This sounds extreme, and orthodoxy often avoids extremes in favor of a *via media*. When facing Judgment Day, however, this theological habit is at once too timid and too complacent. Christian hope is not a tepid medium between presumption and despair. Hope is a daring break with the fallen but familiar "way things are" to risk a new, uncomfortable, and dangerous way of living. Too often, Christians have been led to think that orthodox belief in God's judgment walks a line of guarded optimism, somewhere between despondent dread of damnation and smug certainty of salvation. We are told, "Do not despair; one of the thieves was saved. Do not presume; one of the thieves was damned."[70]

But why should we presume one of the thieves was damned? Deleting the semicolon reveals a more orthodox statement.[71] There is only one shepherd who knows how he will separate the sheep from the goats on "that day." Hanging upon the Cross, he promises one thief, "Today you will be with me in Paradise" (Luke 23:43). But the Good Shepherd does not refuse the other thief the same opportunity. On "that day," the Son of Man will sit in judgment, yet "today" the judge hangs among sinners. By accepting an unjust death, he opens the possibility that the death of sinners—which God never desires—is not the final act of God's justice.[72] Cone reminds us, "The 'Sinner Man' is the one for whom Christ died in order

---

70. People have been attributing this quote to St. Augustine for centuries, though no one has been able to find where he wrote it. It was popularized in the twentieth century by Samuel Beckett in *Waiting for Godot*. See David S. Cunningham, "'Do Not Presume': The Fate of the Other Thief," *The Christian Century*, March 23, 2010, https://www.christiancentury.org/article/2010-03/do-not-presume.

71. Cunningham, "'Do Not Presume.'"

72. See Ezek 18:21–23, 33:11; 2 Pet 3:9.

to set him free."[73] We still have "today" to accept salvation from the Lord of "that day."

Nevertheless, "that day" draws near. Another well-known spiritual declares, "Soon and very soon, we are going to see the King." It is a joyful proclamation of the day of the LORD, but also a reminder of our mortality. Catholic theology distinguishes the *particular judgment* at each person's death from the *general judgment* on the Last Day, but these are two aspects of the one reality of God's justice. The distinction only reinforces the unity of individual salvation with justice for all. The criteria by which each soul is judged at death are the same criteria Jesus will apply when "all the nations" appear before his judgment seat. "And the king will answer them, 'Truly I tell you, just as you did it to one of the least of these who are members of my family, you did it to me.'" The separating of individuals "one from another as a shepherd separates the sheep from the goats" has the final purpose of gathering "the righteous" into one family and bringing them collectively "into eternal life" (Matt 25:31–46).

Justice in society is crucial to eternal salvation because the fruit of God's judgment is *a just people*, not justice in abstraction. Even the particularly Catholic doctrine of purgatory is best understood as a consequence of the communal nature of judgment and hope. In Pope Benedict's telling, purgatory is not some divine bookkeeping mechanism for settling individual debts after death. Rather, the practice of praying for the faithful departed is an acknowledgment that "our lives are involved with one another" in ways that have ultimate, eternal significance beyond earthly death. "No one lives alone. No one sins alone. No one is saved alone."[74]

Following Jesus requires us to ask a man who suffered unjustly at the hands of human power to remember us in mercy when he comes into the power of his kingdom. The glorious reign of "the Lamb that was slaughtered" supplies one and the

---

73. Cone, *The Spirituals and the Blues*, 75.
74. Benedict XVI, *Spe Salvi*, 48.

same answer to every cry for justice and every plea for mercy (Rev 5:12). The power that Nina Simone calls upon to create a new society is the same power—the *only* power—in which sinners may find safety "all on that day." There is no orthodox hope that looks to Jesus for mercy on the Day of Judgment but tolerates injustice today. "Grace does not cancel out justice. It does not make wrong into right"—on the contrary, says Pope Benedict, "the incarnation of God in Christ" has linked God's saving grace so closely to God's righteous judgment of the world that "our hope is always essentially hope for others; only thus is it truly hope for me too."[75]

## The Time Is Late

As Nina Simone's "Sinnerman" shows, the musical and spiritual roots of rock are inextricable from the historical struggle of Black Americans for freedom, equality, and justice. Knowing this, what should you do if you "believe in rock 'n' roll"? Can the right response to Simone's music play a part in saving your immortal soul? Can you answer this question without unjustly appropriating her music for yourself? I believe the way to honor Simone's performance—and the way to prepare for "that day"—is to participate in her struggle for justice.

Simone's own words support this conclusion. At a Long Island concert on April 7, 1968—three days after the assassination of Martin Luther King—Nina stopped singing in the middle of "Mississippi Goddam" and challenged her audience: "If you have been moved at *all*, and you know my songs at *all*, for God sakes join me! Don't sit back there! The time is too late now."[76] Before she finished the song, Nina wanted her audience to know that

---

75. Ibid., 44, 47–48.
76. "Mississippi Goddam," recorded on April 7, 1968, disc 1, track 22 on Nina Simone, *Sugar in My Bowl: The Very Best of Nina Simone 1967–1972*, RCA 07863 67635-2, July 28, 1998. See Cohodas, *Princess Noire*, 210–12.

applause and record purchases are not enough; fans who truly *know* her songs *act* on what she says in them.

The same lesson applies to fans of all kinds of American music. Anyone who knows blues, jazz, R&B, hip-hop, country, or rock knows that we have received the music we love from the music of Black people. We should also know that Black music does not exist to entertain white people or even to educate and awaken them to injustice. Nina Simone didn't record "Sinnerman" to help white folks save their souls. Still, serious music fans and serious Christians are right to honor the soul of the music they love. And by *soul*, I mean the spiritual meaning and power of a song, which doesn't reside in its melody or lyrics alone, nor even in the genius of a performer like Simone, but in the experience of a people whose struggle to survive gave birth to music of sorrow, resistance, and hope.

I have tried to honor the soul of Nina Simone's music, not examine its orthodoxy. Nevertheless, this chapter is also about getting doctrine right—specifically, the intertwined doctrines of judgment and hope. Pope Benedict says judgment is filled with "the splendor of hope," but hope is "often all too well concealed beneath the horrors" of a righteous God dealing with our tremendous injustice.[77] The church teaches that justice and mercy are inseparably united in God, in a way that neither trivializes human responsibility nor leaves us in despair. To discern orthodoxy from heresy in this matter is to discern hope in judgment and justice in redemption. The Sinner Man cannot run to any doctrine of cheap grace to evade responsibility, for how would that be just? The church may not cease to pray for any sinner's salvation, for how would that be hopeful?

In "Sinnerman," Simone calls on God to overthrow the power of white oppressors and hold them accountable for their sins. She sings for herself and for a people who have been enslaved, abused, lynched, and denied the rights and benefits of equal membership in a society enriched by their labor and that of their ancestors. In the end, however, Simone offers a

77. Benedict XVI, *Spe Salvi*, 41.

single piece of advice—a slender thread of hope—to people who admit their culpability and complicity in this historical injustice. She sings, "Oh, Sinnerman, you oughta be prayin'." And if the Savior whose mercy we implore is also the Judge who delivers justice for the oppressed, then along with praying we ought to be working to overcome whatever keeps God's Black children from being fully equal and fully free.

# Hope as Rebellion:
## The Gospel According to Switchfoot

Christian Raab

Christian rock, an industry created by and for Evangelical Christians, and which has its own distinct record labels, radio stations, and music festivals, has existed since at least the 1980s. For much of its history, Christian rock did not garner much respect or interest from secular rock fans. Perhaps this is because Christian rockers always seemed like they were pandering, like they had adopted this heavy sound and rebellious image only in order to catch the ear of an unsuspecting listener long enough that they could proselytize. Most secular rock fans are suspicious of Christian rock and would agree with the sentiments of television cartoon character Hank Hill, that these musicians are "not makin' Christianity any better. [They're] just makin' rock and roll worse."[1]

Furthermore, there is something incongruous in the whole notion of Christian rock. Rock and roll is about rebellion. Fifties stars like Elvis Presley, Chuck Berry, Little Richard, and Jerry Lee Lewis pushed the boundaries of post-war sexual mores and had their records labeled as "devil's music." In the 1960s, rock was transformed by the likes of Bob Dylan and the Beatles into a soundtrack of pushback against the whole of the old order. Rock challenged, sometimes covertly and sometimes openly, everything that one generation typically passes to the next: the family, the government, religion, and traditional values.

Accordingly, "Christian rock" seemed like an oxymoron in the classic rock era because Christianity was an intrinsic part of the institutional edifice that rock was busy trying to tear down. In his book *The Gospel According to the Beatles*, Steve Turner explains that even when rock and roll didn't name Christianity

---

1. *King of the Hill*, s08e02 "Reborn To Be Wild," written by Mike Judge, Greg Daniels, and Tony Gama-Lobo, originally aired November 9, 2003, on Fox TV.

explicitly as a target, rock was against "the restraints of the past," and "it was commonly assumed that the church was on the side" of those same restraints.[2] The Who's Pete Townshend put it plainly and pointedly when he said that, for him at least, rock was about providing an alternative sanctuary "to serve the spiritual needs of the audience" who were abandoning their "parents' church."[3] In this light, Joseph Ratzinger's suspicion that rock provided "a form of worship . . . in opposition to Christian worship" doesn't seem so outlandish.[4]

This is not to say that faith themes have never been part of rock's story. Early on, Elvis Presley and Sam Cooke recorded gospel music as well as rock and roll. Later megastars Leonard Cohen and Bruce Springsteen employed Christian imagery in their lyrics. Dylan underwent a conversion to Evangelical Christianity in the late 70s, and it shone in his subsequent work. U2, meanwhile, has incorporated a Christian social justice message into their music. But all of these were exceptions to rock's main plot, and they weren't products of the Christian rock industry.

There is one band, however, that seems to have been able to stand at the nexus point between Evangelical Christianity and rock music, sell records to both Christian and secular fans, win critical acclaim, and do it consistently for over twenty years. Switchfoot, consisting of Jon Foreman (vocals, guitar), Tim Foreman (bass, vocals), Chad Butler (drums), and Jerome Fontamillas (keys),[5] emerged out of San Diego in the late 1990s. Though they resist the label of "Christian rock" and have explained that they are "Christians by faith, not by genre," they started their career on a Christian music label, won a Grammy in the category of "rock gospel," remain darlings of the Christian contemporary music

---

2.   Steve Turner, *The Gospel According to the Beatles* (Louisville, KY: Westminster, 2006), 58.

3.   David Marchese, "The Who's Pete Townshend grapples with rock's legacy, and his own dark past," *New York Times Magazine*, November 25, 2019.

4.   Joseph Ratzinger, *The Spirit of the Liturgy* (San Francisco: Ignatius Press, 2000), 148.

5.   Drew Shirley (guitar) is a former member.

press, and continue to get played on Christian radio stations. On the other hand, they have earned the right to be acknowledged as transcending the confining label of Christian rock. Their records have achieved top ten status on the Billboard alternative, modern rock, and overall charts. Their music has been heard in the background of Hollywood movies and television shows. They've performed the major network late night circuit, and as an act at the Rose Bowl. They've earned the respect of rock critics and fellow rock artists (One Republic are fans, as is Mötley Crüe's Tommy Lee). In bridging the worlds of Evangelical Christianity and secular rock music, Switchfoot has done what few, if any, other artists have managed.

## Asking the Hard Questions

When so much Christian rock is dismissed by secular fans, why has Switchfoot succeeded in crossing over? That is the mystery this chapter wishes to explore. It seems to me that there are several reasons for it. For one thing, Switchfoot deliberately tries not to come off as preachy. Jon Foreman has acknowledged in interviews that it is not always helpful to give people answers to questions that they have not yet asked, and that it is "a danger within the Body of Christ to pretend like we have it figured out."[6] Instead, the band's usual M.O. is to invite its audience to ask questions and discover mysteries alongside them as fellow sojourners. Foreman sees his role as an artist as facilitating, articulating, and illuminating the questions others have, or should have, but he is clear that these are also his questions. "It's not play-acting,"[7] he has said. Thus, humility and authenticity characterize psalm-like songs like "Vice

6. Beam TV, "SWITCHFOOT INTERVIEW ABOUT BEING IN A 'CHRISTIAN BAND'," YouTube, January 21, 2016, https://www.youtube.com/watch?v=5dGRlYYC8Pk.
7. CCM Magazine, "SWITCHFOOT's Jon Foreman | | Features On Film with Andrew Greer (2 of 2)," YouTube, July 13, 2016, https://www.youtube.com/watch?v=hv-n2LMHB4Q.

Verses" and "The Blues," both of which investigate the meaning of suffering and look for God's presence in times of apparent absence.

The willingness to be honest and confront hard questions is a different kind of posture of faith from those who stand confident in their prepared answers, and indeed forms an implicit critique of a Christianity that arrogantly presents itself as having all the answers. Nonetheless, it *is* a posture of faith. "My view of God is so big that there's no question that I could pose that he's going to be offended by," Foreman says. "As a songwriter, I don't feel like my job is to try and prop up God and make him look good. My job as a songwriter is to be honest."[8] "God doesn't need a lawyer," he said elsewhere.[9] By asking questions, Switchfoot bears witness to faith in a God who can take them.

When the band does offer answers, they are usually presented subtly and humbly. An example of this technique can be found in their song "Stars." The song describes doubtful, anxious thoughts followed by a discovery of one's place in a meaningful cosmos through contemplation of the orderly beauty of the night sky. The scene unfolds:

> I've been thinking about everyone
> Everyone, you look so empty . . .
> But when I look at the stars . . .
> I see someone else
> When I look at the stars, the stars
> I feel like myself

This is typical of Foreman's style. He asks his questions. He empathetically identifies with the loneliness and emptiness of the world. Then the heavens suggest to him the presence of the Other, which leads him to a meaningful sense of himself. The lyrics create a sense of orientation after disorientation and bring a feeling of found serenity that matches the experience of the artist himself.

---

8. *Beam* TV interview.
9. *CCM Magazine* interview.

The same song also provides the fantastic lines: "I've been thinking 'bout the meaning of resistance / Of a hope beyond my own /And suddenly the infinite and penitent / Begin to look like home." Interesting here is the link Foreman makes between hope and resistance (about which I will say more shortly) and the recognition that the hope is going to come from elsewhere, namely "the infinite and penitent," which is a beautiful and subtle but powerful way of expressing the divinity and humanity of Christ. Indeed, the words "Jesus" and "Lord" are few and far between in Switchfoot lyrics, but there are numerous unmistakable references to Christ like this one.

Another attractive aspect of the band's music is their willingness to challenge hypocrisy in the institutional church, but to do so in a way that doesn't just tear down but rather invites people to be more and dream bigger. "The World You Want" echoes both Christ's teaching that just saying "Lord, Lord" won't mean anything if it is not accompanied by action (Matt 7:21), and the words of the epistle of St. James: "Religion that is pure and undefiled before God, the Father, is this: to care for orphans and widows in their distress, and to keep oneself unstained by the world" (1:27). The song emphasizes that our actions change the world for good or ill, and that our actions are the true sign of where our heart lies, i.e., our true religion. Foreman chants:

> What you say is your religion
> How you say it's your religion
> Who you love is your religion
> How you love is your religion
> All your science, your religion
> All your hatred, your religion
> All your wars are your religion

## Hope for Heaven and Earth

From the beginning, however, the band has desired to speak not only to Christians but also to a secular audience. It's why they left their Christian label after three records and signed with the major label Columbia. They've succeeded with that wider audience, in my estimation, by doing what good rock and roll has always done: challenging the old order. What's interesting about Switchfoot, though, is that they are speaking to an audience for whom the old order is no longer traditional Christianity so much as a post-modern, post-Christian world which has failed to provide a meaningful framework of existence for the young. It's a post-modern materialistic metaphysics and its consequent relativistic ethics against which Switchfoot has issued its call to arms.

"Lonely Nation" laments the experience of a generation that is seen only as a "target market" and a culture which has become "slaves of what we want." The song points out that the result of living for material things is emptiness: "I want more than my desperation / I want more than my lonely nation / . . . I'm tired of feeling low / Of feeling hollow." "Gone" unmasks the illusion of transcendence provided by hyper-connected media, and the mirage of satisfaction promised by material gain. It contains the question: "We got information in the information age / But do we know what life is / Outside of our convenient Lexus cages?" In "American Dream," Foreman quips (rather wordily): "When success is equated with excess / The ambition for excess wrecks us," and leads his listeners to the raucous, challenging chorus, "This ain't my American dream / I wanna live and die for bigger things."

Over the years, the band has decried other demons: the cheapening of sex ("Easier than Love," "Enough to Let Me Go"); polarization and stratification of society ("Native Tongue," "Looking for America"); and the constant noise and distraction which prevent a more examined life ("Voices," "Adding to the Noise"). Switchfoot is also, of course, attuned to the timeless force which afflicts the human heart, namely, sin. This is best seen in "The War Inside," with its straightforward lyric: "Ain't no killer like pride / No killer like I / No killer like what's inside."

In response to these demons, Switchfoot articulates a message of hope. A most compelling aspect of Switchfoot's work is that they see hope (as well as faith and charity) as the true form of resistance, of rock and roll rebellion, in a despairing time. Almost since the beginning of their career, they have expressed as a kind of mission statement: "Hope deserves an anthem." They have indeed delivered a series of such anthems.

There are many facets to Switchfoot's message of hope. One is to remind people that they have deep and unique dignity based on the spiritual nature of the *imago dei*. The message takes a philosophical form in the REM-like "4:12," which cautions "You began to believe that all we are is material / It's non-sensical / . . . Souls aren't built of stone and sticks and bones." "All I Need" begs God for the grace to see we are "more than just accidental / more than just inconsequential." "Blinding Light" exhorts listeners not to believe the lies of the culture which reduce persons to material objects of pleasure. Foreman exclaims: "Your skin's more than a pin-up suit / . . . No one else got soul like you."

Another facet is a challenge to the audience to not be content with a shallow, unexamined existence, but to want more. Switchfoot calls their listeners to honor the holy long-ing within that, if they dig deeply, they are sure to find. As "Blinding Light" puts it: "Deep down there's a hope inside / Wake up, wake up." No motif appears so often or with as much conviction in their music as this encouragement to listen to the desire for more than the present despairing world is offering. Examples are ubiquitous, but it was stated well in one of their first hits: "We were meant to live for so much more / Have we lost ourselves? / Somewhere we live inside / Somewhere we live inside" ("Meant to Live").

The desire inside is a gift. This holy longing, with all its discontent, reveals that the world is passing and can never satisfy us. "Nothing is sound," as the name of their 2005 album puts it. At the same time, following the logic of C. S. Lewis, the fact that we have this hunger is a sign that there must be something or someone who can satisfy it. It is a pointer toward the infinite, toward God and toward heaven. Thus, the great lie is that this earthly existence is all there is. The truth is that "the world is flawed, but these scars will heal" ("We Are One Tonight") and "everything will be made new again" ("Golden"). Ultimately, we are made to be whole. It's the future God made us for and which he wants for us.

The promise of heaven is described poetically in the Augustine-inspired "Restless," with its beautiful lines:

Until the sea of glass we meet
At last completed and complete
Where tide of tear and pain subside
And laughter drinks them dry
I'll be waiting

Heaven is also the theme of "Where I Belong," the band's usual live encore. Here heaven is described as a homecoming to a place "where the weak are finally strong" and "where the righteous right the wrongs / . . . a world where I belong."

A focus on the afterlife doesn't mean that Switchfoot is peddling a solely other-worldly Christianity, however. Awareness that we are made to be citizens of the kingdom of God grounds human dignity in its final cause, which requires us to respect it today. The social and moral implications of such an awareness are expressed in songs like "Looking for America," "Dark Horses," and "The World You Want." Meanwhile, experiences of grace, forgiveness, and mercy, which are described in "Redemption" and "Joy Invincible," to name just two, reveal that the kingdom is already breaking through. This provides a solid basis for beginning to live today with hope.

Thus, rather than providing an escape from life, hope empowers one to live it now. In "Dare You to Move," Foreman describes life as a tense stage upon which one must act. One oscillates between the poles of "who you are and who you could be," and between "how it is and how it should be." The future, "what happens next," depends on your choice of action. "I dare you to move / . . . I dare you to lift yourself up off the floor," he sings. The message is to start living in hope rather than to remain weighed down and paralyzed by the internal forces of sin and shame and the external forces of the world's malaise. The song mentions "forgiveness," "redemption," and "salvation" as the present experiences which catalyze hopeful forward movement.

Hope is accompanied by her sisters, faith and charity. As articulated in songs like "The Day That I Found God," the aforementioned "Stars," and the stunning "I Won't Let You Go," faith asserts against nihilism that we live in a meaningfully ordered universe and that our lives have purpose in relation to God. Charity, the theme of "The Hardest Art," "Daisy," "Hello Hurricane," and "The Sound," gives us the strength of Christ, unites us to his cross, and enables us to give ourselves away selflessly, overcoming individualism in the midst of a world that preaches self-interest. These songs are rallying cries to a way of life different from the world's. Against the cultural storms which divide and polarize, Switchfoot sings out, and invites us to sing with them, "Hello hurricane, you can't silence my love." Amidst noisy media messaging which reinforces fear, they exclaim that just as darkness never overcomes light, "there is no song louder than love."

At its origins, Christianity subverted the old order: the pagan values of a violent empire. Today's empire is a world marked by despair and meaninglessness. It is supported by those who live unexamined materialistic lives. Switchfoot provides a soundtrack for a Christian resistance, an anthem of hope against the "new" old order. In doing so they invite us to take up the arms of faith, hope, and charity as non-violent acts of resistance. This is their gospel. It is also their rock and roll.

# From Genesis to Revelation:
## The Eschatology of "Supper's Ready"

Lawrence J. King

Around the year 1160 in Upper Bavaria, Benedictine monks staged a play entitled *Antichristus*. It portrayed the rise of the Antichrist through deception and wonder-working, his conquest of the world, and his ultimate downfall. Medieval clergy and monks often used religious dramas to instruct the Catholic faithful, and the Antichrist soon became one of the more popular topics.[1]

On November 18, 1972, at Brunel University in London, the rock band Genesis premiered its epic composition "Supper's Ready."[2] This seven-section suite portrays the rise of the Antichrist through deception and wonder-working, his conquest of the world, and his ultimate downfall. Peter Gabriel had several reasons for writing the lyrics, but catechizing his audience was not one of them. Nonetheless, the listener might wonder: How orthodox is the theology of "Supper's Ready"?

In this chapter, I begin by describing this song's composition, music, and lyrics. I then examine Catholic teaching regarding the Antichrist, distinguishing between doctrines strongly supported by tradition and the magisterium, and those that remain controverted. Finally, I argue that, interpreted as a piece of eschatological fiction, "Supper's Ready" is indeed compatible with Catholic doctrine.

---

1. Vincent P. Miceli, SJ, *The Antichrist* (Harrison, NY: Roman Catholic Books, 1981), 89–92.
2. Robin Platts, *Genesis: Behind the Lines, 1967–2007* (Burlington, ON: Collector's Guide Publishing, 2007), 58.

## Peter Gabriel and Genesis

While most English rock musicians came from the working classes, Genesis began as a group of upper-middle-class teenagers at Charterhouse School. Founded on the site of a Carthusian priory seized during Henry VIII's dissolution of the monasteries, Charterhouse's alumni include John Wesley, Ralph Vaughan Williams, and nearly a hundred MPs.[3] Peter Gabriel and his songwriting partner Tony Banks loved the rock music sweeping England at the time. Yet they also appreciated England's tradition of classical and church music. As Gabriel later recalled:

> Hymns used to be the only musical moment at Charterhouse. . . . The organ in Chapel was magnificent and the playing was great. . . . Everyone would stand up and scream their heads off. It would be as moving as a Southern spiritual. It was really emotional, and people would come out of Chapel feeling like they were on top of the world.[4]

After leaving school, the boys dithered between going to university or becoming professional rock musicians, and finally chose the band. At this time (1969), a new subgenre of rock music, eventually labeled "progressive rock," was being developed by bands such as Procol Harum, the Nice, and King Crimson. Musicologist Edward Macan lists the "defining features of progressive rock" as "the continuous use of tone colors drawn from symphonic or church music, the employment of lengthy sectional forms such as the song cycle or the multimovement suite, and the preoccupation with dazzling metrical and instrumental virtuosity."[5] The first two are characteristic of Genesis's

---

3. Platts, *Behind the Lines*, 7; Daryl Easlea, *Without Frontiers: The Life and Music of Peter Gabriel* (London: Omnibus Press, 2014), 28.

4. Armando Gallo, *Genesis: I Know What I Like* (Los Angeles: D.I.Y. Books, 1980; Kindle edition, 2014), Kindle location 436.

5. Edward Macan, *Rocking the Classics: English Progressive Rock and the Counterculture* (New York: Oxford University Press,

music in the early and mid-1970s, but they placed less emphasis on virtuosity than some other progressive rock bands.[6]

The members of Genesis were not interested in the life of excess that attracted many rock musicians in that era. Most of them didn't even smoke marijuana. "In their early days on the road, the group traveled with a picnic basket loaded with scones, hard-boiled eggs and tea."[7] In March 1971, the twenty-one-year-old Gabriel married Jill Moore, daughter of Queen Elizabeth's assistant private secretary.[8]

By 1971, Charterhouse alumni Peter Gabriel (lead vocals, flute), Tony Banks (organ, mellotron, piano, 12-string acoustic guitar), and Michael Rutherford (bass guitar, bass pedals, 12-string acoustic guitar) had been joined by Steve Hackett (electric and acoustic guitars) and Phil Collins (drums, harmony vocals). The band became increasingly popular, not only for their music and lyrics, but also for Gabriel's eccentric showmanship. Before each song, he would tell a story; some of these stories explained what the song was about, while others were simply odd. In September 1972, he began wearing costumes and masks to illustrate some of the songs. "Supper's Ready" would eventually involve several costume changes during instrumental passages.[9]

Unfortunately, the popularity of Gabriel's stage persona meant that the music press focused its attention on the singer, even though all members of the band were composing the music. The resulting tension was one of the factors that led to Gabriel's

---

1997), 12–13.

6. There is no evidence that progressive rock bands saw themselves as part of a *movement*. Nonetheless many members of these bands were acquainted with each other. Occasionally their membership overlapped: drummer Bill Bruford played with Yes from 1968 to 1972, with King Crimson from 1972 to 1974, and with Genesis during their 1976 tour.

7. Platts, *Behind the Lines*, 48.

8. Easlea, *Without Frontiers*, 82.

9. Easlea, *Without Frontiers*, 95–100, 106; Platts, *Behind the Lines*, 58–59. Gabriel would later say that the costumes and masks had been a way of compensating for his own shyness.

1975 departure from the band, at which point Collins took over the lead vocals and eventually became more famous than Gabriel ever had been. Nonetheless, many progressive rock fans prefer the band's early LPs.

## The Creation of "Supper's Ready"

"Supper's Ready" is Genesis's longest piece, clocking in at just over 23 minutes and occupying nearly the entire second side of their fourth LP, *Foxtrot*. It is divided into seven sections, each with its own title. All five members contributed to the music, while the lyrics were entirely written by Gabriel.[10]

Peter Gabriel was not someone who would seem likely to write about Christianity. Nominally Anglican, his family were not regular churchgoers. His father was interested in Eastern religions and spirituality, while his mother's passion was music.[11] But sometime during 1971, two frightening incidents occurred. Gabriel said little about them at the time, but many years later, he discussed them with photographer and Genesis chronicler Armando Gallo.

The first occurred when Peter and Jill were at her parents' house, after everyone else had gone to sleep. "We just stared at each other, and strange things began to happen. We saw other faces in each other, and . . . I was very frightened, in fact. It was almost as if something else had come into us, and was using us as a meeting point."[12]

The second incident involved Peter, Jill, and Genesis's producer John Anthony.

> [Gabriel told Gallo:] "And there was a thing later on when Jill suddenly became a medium. Fortunately, it hasn't happened since, because it terrified her, and me in

10. For the composition of the music, see Philip Dodd, ed., *Genesis: Chapter & Verse* (London: Weidenfeld & Nicolson, 2007), 49, 97, 119–23; Gallo, *I Know What I Like*, loc. 493–516, 1492.
11. Easlea, *Without Frontiers*, 24–25.
12. Gallo, *I Know What I Like*, loc. 1431 (ellipsis in original).

a sense, because she started spouting in a different voice. We were with John Anthony . . . and this girl who was an old girlfriend of John was trying to get back at him or something, and she was into magic and that sort of thing. And Jill started speaking in this voice, and it is very strange when someone you live with suddenly starts talking with another voice.

"We'd just been talking with John. . . . There's this strange room in the house in Kensington . . . I can never sleep there. It was decorated in turquoise and purple, which are colours that are both quite high in the frequency range, and I think that it was like an echo chamber for what was going on. The curtain flew wide open, though there was no wind, and the room became ice cold. And I did feel like I saw figures outside, figures in white cloaks, and the lawn I saw them on wasn't the lawn that was outside. It was just like a Hammer horror film, except that it was for real. . . . I was shaking like a leaf, and in a cold sweat. And eventually I made a cross with a candlestick and something and held it up to Jill when she was talking in this voice . . ."

"Was she responding to you?" I asked.

"Oh yes . . . she sort of reacted like a wild animal. John and I had to hold her down. And the rest of the night we eventually quietened [*sic*] her down, and made her a cup of tea, and tried to talk her through. Then she slept downstairs in the sitting room, but neither I nor John slept a wink that night."[13]

After these incidents, Gabriel began to read the Bible, including the Book of Revelation. This reading would shape much of the lyrics to "Supper's Ready":

"Anyway, that's how I got into thinking about good and evil, and the forces working against each other. That's the

---

13. Ibid., loc. 1447 (ellipses in original; these seem to represent pauses rather than editorial omissions).

sort of thing that 'Supper's Ready' was . . . fed on. This was the thing, you see. This is why I was put into this state of mind really, only because the cross had worked. The cross, as a thing, meant nothing to me. I did it because I had seen horror films, and . . . just anything really that might have worked.

"Often I felt that I could talk to the audience through the band's material, and the audience would understand what I was trying to say, and I would have a release, and a conversation with the audience through that. I was singing my heart out there when I used to sing the 'New Jerusalem'. . . I was singing for my life. I was saying this is good over evil, and . . . you know, it was an old-fashioned gesture, but I meant it, and I was fighting."[14]

The album *Foxtrot* was released in October 1972, with lyrics to "Supper's Ready" and the other tracks printed on the gatefold sleeve. The piece was first played live on November 18, and quickly became a highlight of Genesis's shows. Before the concert, the band would pass out a program with its lyrics (all 128 lines!), accompanied by a brief explanation of the piece, written by Gabriel.[15] Some of this "explanation" helps to illuminate the song's meaning, but other parts are clearly tongue-in-cheek. Therefore, the lyrics themselves will be taken as the primary source for my analysis.

## Lyrics and Music

The lyrics to "Supper's Ready" are written in the first person.[16] The initial verses establish that this is a man speaking to his

14. Ibid., loc. 1461 (ellipses in original).
15. Easlea, *Without Frontiers*, 105; "Genesis Programmes," Genesis Museum, http://www.genesismuseum.com/programs1.htm. The program contained the lyrics to "Supper's Ready," but none of their other songs.
16. For my musical analysis, I am indebted to Mark Spicer, "Large-

lover. Neither is given a name (he calls her "babe"). Nearly all the lyrics are in the present tense. The overall impression is that the singer is narrating what he sees, without knowing what will happen next.

"Lover's Leap" (section one of the suite) is free verse, with almost no rhyme. The story begins in a thoroughly mundane place: "Walking across the sitting-room / I turn the television off." The line "And it's 'Hey, babe, your supper's waiting for you'" sounds like an ordinary summons to a meal.

The music of "Lover's Leap" is stark: acoustic guitars, a subdued bass guitar, and voice. The vocals are double-tracked—Gabriel is singing the melody in two different octaves—which generates a sense of foreboding.[17] Then the story takes a frightening turn, adopting several elements from the mystical experiences described earlier. One significant difference is the cross: Gabriel told Gallo that he made the cross himself, but the song describes it outside the house: "Six saintly shrouded men move across the lawn slowly / The seventh walks in front with a cross held high in hand."

"Lover's Leap" ends and the scene changes. The woman is no longer mentioned, apparently because the narrator is now elsewhere. "Supper's Ready" draws from the Book of Revelation, so we might speculate that the narrator is now about to behold several visions, and perhaps the woman is still present but the man is unaware of her.[18]

Two new figures appear. One is a hard-working farmer, who is soon forgotten. The other is "The Guaranteed Eternal

---

Scale Strategy and Compositional Design in the Early Music of Genesis," in *Expression in Pop-Rock Music: Critical and Analytical Essays*, 2nd ed., ed. Walter Everett (Abingdon-on-Thames: Routledge, 2008), 313–44.

17. In concert, Collins sang the higher part.
18. The program indicates that "the lovers" remain the point-of-view characters for the entire piece, but the lyrics do not support this. In sections two through six, the narrator uses the word "you" to address a multitude, not a single person. At the end of section six, the narrator is overjoyed to be "back again" with his lover.

Sanctuary Man" (the title of section two). The program describes him as "the head of a highly disciplined scientific religion."[19]

When the Sanctuary Man appears, the music becomes extremely powerful, led by fanfares on the Hammond organ. According to musicologist Edward Macan, progressive rock uses the Hammond as a substitute for the pipe organ in the Anglican tradition, allowing the music to play "a quasi-liturgical role for its listeners."[20] Here, the soaring and majestic music is in a major key, creating a sense of awe and perhaps even worship. But the lyrics speak of danger. The narrator is desperately trying to warn the Sanctuary Man's followers about him:

> You, can't you see he's fooled you all?
> Yes, he's here again
> Can't you see he's fooled you all
> Share his peace, sign the lease
> He's a supersonic scientist
> He's the guaranteed eternal sanctuary man

When the song was performed in concert, Gabriel wore a crown of thorns during this section. But the thorns were shiny silver, not wooden. Combined with his reverse-mohawk haircut and pale makeup, the crown suggested not Christ but a dangerous imitation.

At the end of the second section, the music cuts off abruptly. The only sound is a group of children singing a lullaby to a "little snake." Despite the narrator's warnings, the Sanctuary Man appears to have deceived the people.

A comforting interlude follows, in which the flute reprises the melody from "Lover's Leap." Then section three begins. For the first time, the music is actually upbeat. "Ikhnaton and Itsacon and Their Band of Merry Men" tells the story of a battle. The narrator's role is unclear—in the first verse he is an observer, but in the second he seems to be one of the soldiers. According to the program, the Sanctuary Man has launched this war "to attack all

---

19. Programme.
20. Macan, *Rocking the Classics*, 32; see also 150.

those without an up-to-date 'Eternal Life Licence,' which were [*sic*] obtainable at the head office of the Sanctuary Man's religion."[21] The soldiers have been drugged by a "wonderful potion" that controls their emotions. But the narrator does not succumb to this mind control: "And even though I'm feeling good / Something tells me I'd better activate my prayer capsule." (During section three, Gabriel did not wear a costume or mask, except for a few months in 1974 when he wore a strange headdress which may have been intended to represent the pharaoh of the title.)

The Sanctuary Man's army wins the battle. There is "rejoicing and dancing," but the narrator does not share in the joy. Accompanied by slow, dirge-like music, he wanders the battlefield, mourning the dead. The lyrics take a surrealistic turn: atop a mountain of corpses he finds a young Narcissus staring into a pool. ("How Dare I Be So Beautiful?" is the title of this section.) The narrator watches as Narcissus transforms into a flower.

"A flower?" the outro asks. Gabriel is suddenly wearing a bright yellow and orange flower mask, and the fifth section, "Willow Farm," hits the audience with its upbeat tempo. This song was not originally intended to be part of a longer piece. When the band was composing and assembling what would become "Supper's Ready," Tony Banks felt that a sudden change of mood was needed at this point.

> So I thought after this really romantic bit, which became "How Dare I Be So Beautiful?," why don't we do something really stupid, and go straight into "Willow Farm." Just bang . . . stop the song, and instantly go into it. This was a little song that Peter had, lyrics and everything. And once we all got used to the idea and slotted "Willow Farm" in, it gave us great momentum to write the rest of the thing.[22]

"Willow Farm" is full of wordplays and strange rhymes with no particular meaning. Musically, it functions as a break from

---

21. Programme.
22. Tony Banks, quoted in Gallo, *I Know What I Like*, loc. 1492 (ellipsis in original).

the menace: a respite so we can forget our troubles. The song's bouncing pace and humorous lyrics make it jolly, despite the A♭ minor key. After a brief switch to the parallel major, the song returns to the minor for the final verse. The music is the same as the earlier verses, but after the major-key bridge, the minor key feels ominous.

An instrumental interlude follows: Hackett makes eerie sounds with his electric guitar, then Gabriel plays a calming melody on his flute. This moment is interrupted by a trumpet-like fanfare, reprising the opening melody from the second section—the melody which announced the appearance of the Guaranteed Eternal Sanctuary Man.

In section two, this melody became a soaring organ piece. In section five, it becomes a thunderous, pulsing beat in compound triple meter: "Apocalypse in 9/8 (Co-Starring the Delicious Talents of Gabble Ratchet)." While the bass and guitar repeat an ominous nine-note sequence,[23] Gabriel delivers his harshest vocal yet. In section two, the Sanctuary Man had deceived the world into believing he was good. Now he reveals his true nature. Some of the lyrics are taken from the Book of Revelation, annotated here:

> With the guards of Magog [Rev 20:8], swarming around
> The Pied Piper takes his children underground
> Dragon's [Rev 12:3] coming out of the sea [Rev 13:1]
> Shimmering silver head of wisdom looking at me
> He brings down the fire from the skies [Rev 13:13]
> You can tell he's doing well by the look in human eyes
> Better not compromise
> It won't be easy

An organ interlude gives Gabriel the chance to change into his "Magog" costume, consisting of a red polyhedral mask and a black robe. It's not clear what this geometric object has to do

---

23. Spicer compares this to Stravinsky's use of a repeating three-note ostinato in "The Augurs of Spring" ("Large-Scale Strategy," 329–331.)

with the Magog of Ezekiel and Revelation, but the costume
was so striking that the band put it on the cover of their next
LP, *Genesis Live*.

The final verse of section six consists of six lines, and begins
with "666 is no longer alone, / He's getting out the marrow in your
back bone."[24] The words "no longer" seem to indicate that this is
someone we have seen before, which in turn suggests that this
"666" is the Sanctuary Man. The relentless 9/8 beat continues,
now backed by the sound of an orchestra (actually, Banks's
mellotron).[25] Finally the verse ends, the keyboard modulates
downward, and the beat falters. The evil theme makes one final
attempt to assert itself, and then collapses as church bells ring
out. The final act has begun.

The conclusion to "Supper's Ready" consists of two parts.
The first, which reprises the melody from section one, is not given
its own name, perhaps to preserve the sevenfold symbolism. The
second, which reprises the melody from section two, is entitled
"As Sure As Eggs Is Eggs (Aching Men's Feet)."

The narrator's lover, unseen since the first section, returns
in the first part of this conclusion. The melody from that section
returns with her, but instead of a mellow acoustic piece, it is
recast as a dramatic, even overwhelming, song. "And it's 'Hey
babe, with your guardian eyes so blue' / ... Now I'm back again,
and babe it's gonna work out fine." The lovers are reunited, but
even greater things are in store. The melody and harmony from
section two return in the transition to "As Sure As Eggs," in the

---

24. Gabriel sings this as "six six six," rather than the King James' "six
hundred threescore and six."
25. The mellotron was a keyboard instrument containing a variety
of single-note magnetic tapes. The keyboardist could choose a
setting (orchestra, three violins, vocal chorus, etc.), and each key
would trigger a tape of a single note. For example, if he chose
the chorus setting and pressed the C, E, and G keys, it would
sound like a chorus singing three notes in harmony. Moving
from one note to another sounded artificial, so the mellotron
was rarely used as a lead instrument, but it could provide a lush
background while other instruments took the lead.

same key as before (A major), but with important changes. In section two, the music was dominated by organ fanfares, full of menace, as the Sanctuary Man appeared. This time, it features fluid guitar lines over a Hammond organ sounding like a church organ.[26] The lyrics, which began twenty minutes earlier with a mundane domestic scene, have now reached the sublime:

> There's an angel standing in the sun
> And he's crying with a loud voice
> "This is the supper of the mighty one" [Rev 19:17]
> Lord of lords, king of kings [Rev 19:16]
> Has returned to lead his children home
> To take them to the new Jerusalem [Rev 21:2]

For the finale, Gabriel wore a silver bodysuit that blazed white in the stage lights. When Genesis played at London's Theatre Royal, Drury Lane, the singer "flew" with the assistance of stage wires, but this dangerous stunt was rarely repeated.[27]

Genesis released "Supper's Ready" several times. The studio version appears on the album *Foxtrot*. The recording is clear, but the sound engineering does not fully capture the strength of the band. A remixed stereo version and a 5.1 surround sound version were released in 2008 as part of the *Genesis 1970–1975* box set. This set also includes a DVD of a concert filmed at Shepperton Studios in 1973, with a full performance of "Supper's Ready." The film is far from perfect—the band decided against releasing it at the time—but it's worth watching for Gabriel's costume changes alone. Another live version of "Supper's Ready" was released in 1998 on the *Genesis Archive 1970–1975* box set, but Gabriel insisted on re-recording all the vocals. The instrumental tracks (recorded

26. Nors S. Josephson writes, "Indeed, section 7 may be viewed as a Lisztian, symphonic apotheosis (with added high lead guitar countersubjects that restress the high F#") of both the A matrix and its related cyclical fanfares that originated in section 2" ("Bach meets Liszt: Traditional Formal Structures and Performance Practices in Progressive Rock," *Musical Quarterly* 76/1 [Spring 1991]: 67–92, at 84).
27. Easlea, *Without Frontiers*, 124.

in 1973) are the strongest of any version, but the 48-year-old Gabriel's voice sounds quite different from his younger voice.

After Gabriel left the band, Phil Collins did not attempt to replicate the costumes or other visuals, relying instead on his natural rapport with the audience. "Supper's Ready" remained a highlight of Genesis concerts for several years, and a version with Collins on vocals appears on their 1977 live album *Seconds Out*. After 1982 they never played the entire suite, although pieces of it occasionally appeared in medleys. Peter Gabriel-era Genesis, including the costumes, is recreated today by the Montreal-based tribute band The Musical Box.

But let us return to the original question. What can be said of the theology of "Supper's Ready"? Does it have anything worthwhile to say to Christians about the last days, or is it merely a long rock song with random biblical references thrown into the lyrics?

## The Antichrist in Catholic Tradition

"Supper's Ready" draws from the Apocalypse to St. John, but Catholic teaching on the Antichrist and the end-times begins with the Gospels and Paul's epistles. In this section I will examine passages in the Gospels and epistles, then their interpretation throughout history, and finally turn to the last book in the Bible.

### The Gospels and Epistles

First and foremost is the eschatological discourse (Matt 24—25 and parallels). Jesus and his disciples are at the Temple, and Jesus predicts that it will be destroyed. The disciples ask him, "When will this be, and what will be the sign of your coming and of the end of the age?" (Matt 24:3). He replies to all these questions together, making it difficult to determine which parts of his reply concern the destruction of the Temple, and which parts concern his return and the end of the age.[28]

---

28. Even in patristic times, it was understood that the eschatologi-

Jesus begins by speaking of false messiahs who will come in his name, wars, famines, and earthquakes, and yet these are only "the beginning of the birth pangs" (24:4–8). His followers will suffer horrible persecutions, and be "hated by all nations." People will be deceived by false prophets and seduced by sin, so that "the love of many will grow cold. But the one who endures to the end will be saved. And this good news of the kingdom will be proclaimed throughout the world, as a testimony to all the nations; and then the end will come" (24:9–14).

In the next passage, Christ refers to Daniel's prophecy of the abomination of desolation that will desecrate the holy place in Judea (Dan 9:27, 12:11; Matt 24:15–20). Some interpret this as the destruction of the Temple in AD 70, others as a later event, and some assign it both meanings. The next passage (24:21–31) clearly refers to the last days. The "great tribulation" (NABRE) will end when Christ returns in glory, manifested for all to see:

> All the tribes of the earth will mourn, and they will see "the Son of Man coming on the clouds of heaven" with power and great glory. And he will send out his angels with a loud trumpet call, and they will gather his elect from the four winds, from one end of heaven to the other. (24:30–31)

This eschatological discourse mentions false Christs, but always in the plural: "False messiahs [*pseudochristoi*] and false prophets will appear and produce great signs and omens, to lead

---

cal discourse combines statements about the destruction of the Temple alongside statements about the end times and Christ's return. John Chrysostom suggests that the disciples mistakenly believed that Christ's return would be at the same time as the destruction of the Temple, so in his reply he addressed both events: Chrysostom, "Homily 75 on Matthew," trans. George Prevost and M.B. Riddle, New Advent, https://www.newadvent.org/fathers/200175.htm. Chrysostom's exposition is repeated in Thomas Aquinas, *Catena aurea in quatuor Evangelia: Expositio in Matthaeum*, cap. 23, lect. 6, Corpus Thomisticum, https://www.corpusthomisticum.org/cmt21.html#85574.

astray, if possible, even the elect" (24:24). But there is no mention of one particular false Christ who towers above the others.

Paul discusses the return of Christ in his two letters to the Thessalonians. In the first, he writes that Christ will return suddenly, "like a thief in the night" (1 Thess 4:13–5:11). His second letter is written in response to reports that many in Thessalonica are alarmed that that day is imminent. Paul reminds them that Christ will not return until after certain events occur. There will be a great apostasy, and "the lawless one . . . the one destined for destruction," will be revealed. This man,[29] aided by Satan, will deceive many with "lying wonders." Finally, Jesus himself "will destroy [him] with the breath of his mouth, annihilating him by the manifestation [*epiphaneia*] of his coming [*parousia*]" (2 Thess 2:1–12).

The word "antichrist" appears only in the letters of John. It can refer to one particular individual or to multiple individuals. Indeed, sometimes both usages appear in a single sentence: "Children, it is the last hour! As you have heard that the antichrist [*antichristos*] is coming, so now many antichrists have come" (1 John 2:18). The Greek does not include the definite article, as if John were using "Antichrist" as a name. In English, use of the definite article varies from writer to writer.

## Consensus of Catholic Tradition

Although Paul does not use the term "antichrist," the Church Fathers equated this term with the "son of perdition" or "lawless one." They nearly always use it in the singular to refer to one specific person. Even when used in the plural, its meaning was often linked to the singular. In *City of God*, Augustine quoted the passage from Second Thessalonians, and stated, "No one can doubt that Paul is here speaking of Antichrist." He then distinguished two meanings of "Antichrist": it can mean "the

---

29. The NRSV's term "the one destined for destruction" is gender-neutral, but the Greek has *ho huios tēs apōleias*, "the son of perdition."

leader himself," or the multitude "who belong to him, together with himself"—"what we may call his whole body."[30]

In the tenth century, Adso, a Benedictine monk in Montier-en-Der, France, collected patristic teachings on the Antichrist in his *De ortu et tempore Antichristi*, the first of many medieval monographs on this topic.[31] In the sixteenth century, Robert Bellarmine used the third book of his *De Romano Pontifice* to expound on the Antichrist in Christian tradition. Against those Reformers who identified the Antichrist with the papacy as an institution, Bellarmine stated, "All Catholics think that Antichrist is one specific man."[32]

John Henry Newman wrote, "That Antichrist is one individual man, not a power,—not a mere ethical spirit, or a political system, not a dynasty, or succession of rulers,—was the universal tradition of the early Church."[33] Newman gave a series of lectures on the Antichrist during his Anglo-Catholic phase. He defended the traditional view that the Antichrist will persecute the Church in the years immediately prior to Christ's return, and accepted the identification of the Antichrist with Paul's "son of perdition" as settled.[34]

In the nineteenth and twentieth centuries, many scholars questioned the traditional interpretations of these New Testament texts. Some exegetes argued that the eschatological discourse was composed after the destruction of the Temple, and simply placed on the lips of Jesus to make it appear as if he had predicted this event. Others saw it as an authentic teaching of Jesus, who had, however, mistakenly believed that his return in glory was only

---

30. Augustine, *Concerning the City of God against the Pagans*, trans. Henry Bettenson (New York: Penguin, 2003), 932 (XX.19).

31. Miceli, *The Antichrist*, 83–101.

32. Robert Bellarmine, SJ, *Antichrist*, trans. Ryan Grant (Post Falls, ID: Mediatrix Press, 2018), 7 (*De Romano Pontifice*, book III, c. 2). He identifies the Antichrist with Paul's "son of perdition" on p. 10.

33. John Henry Newman, "The Patristical Idea of Antichrist," in *Discussions and Arguments on Various Subjects* (Notre Dame, IN: Notre Dame Press, 2004), 44–108, at 55–56.

34. Ibid., 51–57, 98.

a few years away. First Thessalonians was taken as proof that Paul believed that Christ's return was imminent, and therefore Second Thessalonians must have been written by someone else after Paul's death, in order to tamp down the end-times fever that had been spawned by the first letter. There have also been theologians who have argued that there will be *no* tribulation prior to Christ's return: Instead, human society will gradually become more just, more loving, and more Christ-like, until Christ returns to confirm this work of his body on earth.

The Catholic Church allows scholars to teach these interpretations of Scripture. Nevertheless, there has been no change in the Church's teaching regarding the end times. The *Catechism* states that "before Christ's second coming the Church must pass through a final trial that will shake the faith of many believers," and that this trial involves the "supreme religious deception" of the Antichrist.[35] Pope Benedict XVI cited St. Paul's teaching on the events that will occur before Christ's parousia: "Before the Lord's arrival there will be apostasy, and one well described as the 'man of lawlessness,' 'the son of perdition' ([2 Thess] 2:3) must be revealed, who tradition would come to call the Antichrist."[36] Most recently, Pope Francis offered a meditation on the last judgment and the resurrection of the body:

> Perhaps we do not have much fear of the Apocalypse of the Evil One, of the Antichrist who must come first; perhaps we do not have much fear. Perhaps we do not have much fear of the call of the Archangel or of the sound of the trumpet: but, the victory will be the Lord's.[37]

---

35. *Catechism of the Catholic Church*, 675; see 673–677. These passages are terse, and do not explain who or what this Antichrist is.
36. Pope Benedict XVI, "General Audience," November 12, 2008, http://www.vatican.va/content/benedict-xvi/en/audiences/2008/documents/hf_ben-xvi_aud_20081112.html.
37. Pope Francis, "Morning Meditation: Fear of resurrection," September 19, 2014, https://www.vatican.va/content/francesco/en/cotidie/2014/documents/papa-francesco-cotidie_20140919_fear-of-resurrection.html.

Catholic teaching regarding the Antichrist traditionally includes the following points:

- Before Christ returns, the Gospel will be preached throughout the world.[38] (Cf. Matt 24:14)

- In the last days, many Jews will recognize Jesus as the Messiah.[39] (Cf. Rom 11:1–27)

- Elijah, the prophet who never died, will return.[40] (Cf. 2 Kings 2:1–14; Mal 3:23–24; Sir 48:10–11; Matt 17:11)

- The Antichrist will mimic Christ in many ways, pretending to be meek and humble. Gregory the Great refers to his "apparent holiness." Origen contrasts "all the virtues personified in Christ" with "all the counterfeit virtues incarnated in the Antichrist." At first he will seem benevolent and deceive many, but eventually his wickedness will be made manifest.[41]

- The Antichrist will appear to work miracles. Augustine, Thomas Aquinas, and Newman say they do not know whether these will be supernatural and diabolical, or merely fraudulent.[42]

---

38. Joseph Pohle, *Eschatology, or, The Catholic Doctrine of the Last Things: A Dogmatic Treatise*, ed. Arthur Preuss (St. Louis: B. Herder, 1920), 104–5; Newman, "The Patristic Idea," 48.

39. Pohle, *Eschatology*, 104–7; Augustine, *City of God*, 957, 963 (XX.29,30); *Catechism of the Catholic Church*, 674.

40. Pohle, *Eschatology*, 104, 107–9; Miceli, *The Antichrist*, 78–79, 87; Augustine, *City of God*, 957, 963 (XX.29,30); Bellarmine, *Antichrist*, 46 (III.6). Some assert that Enoch will accompany Elijah, but this was less widely accepted in Catholic tradition and probably should not be included in a list of "consensus" teachings.

41. Miceli, *The Antichrist*, 57, 77, 86–88 (quotes on 77, 88); *The Church Fathers on the Bible: Selected Readings*, ed. Frank Sadowski, SSP (New York: Alba House, 1987), 48.

42. Miceli, *The Antichrist*, 57, 87; Augustine, *City of God*, 934 (XX.19); Newman, "The Patristic Idea," 75, 98; Thomas Aquinas, OP, *Summa Theologica*, trans. Fathers of the English Do-

- He will control a vast realm, possibly the entire world.[43]

- His persecution of the Church will be the worst in history. Domingo de Soto suggests that the Apostolic See itself will defect from the faith, but Bellarmine disagrees. Alphonsus Liguori states that the Mass will be completely suppressed during this time.[44]

- Finally, Christ will return and destroy the Antichrist and his works.[45]

These doctrines date back to the early Church. Later theologians—medieval, Tridentine, and modern—have usually been content to cite the consensus of the Fathers on these points. With regard to more precise details, some theologians have made elaborate assertions, while others argue that much will remain unknown until the events occur.[46]

## The Book of Revelation

Now we turn to the Book of Revelation, traditionally known as the Apocalypse of St. John. Each of the authorities mentioned above hold that *some* of its passages refer to the end times, but they do not agree on which. The primary reason for this disagreement, of course, is the difficulty in interpreting the book's apocalyptic symbolism. But another reason is that this

---

minican Province (Allen, TX: Christian Classics, 1981), I, q. 114, a. 4, ad 1.
43. Miceli, *The Antichrist*, 87; Newman, "The Patristical Idea," 56–57; Sadowski, *The Church Fathers*, 49; Augustine, *City of God*, 910 (XX.8); Bellarmine, *Antichrist*, 128 (III.16).
44. Miceli, *The Antichrist*, 57, 276; Augustine, *City of God*, 838, 910, 921 (XVIII.53; XX.8,13); Bellarmine, *Antichrist*, 53, 140 (III.7,17); Newman, "The Patristical Idea," 97–102.
45. Sadowski, *The Church Fathers*, 49, 231; Augustine, *City of God*, 838 (XVIII.53);
46. Augustine, *City of God*, 963 (XX.30); Newman, "The Patristical Idea," 67–68; Miceli, *The Antichrist*, 18–19.

book seems to depict *two* great persecutions of the Church, each of which is ended by a public manifestation of Christ's power.

From chapters 11 to 20, three fearsome monsters are prominent. One is "a great red dragon" (12:3). Its identity is stated explicitly: it is "that ancient serpent, who is called the Devil and Satan" (12:9; also 20:2).

The second creature is a beast with ten horns and seven heads that comes out of the sea. "And the dragon gave it his power and his throne and great authority" (13:2). For forty-two months, this beast is "allowed to make war on the saints and to conquer them."

> It was given authority over every tribe and people and language and nation, and all the inhabitants of the earth will worship it, everyone whose name has not been written from the foundation of the world in the book of life of the Lamb that was slaughtered. (13:7–8)

> All men and women are required to be marked on their right hand or forehead with the name of the beast or the number of its name. This calls for wisdom: let anyone with understanding calculate the number of the beast, for it is the number of a person. Its number is six hundred sixty-six. (13:17–18)

In subsequent chapters, this creature—which may also appear in the Book of Daniel[47]—is often just called "the beast."

The third monster is a beast that comes out of the earth; it has "two horns like a lamb and it spoke like a dragon" (13:11). This beast is called "the false prophet" (16:13; 19:20). It "makes

---

47. The prophet Daniel had a vision of four beasts from the sea (Dan 7). The fourth of these had ten horns, and then an additional horn appeared. Daniel is told that these horns are ten kings, and the other horn is another king who shall displace them. This king will "wear out the holy ones," until God appears in judgment (7:19–27). The Church Fathers saw connections between Daniel's prophecy and Revelation, but they disagreed on the details.

the earth and its inhabitants worship the first beast, whose mortal wound had been healed. It performs great signs, even making fire come down from heaven to earth in the sight of all" (13:12–13).

The beast, the false prophet, and the dragon perform miracles, but God smites their kingdom with many plagues. They assemble a great army "in the place that is named Armageddon in Hebrew" (16:16, NABRE). The next two chapters focus on the fall of Babylon. Finally, Christ appears (his name is given as "The Word of God" and as "King of kings and Lord of lords"). He defeats the armies, and then the beast and the false prophet are thrown alive into a lake of fire (19:11–21). The dragon—again identified as Satan—is chained for a thousand years (20:1–3).

"Those who had been beheaded for their testimony to Jesus" are raised, while the rest of the dead are not. "This is the first resurrection." For a thousand years, these martyrs reign with Christ (20:4–6).

> When the thousand years are ended, Satan will be released from his prison and will come out to deceive the nations at the four corners of the earth, Gog and Magog, in order to gather them for battle; they are as numerous as the sands of the sea. They marched up over the breadth of the earth and surrounded the camp of the saints and the beloved city. And fire came down from heaven and consumed them. And the devil who had deceived them was thrown into the lake of fire and sulfur, where the beast and the false prophet were, and they will be tormented day and night forever and ever. (20:7–10)

Then the second resurrection takes place: all are raised and "judged according to their works" (20:12). God creates a new heaven and a new earth, and establishes "the holy city, a new Jerusalem," where God will dwell with his people forever, and where "Death will be no more; mourning and crying and pain will be no more" (21:1–4).

Prophetic and apocalyptic passages in Scripture often jump back and forth in time, so the chronology of these events—if indeed they *are* events—should not be assumed to match the narrative order. Yet the events described above are narrated as if they were sequential. The beast and false prophet rule for forty-two months, and then Christ defeats their armies and casts the two into the lake of fire. After this, Christ reigns with the martyrs for a thousand years. Then, "when the thousand years are completed," there is another battle, this time involving Gog and Magog.[48] Again, God defeats the evil forces, and throws the devil into the pool of fire, where the beast and false prophet *already are*. So the most natural reading of this text involves two distinct conflicts, a thousand years apart from one another, each of which ends when evil is defeated by Christ. What should we make of this?

### Disagreement Among the Church Fathers

The earliest Church Fathers interpreted these passages sequentially. The beast—identified with Paul's "son of perdition" and John's "antichrist"—will persecute the Church and rule for forty-two months. Then Christ will return in glory, destroy the beast, raise Christian martyrs from the dead, and reign for one thousand years. This millennium will be fully terrestrial: if someone living in Athens wants to see Christ in person, he will have to travel to Jerusalem. At the end of this time, Gog and Magog will rebel, and Christ will defeat them. Then the general resurrection and general judgment will occur, and the wicked will be punished, and God's people will be given glorified bodies to live with the Lamb in the New Jerusalem forever.

This interpretation—known as *chiliasm* or *millenarianism*—was taught by Irenaeus, Justin Martyr, Papias, Tertullian, Victorinus, Hippolytus (in his early writings), Apollinaris,

---

48. Gog and Magog first appear in Ezekiel 38–39, where Gog is an evil prince, and Magog might be his kingdom (translations vary). This passage predicts that Gog will invade Israel, and the Lord will destroy his armies with earthquakes and fire from heaven.

Lactantius, and probably the Letter of Barnabas.[49] They agreed on the basic outline of this system, but disagreed on the identity of Gog and Magog. Some held that Gog and Magog will be nations who chafe under the thousand-year reign of Christ, and finally revolt.[50]

In the third century, chiliasm was rejected by Origen in the east, and by the Church of Rome in the west. Hippolytus appears to have retreated from this view as well in his later years. In the fourth and early fifth centuries, opposition from Jerome and Augustine cast a permanent cloud upon this view. By the late patristic age, chiliasm had mostly died out.[51]

The alternative interpretation, proposed by Tychonius and supported by Jerome and Augustine, was that Revelation's "thousand years" was not intended literally. As Augustine writes, the thousand years represent the era of the Church, "from the first coming of Christ to the end of the world, which will be Christ's second coming." The "first resurrection" refers to our salvation, using a metaphor that appears elsewhere in Scripture, for Paul himself describes salvation as being "raised" from death with Christ (Rom 6:4, 13). The chaining of Satan represents the victory won by Christ, using a metaphor attested in Scripture (the binding of the strong man in Matt 12:28–29). Satan can still tempt us, but the victory of Christ's cross restrains him from

---

49. J. N. D. Kelly, *Early Christian Doctrines*, rev. ed. (New York: HarperSanFrancisco, 1978), 465–466, 469; William C. Weinrich, ed., *Revelation*, "New Testament Volume XII" in *Ancient Christian Commentary on Scripture* (Downers Grove, IL: InterVarsity Press, 2005), xxii, xxiv, 333; Bellarmine, *Antichrist*, 132 (III.17). The heretic Cerinthus taught that this millennium would be a time of unbridled sensuality, but this was not held by any of the Fathers: see Kelly, *Early Christian Doctrines*, 466, 473; Augustine, *City of God*, 906–7 (XX.7). The word *chiliasm* comes from the Greek *chilioi*, "one thousand," which also gave us the metric prefix "kilo."
50. Bellarmine, *Antichrist*, 132 (III.17).
51. Kelly, *Early Christian Doctrines*, 469, 473; Weinrich, *Revelation*, xxiv–xxv; Augustine, *City of God*, 906–7 (XX.7).

"exert[ing] his whole power of temptation either by force or by guile," and this is what the chains represent.[52]

Thus the defeat and chaining of Satan (Rev 20:1–3) have already occurred. The unchaining of Satan and the subsequent conflict (Rev 20:7–10) still lies in the future, and is identified with the time of the Antichrist, who will gain power when his master Satan is unchained, and will persecute God's holy ones. But Christ will return and destroy him (Rev 20:9; 2 Thess 2:8), and then the "second resurrection" —the actual bodily resurrection—will occur.[53]

This interpretation avoided the double return of Christ (which would seem to contradict the Gospels and Paul's epistles), and it had the authority of Augustine and Jerome behind it. It soon became dominant in both east and west, and the millennial interpretation died out. By AD 600, Andrew of Caesarea would dismiss chiliasm as absurd: "It is unnecessary to say that the church receives nothing of this."[54] In the sixteenth century, Bellarmine claimed that "all Catholics understand the thousand years as the whole time which is from the arrival of Christ even to Antichrist."[55]

Yet many questions remained. First, who are Gog and Magog? Ambrose identified them with the Goths; Theodoret with the Scythians or Huns. Andrew of Caesarea and Oecumenius saw them as future nations, currently unknown, who will follow the Antichrist. Augustine was torn between two possibilities: either Gog and Magog collectively refer to the nations that follow Satan, or Magog refers to these nations while Gog refers to Satan himself. Bellarmine saw Gog as the Antichrist, and Magog as his army. Newman takes Magog to refer to "the nations of the

52. Augustine, *City of God*, 903–4, 907–11, 914 (XX.6–9), quotes on 911; Weinrich, *Revelation*, xxiii.
53. Augustine, *City of God*, 910–12, 923 (XX.8,14); Bellarmine, *Antichrist*, 129 (III.16).
54. Weinrich, *Revelation*, xxv, xxviii, 323–24, 339, 341, quote on 339; Kelly, *Early Christian Doctrines*, 479; Pohle, *Eschatology*, 158.
55. Bellarmine, *Antichrist*, 137 (III.17).

North," but with a very broad understanding of "north"—he wonders if it might refer to China.[56]

Second, if the binding of Satan in Revelation 20:1–3 occurred when Christ died and rose from the dead, then how should we interpret the beasts, plagues, and persecutions of chapters 13 to 19? Some contemporary scholars identify these with the early persecutions of the Church under the Herodians, ending with the destruction of the Temple.[57] Other scholars identify them with Roman persecutions, either Nero's or Domitian's. Some of these scholars see Revelation as a supernatural prediction written before these events, while others take the descriptions as written after the fact and retrojected into the mouth of John.[58] Adso and Bellarmine identify the Antichrist with the beast whose number is 666. In this view, chapter 13 will take place after the events of 20:1–6.[59] Many others interpret these things as spiritual allegories. Augustine suggests that the beast might represent "the godless city itself." More recently, Scott Hahn has proposed that the structure of the whole book represents a Mass.[60]

Scripture scholars have assigned names to different paradigms of interpreting Revelation. The *historicist* sees the Book of Revelation as a prediction of events that were in the future

---

56. Weinrich, *Revelation*, 339 n14, 340, 340 n20; Augustine, *City of God*, 919–920 (XX.11); Bellarmine, *Antichrist*, 137 (III.17); Newman, "The Patristical Idea," 104–5.

57. David B. Currie, *Rapture: The End-Times Error that Leaves the Bible Behind* (Manchester, NH: Sophia Institute Press, 2003), 230–31, 267, 357, 372, 454–56 argues for this view, and in his introduction (vii-xi), Scott Hahn appears to agree. Currie holds that only the last two chapters of Revelation refer to future events.

58. The commentary and footnotes in the New American Bible are a good example.

59. Miceli, *The Antichrist*, 87; Bellarmine, *Antichrist*, 12, 69–78 (III.2,10). Newman ("The Patristical Idea," 72–74) mentions this view, but it's unclear whether he endorses it.

60. Augustine, *City of God*, 917, 923 (XX.9,14); Scott Hahn, *The Lamb's Supper: The Mass as Heaven on Earth* (New York: Doubleday, 1999), 73, 115–29.

when it was written, most of which are now in our past. The *futurist* sees chapters 4–21 as referring to events still in our future. The *preterist* sees the entire book as describing past events (although some hold that chapters 20–21 remain in the future). The *idealist* or *spiritualizing* interpretation sees the book as a symbolic depiction of the battle between good and evil that Christians encounter every day.[61] And within each of these paradigms there is argument about the details.

## Dispensationalism

Among American Protestants today, the most widely held eschatology is known as *dispensationalism*, or more precisely, *pretribulational premillennial dispensationalism*. In most respects this is identical to the chiliasm attested by some of the early Fathers: The Antichrist will rule the world for forty-two months while the Church undergoes a great tribulation; then Christ will appear, destroy him, and rule on earth for a thousand years; then Gog and Magog will revolt and be destroyed; then the general resurrection and last judgment will take place. To this scheme, dispensationalism adds one more event: immediately before the tribulation begins, Christians will be whisked away from this world and taken to heaven with Christ, where they will be safe from the Antichrist's persecution.

This event, known as the rapture,[62] seems to have originated in the speculations of a Chilean Jesuit named Manuel de Lacunza y Díaz around the year 1800. It was taken up by the English

---

61. Steve Gregg, *Revelation: Four Views*, rev. ed. (Nashville: Thomas Nelson, 2013), 12–13; Tim LaHaye, *Revelation Unveiled* (Grand Rapids: Zondervan, 1999), 19, 26–28; Hahn, *The Lamb's Supper*, 65–66, 73; Carl E. Olson, *Will Catholics Be "Left Behind"? A Catholic Critique of the Rapture and Today's Prophecy Preachers* (San Francisco: Ignatius, 2003), 77–81.

62. From the Vulgate translation of 1 Thess 4:17: *rapiemur cum illis in nubibus obviam Christo in aera*, "we shall be caught up with them in the clouds to meet Christ in the air."

preacher John Nelson Darby around 1830, popularized in the United States by the *Scofield Reference Bible* (1909), and made famous in the 1970s by the writings of evangelical preachers such as Hal Lindsey and Tim LaHaye. In addition to works of exegesis, LaHaye also co-authored the fictional *Left Behind* series, which became best-sellers and spawned multiple movies.[63]

## Magisterial Teaching

Earlier, I listed eight doctrines about the Antichrist that the Church Fathers and Catholic tradition have agreed on. Dispensationalist Protestant theologians agree with these as well. But there are two questions on which there is significant disagreement between Catholics and dispensationalists.

The first concerns the rapture. There have been no magisterial pronouncements on this topic, probably because discussion about this idea has been largely confined to Protestant churches in America and Britain. So the rapture doctrine is not heresy. Yet it postulates two future comings of Christ: one in secret before the tribulation, and one in public a few years later. This seems incompatible with longstanding Catholic teaching about Christ's return, so it is reasonable to grade it as *haeresi proxima* (close to heresy). At the very least, it is a theological error.[64]

---

63. For the history of dispensationalism and the rapture, see Olson, *Will Catholics Be "Left Behind"?*, 151–201; Paul Thigpen, *The Rapture Trap: A Catholic Response to "End Times" Fever* (West Chester, PA: Ascension Press, 2001), 143–48; Gregg, *Revelation: Four Views*, 53–55. Lindsey's *The Late Great Planet Earth* (1970) and LaHaye's *Revelation Unveiled* are helpful one-volume defenses of this view.
64. LaHaye responds to this criticism by arguing that "there is only one 'Second Coming,' but it occurs in two phases" (*Revelation Unveiled*, 105). For a more elaborate argument that a pre-tribulation rapture is incompatible with Catholic doctrine, see Olson, *Will Catholics Be "Left Behind"?*, 286–340, and Currie, *End-Times Error*, 399–403.

The second question concerns the millennium. After Christ returns, will there be a thousand-year kingdom on earth, followed by another rebellion? Or will Christ's return lead immediately to the final judgment and the separation of the saved and the damned? Many issues on which the Church Fathers disagreed are still considered open questions by Catholic theologians. But in this case, although the early Fathers were divided, the later Fathers were unanimously opposed to this view. From the fifth century to the present, Catholic tradition has consistently rejected the idea that Christ will reign bodily on earth for one thousand years. So chiliasm probably should be considered a heresy, and is certainly *haeresi proxima.*[65]

A third topic is also disputed, but here the opinions cross confessional lines: *When* will these things occur? Will it be tomorrow, or next year, or ten thousand generations from now? The Church, following her Lord, has always taught that we do not know the day or the hour (Matt 24:36). Yet throughout Christian history this has been a topic of speculation. From Joachim of Fiore to Savonarola to the Seventh Day Adventists, some teachers and pastors have made rash predictions. Hal Lindsey asserted that Christ's return would occur within a generation of the 1948 founding of the State of Israel.[66] Even some popes—including St. Gregory the Great and St. Pius X—believed that they were *probably* living in the last days.[67] However, this fascinating topic

---

65. There have been no recent statements about chiliasm by popes or councils, probably because there was no need. Indeed, Gregory the Great (590–604) might be the most recent pope to condemn this doctrine! In 1944, the Holy Office (the Vatican congregation responsible for the defense of doctrine) condemned chiliasm, even in "mitigated" form, apparently because de Lacunza's book was still being circulated in Chile (DS 3839). But the censure used ("this doctrine cannot be safely taught") is one of the weaker theological notes, and adds little to this doctrine's status.
66. Hal Lindsey, *The Late Great Planet Earth* (London: Lakeland, 1970), 54.
67. Miceli, *The Antichrist*, 77–80; Pope Pius X, *E Supremi* (On the Restoration of All Things in Christ), October 4, 1903, 5, http://

will not be pursued in this chapter, as "Supper's Ready" has nothing to say about the timing of these events.

## Assessing the Orthodoxy of "Supper's Ready"

Suppose that Peter Gabriel sent the lyrics of "Supper's Ready" to a Catholic bishop and requested an imprimatur.[68] Should it be granted?

Let us first look at the suite as a whole. The first section, which incorporates Gabriel's own mystical experience, serves merely as the launching point for the story.[69] The story itself involves at least three major figures: the narrator, who functions mostly as an observer; the Guaranteed Eternal Sanctuary Man, who is later revealed to be "666" and has the upper hand for most of the suite; then "the mighty one, / Lord of lords, king of kings," who appears in the seventh section and has the final victory.

Who is this Lord of lords, king of kings? In Christian usage, this title could refer to the Triune God or to Jesus, the Second Person of the Trinity. In this case, the lyrics' connection to Revelation tells us who is meant. Revelation 19:16–17 (in the King James Version familiar to Gabriel) reads:

---

www.vatican.va/content/pius-x/en/encyclicals/documents/ hf_p-x_enc_04101903_e-supremi.html.

68. There is no reason to expect such an event.

69. Sarah Hill compares the first section of "Supper's Ready" to the prologue of the Book of Revelation (where John is caught up in a vision). However, she also argues that the seventh section corresponds to the epilogue of Revelation (where the angel and John discuss the book that he has written about these visions), and on that point I disagree. In the song, the narrator does not return to the mundane world after the drama ends. Hill's analysis of the piece is interesting, but her overall focus is on the formalist and narrative structure of the seven-part suite, not on its meaning and content (Sarah Hill, "Ending It All: Genesis and Revelation," *Popular Music* 32/2 [2013]: 199–224, at 212–13, 218 note 18).

And he hath on his vesture and on his thigh a name written, King Of Kings, And Lord Of Lords. And I saw an
angel standing in the sun; and he cried with a loud voice,
saying to all the fowls that fly in the midst of heaven,
Come and gather yourselves together unto the supper of
the great God.

The final lines of "Supper's Ready" are simply a rearrangement
of this text:

There's an angel standing in the sun
And he's crying with a loud voice
"This is the supper of the mighty one"
Lord of lords, king of kings
Has returned to lead his children home
To take them to the new Jerusalem

In the Book of Revelation, this person is identified as the
rider of a white horse. His name is "The Word of God" (19:13).
He will rule the nations "with a rod of iron" (19:15), identifying
him with the child born of the woman who will "rule all the
nations with a rod of iron" (12:5). So there can be no doubt
that this is Christ.

Then who is the Guaranteed Eternal Sanctuary Man?
"Supper's Ready" portrays him as an evil deceiver, and yet
he has resemblances to Christ. The music in section two that
announces his appearance is the same as that which announces
Christ in section seven, except that the tone of the former is
frightening while the latter's is uplifting. Gabriel wore a distorted
silver crown of thorns during performances of section two.
These facts identify the Sanctuary Man as a pseudo-Christ who
deceives the world, wages war, and is destroyed when the real
Christ returns. Clearly this is the "son of perdition" described
in Second Thessalonians: the Antichrist of Christian tradition.

What does the song say about the Antichrist's attributes?
He claims to offer "peace" and unity (his followers walk "hand
in hand"), but then becomes a "warlord." He is a deceiver ("can't
you see he's fooled you all"), especially of "all the children lost
down many paths." We even hear the children singing a lullaby
to a "little snake."

The Sanctuary Man also appears to work miracles, but it is unclear whether these are truly supernatural workings, or only scientific tricks. The program handed out at concerts describes him as "the head of a highly disciplined scientific religion."[70] In section three, his soldiers are given a "wonderful potion" to control their emotions. The term *potion* has magical connotations, but in the psychedelic hippie culture of 1972, who could guess whether a given potion was created in a pharmaceutical lab or a witch's cauldron? The ambiguity between magic and science reappears in section six, when the dragon "brings down the fire from the skies," just as the false prophet in Revelation "performs great signs, even making fire come down from heaven to earth in the sight of all" (13:13). The first-century reader would assume that fire from the skies must be supernatural, but today we accomplish such a feat on a regular basis. In 1838, Newman anticipated this blurring of the line between magic and science:

> Moreover the reign of Antichrist will be supported, it would appear, with a display of miracles, such as the magicians of Egypt effected against Moses. On this subject, of course, we wait for a fuller explanation of the prophetical language, such as the event alone can give us. So far, however, is clear, that whether false miracles or not, whether pretended, *or the result, as some have conjectured, of discoveries in physical science*, they will produce the same effect as if they were real,—viz., the overpowering the imaginations of such as have not the love of God deeply lodged in their hearts,—of all but the "elect." Scripture is remarkably precise and consistent in this prediction.[71]

The Sanctuary Man's dictatorship resembles that of the beast. According to the program, as we have seen, his armies were ordered "to attack all those without an up-to-date 'Eternal Life Licence,' which were obtainable at the head office of the

---

70. Programme.
71. Newman, "The Patristical Idea," 98 (emphasis added).

Sanctuary Man's religion."[72] In Revelation, the false prophet requires all people to worship the beast upon pain of death, compelling them "to be marked on the right hand or the forehead, so that no one can buy or sell who does not have the mark, that is, the name of the beast or the number of its name" (13:16–17).

On all these points, Genesis's depiction of the Antichrist matches those attested by Scripture and by Catholic tradition. But what of the disputed topics mentioned earlier?

The sudden disappearance of millions of people from the earth—the rapture—makes excellent drama. The protagonists in the *A Thief in the Night* film series (1972–1983) and the *Left Behind* book series (1995–2007) are non-Christians stunned by the disappearance of their loved ones. They had heard Christians preach about the rapture, but they didn't believe until it was too late. Now they must witness to Christ in a world ruled by the Antichrist. Is there any hint of this drastic shift in "Supper's Ready"?

Not at all. There is certainly no mention of widespread disappearances—or any other major event—prior to the appearance of the Sanctuary Man. When Christ appears in section seven, his purpose is explicitly stated: He "has returned to lead his children home / To take them to the new Jerusalem." So his "children" have been suffering under persecution. They were not raptured away to safety before the Antichrist's rise. So on the question of the rapture, "Supper's Ready" stands with Catholic doctrine against the dispensationalist view.

What about the thousand-year reign? According to millenarian theology, the reign of the Antichrist (whose number is 666) will not end in Christ's *final* triumph, but in a temporary victory. Christ will establish an earthly kingdom which will last for a thousand years. After this will be the revolt of Gog and Magog, Christ's final victory, and then the establishment of the New Jerusalem. This view is rejected by the Catholic Church. It is also rejected by "Supper's Ready," whose lyrics clearly contradict this theory. In the sixth section ("Apocalypse in 9/8"), Magog

72. Programme.

appears alongside "666"; they are not separated by a thousand years. And the New Jerusalem immediately follows the triumph of "the mighty one."

The music itself points in the same direction. In their early years, Genesis recorded several epic tracks in which the lyrics and music told a complicated story. These pieces usually ended in one of two ways. Some ended with a dramatic cadence—a firm, unambiguous conclusion.[73] Others ended with a return of the very first theme, bringing the music full circle.[74] "Supper's Ready" is their longest epic by far, and yet it ends with a fade-out. On the LP this might not be significant; many pop songs in the 70s ended with fade-outs. This was a radio-friendly choice; it helped the melody to stick in the listener's brain, and allowed the DJ to fade each song into the next to prevent the listener from turning the dial. But a fade-out is a studio creation, and difficult to replicate live. Pop bands end their songs decisively in concert, so that the audience knows when to clap. Yet "Supper's Ready" ended with a fade-out even in concert. That this was a deliberate choice is shown by the fact that it ended with a dramatic cadence the first few times Genesis performed it, after which the band changed the ending to mimic the fade-out from the studio version.[75]

Why would the songwriters attach so much importance to the fade-out? When we look at music and lyrics together, the answer seems clear. Amid soaring guitar lines, the singer proclaims that the Lord of lords has come to take his people to the New Jerusalem. If the music then came to a solid end,

---

73. Examples include "Stagnation" (1970), "The Knife" (1970), "The Musical Box" (1971), "The Fountain of Salmacis" (1971), "Watcher of the Skies" (1972), "Can-Utility and the Coastliners" (1972), "Robbery, Assault and Battery" (1976), and "Eleventh Earl of Mar" (1976).
74. Examples include "Firth of Fifth" (1973), "Mad Man Moon" (1976), and "One for the Vine" (1976).
75. The ending changed sometime between the 1/22/1973 concert in Rome and the 2/9/1973 concert in London, as can be heard on bootlegs from that era.

the story would be over. Instead, the guitar continues after the singing stops, and continues without end. This is not a kingdom that will last merely a thousand years. This is a kingdom that will last forever. So both music and lyrics are incompatible with millenarianism as well.

We should also take note of what does *not* happen during the song: At no point does the narrator attempt to *fight* the Sanctuary Man. In section two, he tries to warn the people about his true nature. In section three, when he feels himself being overcome by the "wonderful potion," he uses his "prayer capsule." In section six, he urges his listeners, "Better not compromise, it won't be easy." These lines bring to mind how Christians responded to the Roman persecutions. They did not try to overthrow the government or assassinate the Caesars. Rather, they preached the gospel, prayed, and encouraged their brothers and sisters in Christ to remain faithful even in the face of death.

From a Catholic perspective, many details within this song are imprecise, to say the least. In Revelation chapter 13, the dragon gives his power to the beast that comes out of the sea, and the false prophet (the second beast) brings down fire from the skies. "Apocalypse in 9/8" seems to jumble all of these together. It is also unclear who Magog is, but there is no consistent Catholic tradition on this question anyway.

Finally, what does the title signify? The word "supper" appears twice in the suite. In the beginning, it indicates mundane domestic life. At the end, the angel standing in the sun announces "the supper of the mighty one." This line is taken from Revelation 19:17–18, where the supper in question is grotesque but triumphant: the "angel standing in the sun" summons birds to feast on the Antichrist's dead soldiers and their horses.[76] In concert, Peter Gabriel often introduced this piece with an eccentric story about a man who summons worms from the ground so that the birds could have their supper, which was

---

76. This is the same passage that gave Julia Ward Howe the image of Christ "trampling out the vintage where the grapes of wrath are stored" (cf. Rev 19:15).

probably an allusion to this passage in Revelation. But Gabriel told this story for laughs (and to keep the audience's attention while the band tuned their 12-string guitars); the birds are not mentioned in the song itself. Moreover, Gabriel told Armando Gallo how seriously he took the conclusion to "Supper's Ready," as we heard: "I was singing my heart out there when I used to sing the 'New Jerusalem' . . . I was singing for my life. I was saying this is good over evil, and . . . you know, it was an old-fashioned gesture, but I meant it, and I was fighting."[77] So it seems likely that the supper of the title should be identified instead with the arrival of the New Jerusalem, "coming down out of heaven from God, prepared as a bride adorned for her husband" (Rev 21:2). It is the wedding supper of the Lamb.

I propose, then, that there is no reason that this song could not be granted an imprimatur. A novel of historical fiction is judged by the accuracy of its historical setting, even though the characters themselves are fictional. Just so, *eschatological* fiction should be judged by the orthodoxy of its end-times setting. By that standard, "Supper's Ready" is fully orthodox.

Of course, this twenty-three-minute work of progressive rock should not be taken as a definitive interpretation of eschatological prophecy. But even the Church herself does not offer such an interpretation. Some of these prophecies will not be understood until the events themselves occur. Bellarmine, following Irenaeus, made this very point: "It is common to all prophecies of the prophets to be ambiguous and obscure until they are fulfilled."[78]

---

77. Gallo, *I Know What I Like*, loc. 1461 (ellipses in original).
78. Bellarmine, *Antichrist*, 77 (III.10).

# About the Authors

**Robert E. Alvis** serves as a professor of Church history at Saint Meinrad Seminary and School of Theology. His publications include two books: *Religion and the Rise of Nationalism: A Profile of an East-Central European City* (Syracuse University Press, 2005) and *White Eagle, Black Madonna: One Thousand Years of the Polish Catholic Tradition* (Fordham University Press, 2016). He also edited *A Science of the Saints: Studies in Spiritual Direction* (Liturgical Press, 2020). His current research focuses on the Divine Mercy devotion.

**Dawn Eden Goldstein** received her S.Th.D. in systematic theology in 2016 from the University of St. Mary of the Lake. She has written about music for the *Village Voice*, *Billboard*, and *Mojo*, and has written liner notes (historical booklets) for more than eighty albums of 1960s rock and roll. Her Catholic books include *My Peace I Give You: Healing Sexual Wounds with the Help of the Saints* (Ave Maria Press, 2016), *Sunday Will Never Be the Same: A Rock and Roll Journalist Opens Her Ears to God* (Catholic Answers Press, 2019), and *Father Ed: The Story of Bill W.'s Spiritual Sponsor* (Orbis Books, 2022).

**William C. Hackett** is an assistant professor of philosophy at Saint Meinrad Seminary and School of Theology. He is the translator of several works, including *The Expansion of Metaphysics* by Miklós Vetö (2018), co-author of *Quiet Powers of the Possible: Interviews in Contemporary French Phenomenology* (2016), and author of *Philosophy in Word and Name* (2020) and *Anthropomorphism and Theology: The Apophatics of the Sensible* (forthcoming, 2023), as well as *Outside the Gates*, a novella based on the life of Jewish philosopher Jean Wahl during the Occupation.

**Lawrence J. King** is a part-time lecturer for Saint Meinrad Seminary and School of Theology, and also works in the tech industry. He holds a Ph.D. in systematic theology from the Catholic University of America, an M.A. in theology from the

Dominican School of Philosophy & Theology, and an M.S. in mathematics from the University of Washington. His writing has appeared in *Newman Studies Journal, Eastern Churches Journal, Theological Studies,* and *Public Discourse.*

**Keith Lemna** is an associate professor of systematic theology at Saint Meinrad Seminary and School of Theology. He is the author of *The Apocalypse of Wisdom: Louis Bouyer's Theological Recovery of the Cosmos* (Angelico Press, 2019) and *The Trinitarian Wisdom of God* (Emmaus Academic Press, 2022). He has published articles in *Gregorianum, The Heythrop Journal, Communio, Irish Theological Quarterly,* and several other academic and non-academic journals.

**Thomas E. Malewitz** is an assistant professor and the director of the Ed.D.: Leadership program at Spalding University. He has also served as a lecturer at Saint Meinrad Seminary and School of Theology and Bellarmine University. He is the author of *Authenticity, Passion, and Advocacy: Approaching Adolescent Spirituality from the Life and Wisdom of Thomas Merton* (Wipf & Stock, 2020) and co-editor of *Hollywood or History?: An Inquiry-Based Strategy for Using Film to Teach World Religions* (Information Age, 2023). He has published articles in *The Journal of Catholic Education, The Merton Annual,* and the NCEA's *Momentum.*

**Nathaniel Marx** is an associate professor of liturgical and sacramental theology at Saint Meinrad Seminary and School of Theology. He is the author, most recently, of *Authentic Liturgy: Minds in Tune with Voices* (Liturgical Press, 2020), which won an honorable mention in the 2021 Catholic Media Association Book Awards. He contributes to the Liturgy and Culture seminar at the North American Academy of Liturgy and serves as treasurer for the organization. He is currently leading an initiative to invigorate children's participation at Sunday Mass.

**Brian Pedraza** is an associate professor of theology at Franciscan Missionaries of Our Lady University in Baton Rouge, Louisiana. He has published articles in *Church Life, The Catechetical*

*Review, First Things, The Josephinum Journal of Theology,* and *The International Journal of Evangelization and Catechesis.* His recent book, *Catechesis for the New Evangelization: Vatican II, John Paul II, and the Unity of Revelation and Experience,* was published by CUA Press (2020).

**Christian Raab, OSB**, is an associate professor of theology at Saint Meinrad Seminary and School of Theology and an associate pastor at Saint Joseph Parish in Jasper, Indiana. His writing has appeared in *Logos, American Benedictine Review, Commonweal, The Priest,* and *Review for Religious.* He is co-editor of *The Tradition of Catholic Prayer* (Liturgical Press, 2007), and author of *Understanding the Religious Priesthood: History, Controversy, Theology* (CUA, 2021).

**Joseph Q. Raab** is a professor of religious studies and theology at Siena Heights University in Adrian, Michigan. He is the author of the recent book on Merton's dialogue with D. T. Suzuki entitled *Opening New Horizons* (Pickwick, 2021). He also served as co-editor of *The Merton Annual: Studies in Culture, Spirituality, and Social Concerns* for volumes 25 (2012) through 33 (2020).

**Elizabeth Scalia** is a Benedictine Oblate and the culture editor at OSV News. She is the author of several award winning books, including *Strange Gods: Unmasking the Idols in Everyday Life* (Ave Maria Press, 2013) and *Little Sins Mean a Lot* (Our Sunday Visitor, 2016). A widely read blogger known as "The Anchoress" (www.theanchoress.com), she has also served as editor-at-large for Word on Fire Ministries and editor in chief at Aleteia.org.

**Elizabeth Woodard** holds a Ph.D. in systematic theology from the Catholic University of America. She is a lecturer in systematic theology at Saint Meinrad Seminary and School of Theology. She works as a pastoral associate in the Archdiocese of Boston. Her work as an ecumenist and spiritual director is carried out though her web-site, unityhopeful.com. She is the author of *Cruciform Ecumenism: The Intersection of Ecclesiology, Episcopacy, and Apostolicity from a Catholic Perspective* (Fortress Academic, 2019). Also a sacred musician, she directs the Alumni Chorus at Regis College.

# FOCOLARE MEDIA

*Enkindling the Spirit of Unity*

The New City Press book you are holding in your hands is one of the many resources produced by Focolare Media, which is a ministry of the Focolare Movement in North America. The Focolare is a worldwide community of people who feel called to bring about the realization of Jesus' prayer: "That all may be one" (see John 17:21).

Focolare Media wants to be your primary resource for connecting with people, ideas, and practices that build unity. Our mission is to provide content that empowers people to grow spiritually, improve relationships, engage in dialogue, and foster collaboration within the Church and throughout society.

 Visit www.focolaremedia.com to learn more about all of New City Press's books, our award-winning magazine *Living City*, videos, podcasts, events, and free resources.

**NEW CITY PRESS**